First-Grade Math

1

A Month-to-Month Guide

First-Grade Math

A Month-to-Month Guide

Vicki Bachman

Math Solutions Publications

Sausalito, CA

Math Solutions Publications
A division of
Marilyn Burns Education Associates
150 Gate 5 Road, Suite 101
Sausalito, CA 94965
www.mathsolutions.com

Library of Congress Cataloging-in-Publication Data

Bachman, Vicki.
  First-grade math : a month-to-month guide / Vicki Bachman.
      p. cm.
Includes bibliographical references and index.
    ISBN 0-941355-54-3 (alk. paper)
  1. Mathematics—Study and teaching (Elementary) I. Title.
  QA115.B33 2003
    372.7'049—dc22

                                    2003020180

Editor: Toby Gordon
Production: Melissa L. Inglis
Cover and interior design: Catherine Hawkes/Cat and Mouse
Composition: Argosy Publishing

Printed in the United States of America on acid-free paper
07 06 05 04 03 ML 1 2 3 4 5

A Message from Marilyn Burns

We at Marilyn Burns Education Associates believe that teaching mathematics well calls for increasing our understanding of the math we teach, seeking greater insight into how children learn mathematics, and refining lessons to best promote children's learning. All of our Math Solutions Professional Development publications and inservice courses have been designed to help teachers achieve these goals.

Our publications include a wide range of choices, from books in our new Teaching Arithmetic and Lessons for Algebraic Thinking series to resources that link math and literacy; from books to help teachers understand mathematics more deeply to children's books that help students develop an appreciation for math while learning basic concepts.

Our inservice programs offer five-day courses, one-day workshops, and series of school-year sessions throughout the country, working in partnership with school districts to help implement and sustain long-term improvement in mathematics instruction in all classrooms.

To find a complete listing of our publications and workshops, please visit our Web site at *www.mathsolutions.com*. Or contact us by calling (800) 868-9092 or sending an e-mail to *info@mathsolutions.com*.

We're eager for your feedback and interested in learning about your particular needs. We look forward to hearing from you.

A DIVISION OF MARILYN BURNS EDUCATION ASSOCIATES

To the memory of fellow educator Diane McConnahay;
with deep appreciation for her unwavering belief
in children and their teachers.

Contents

Contents

Foreword

One of the challenges of teaching mathematics is planning a coherent year of instruction. Not only must we address the important mathematics children need to learn, we also need to help children learn to think, reason, and become proficient problem solvers. And we also want to inspire children to enjoy mathematics and see it as useful to their lives. Accomplishing this is a tall order that calls for understanding the full scope of the mathematics curriculum, having a rich repertoire of instructional options, being skilled at managing instruction in the classroom, and understanding the needs of the individual students in your class.

This book offers a month-by-month guide for planning a year of math instruction. It is one of a three-book series, each written by a master teacher to address teaching mathematics in grades one, two, and three. The author of each book acknowledges that her suggestions do not comprise the only approach to accomplish planning, or necessarily the best approach for others to follow. Rather, each suggests a thoughtful, practical, and very personal approach to planning that has grown out of her years of experience in the classroom.

The three authors of this series are truly master teachers—experienced, caring, hard-working, and incredibly accomplished. They bring their wisdom and experience to their books in unique ways, but as teachers they share common experiences and outlooks. Each has offered many professional development classes and workshops for teachers while also choosing to make classroom teaching the main focus of their careers. For all three of them, mathematics was not their initial love or strength. However, they each came to study and learn to appreciate mathematics because of their need to serve their students. They are committed to excellence in math instruction, they understand children, they know how to manage classrooms, and they are passionate about teaching. It is a great pleasure to present these books to you.

MARILYN BURNS

Introduction

Children begin their long school careers in our care. The feelings and self-perceptions they establish during this time will likely exert a long-term impact on their lives. In the area of mathematics, being able to reason confidently with numbers and to develop understanding in all of the other areas of the mathematics curriculum are critical for students' mathematical literacy and later success. By carefully planning students' first year in math, we teachers can boost our chances of helping students become flexible, resourceful problem solvers. Also, just as we encourage young learners to seek and notice printed language around them as they are learning to read, we can help them identify the math that is all around them and see mathematics as inextricably connected with the real world.

I've written this book to provide practical support to first-grade teachers for planning a year of mathematics instruction. Long-range planning enhances our ability to be responsive to individual children during daily math lessons. It enables us to provide broad and deep support through enjoyable mathematical experiences. And it gives us the capacity to build on what our students have accomplished and to anticipate the work that lies ahead.

Several years ago, the first-grade teachers at my school worked together to create a timeline for an entire school year that would offer an overall framework for the teaching we did in specific areas of the curriculum. Like most first-grade teachers, we teach a curriculum defined by set objectives. Our new timeline would augment the month-by-month planning we had already done to establish the timing for teaching the various topics in our curriculum. We identified significant and predictable events that occurred each month that we could incorporate into our content-area instruction. We were not striving to teach through calendar themes, but rather to capitalize on what our students would encounter during a typical month and make connections whenever possible to what we were teaching. For instance, here in Iowa, our classes collect a variety of leaves and seeds each fall, so we brainstormed specific math possibilities that involve sorting, making patterns, and graphing, and that tie to the math strand we had already identified for the month. (We identified possibilities for other subject areas as well; for instance, reading and writing about autumn, working with science content relating to life cycles, engaging in art activities, and so on.) I am grateful to my colleagues for all of the rich conversations and collaboration that came out of this planning process. Many of our collective ideas appear in this book.

The chapters in this book are presented in a month-by-month format. The beginning of each chapter identifies the mathematical strand featured for the month, such as geometry, measurement, and so on. As much as possible, the strand for each month has been selected to enhance connections with the ideas from the calendar events that my colleagues and I identified for the year. In addition to the featured strand, and because the topic of number overarches all areas of mathematics for first graders, each month also identifies specific numerical understandings to focus on, such as keeping track of quantities, putting amounts together, taking amounts apart, and so on. Also, each chapter provides a variety of practical routines, literature-based lessons, and activities that specifically support that month's content goals. The lessons include individual, partner, and class explorations of topics, and they offer enough flexibility to engage diverse learners. Throughout the book, students are encouraged to solve problems in a variety of ways and to communicate about their work verbally and in written form.

I hope this book will help you enjoy exploring math with your students while you facilitate their mathematical understanding. I also hope that through experiencing some of the possibilities offered here, you'll discover, imagine, and create many of your own avenues through which to enjoy mathematics with your first graders.

Chapter 1

BEFORE THE CHILDREN ARRIVE

Thinking through your math program before the first day of school enables you to set the stage for a productive beginning and a purposeful year. In planning your year, you'll want to consider the following:

- setting up the classroom for mathematics learning
- planning daily instruction
- helping children develop number sense
- organizing student work
- integrating assessment into instruction ■

Setting Up the Classroom for Mathematics Learning

The practical task of arranging furniture and designing your classroom space will influence everything from traffic patterns to accessibility of materials. Keep in mind that various math activities will involve several different groupings of children—including group, partner, and individual work. As you arrange the room, reserve a space that is large enough for whole-class interaction. This *circle-time* area will enable you to share information and orchestrate class interactions in a relaxed and comfortable setting. The area can also provide space for partner activities.

A classroom set of first-grade math materials will ideally include sorting and counting sets, pattern blocks, and interlocking cubes (Unifix, Multilink, or Snap Cubes). Geo blocks and Cuisenaire rods are also versatile and useful. During the year, you will also want access to face (analog) clocks, rulers, plastic or real coins, and balance scales. Many schools have limited collections of math materials and expect that teachers will share them among classrooms. Sharing requires careful planning and coordination so that you have the necessary materials when you need them.

Reserve some wall space in order to display materials, like calendars, that you plan to use throughout the year. Also reserve wall space for attendance and lunch-count information. In addition, the calendar area is a good place to mount a 1–100 pocket chart that can be used throughout the year. As your students' math vocabulary develops throughout the year, keep a list of math words and ideas to remind children about relevant terms and symbols. Reserve some wall space—your class's "math wall"—for this list and for photos of student work, graphs, and other math products created by students throughout the school year. The children will begin to expect their work to appear in this designated area, and will take pride in seeing it displayed.

The room's layout should also reflect first graders' increasing independence and ability to follow directions. Easy accessibility of clearly marked materials will allow children to get what they need when they need it, and will encourage them to return the materials in an orderly way. Students will gain confidence when they realize they can consistently find needed materials in a predictable place. In your classroom, you may have some math materials—such as connecting cubes, counting sets, and pattern blocks—always out in the open and available to children, while others will be stored and brought out for occasional use. Organization is a key to success in either circumstance.

Planning Daily Instruction

Each day in the classroom should ideally include about sixty total minutes devoted to math. As you plan instruction for the upcoming year, think about the structure of your lessons. What math routines, such as calendar and warm-up activities, will you include on a daily basis? How will you balance the rest of instruction with whole-class discussions, partner work, and individual assignments? How can you draw on different types of experiences—such as building lessons on children's books, using particular manipulative materials, or drawing on classroom experiences—to pose problems?

Make class discussion part of your regular schedule. Through discussion and conversation, children hone their listening skills and learn to articulate their mathematical thinking. But avoid always scheduling class discussions for the end of the day's math session. Children are often better able to focus at the beginning of a lesson, so plan a variety of processing times to maximize these exchanges.

Helping Children Develop Number Sense

Children who have number sense make reasonable estimates, see the usefulness of numbers, and understand relationships among numerical quantities. Throughout the year, you'll introduce a wide range of contexts to help students expand their understandings about numbers and the interrelationships among them. Specifically, first graders focus on:

- counting objects with accuracy.
- grouping quantities (e.g., by 2s, 5s, and 10s).
- developing understandings of the relationships between amounts (greater than, less than, equal to).
- adding and subtracting quantities.

Children need opportunities to revisit these same ideas again and again by encountering mathematical situations and solving problems.

Keep in mind, however, that young children's ability to understand sophisticated ideas is complicated by limitations to their thinking. These constraints are normal aspects of human cognitive development. For example, young children need time to develop *conservation of number*. When a child conserves number, he or she realizes that amounts don't change just because the arrangement or position of the objects involved has changed. A child who does not conserve might think that there are more marbles when they are spread out than when they are packed closely together, or vice versa. If a child believes that the *number* of objects changes because the objects' positions have changed, he or she may struggle with other numerical understandings. For instance, if Mona does not conserve number, she may not understand that 5 + 1 represents the same total as 3 + 3.

You can support your students' development of conservation by offering contexts and problems that help them make sense of numbers, respecting the fact that maturation is a natural and predictable part of this process. Asking questions of, listening to, and carefully observing children while they work will help you select appropriate activities for them and challenge them without overwhelming them. Throughout this book, you'll find routines and activities that provide choices and varied levels of complexity. Use what you know about your students to design your specific plans.

Organizing Student Work: Math Folders and Notebooks

First graders are just beginning to develop the ability to put their ideas on paper. Every effort to communicate mathematical thinking in written and symbolic form is a step forward for these young learners. It's useful for each child to have a pocket folder labeled for math work that he or she uses to store papers.

You'll also find references to math notebooks throughout this book. These notebooks serve several purposes. Children use them to write and draw about math ideas as they're working to solve problems. They also use them to record new symbols they've learned. You can also provide materials that the students will tape into these books; for instance, trimmed copies of 1–100 charts and copies of math menu choices so they can keep track of their personal selections.

As the children record and organize their ideas, don't expect the resulting contents of their math notebooks to look orderly and polished. It may help, however, if each time children make a new entry, you specifically remind them to turn to the next blank page in their notebooks and put the date at the top of the page. The main purpose of the notebooks is to give children a personal and comfortable place to try out and record mathematical ideas.

Math notebooks can be simple spiral-bound notebooks labeled *Math*. You might write the word *Math* on some sticky labels ahead of time and have each child attach one on the front of his or her notebook. If spiral-bound or composition notebooks are not available, create notebooks using standard-sized notebook paper with construction-paper covers.

Integrating Assessment into Instruction

Teachers participate in countless spontaneous exchanges with their students. Listen carefully and observe the ways children are responding to problem-solving situations. The exchanges between your students and you shed constant light on young learners' abilities. In addition, regularly conduct specific assessments that gauge students' mathematical capacities; for example, finding out if they can sort with consistent criteria or count objects one at a time. You can use these same assessments to gauge students' comfort levels, strengths, and limitations, and to see how specific individuals respond when something doesn't make sense. You can also observe the ways in which children cope with their peers, with their own reactions to competition, or with uncertainties about their adequacy.

Moreover, you can use information about your students to extend their thinking and fuel their curiosity. It is a simple thing to take a few minutes now and then to discuss with an individual child what he or she has been working on or is thinking about. Listening carefully to responses and then asking further questions can provide powerful encouragement to students.

Of course, asking effective questions can prove more challenging than we might imagine. Good questions are often open ended; that is, they do not call for a "yes" or "no" response or a predetermined "answer." Open-ended questions require genuine interest in the child's response. As teachers, we often have an academic "destination" in mind, and it's easy to fall into the habit of listening for "the right answer." Try to resist this habit. Though it's important to introduce the concepts students will need to master math, each child travels a unique path to those understandings. Following a *learner's* train of thought can help you make thoughtful choices about lessons and activities.

Chapter 2

September

SORTING AND COUNTING

The Learning Environment

Whyen the first day of school finally arrives, expectations and apprehensions are running high for children, teachers, and parents alike. The first weeks of school stir up a unique blend of nervous excitement, countless details, and possibilities for the new academic year. As a teacher, you face the challenge of helping your students to feel welcomed and comfortable as you define expectations that will support a productive community of learners. During these first weeks, most of your time is devoted to establishing routines and procedures. This is when all of your preparations will really pay off. Keeping daily activities short and simple, and giving children time to practice procedures, will boost the children's sense of confidence and control. Take your time when introducing new routines and pay close attention to detail and to students' reactions. It's easy to introduce too many things at once, or to spend too much time on a topic and find that the children have lost their focus. ■

The Mathematics

Beginning the year with sorting and counting can be advantageous in a variety of ways. These activities convey important mathematical content and can shed light on how children approach the task of keeping track of quantities. Sorting activities for the month will include:

- identifying similarities and differences between objects.
- discriminating among attributes within a set of objects (like color and shape).
- developing awareness of part/whole relationships.
- making a one-to-one correspondence when counting.
- comparing quantities and accurately using the terms *more*, *same*, and *less*.

Counting and sorting materials can be quite varied and are often easily obtained. Select materials that can be sorted in at least two ways (e.g., by color and shape). Popular examples of sorting sets include small toy animals, decorative erasers, the lids from used markers, barrettes, small mosaic tiles, keys, shells, polished stones, plastic bread ties, jar lids, or baseball cards. Colorful and interesting, sorting sets engage children in the work of comparing, organizing, and arranging materials. During the first month of school, youngsters will sort, count, and organize these sets of objects on a regular basis. You can facilitate this their work by asking questions such as:

"Which ones go together? Which ones are alike in some way?"

"Which group has the most, and how many does it have?"

"Which group has the least, and how many does it have?"

"How many more do you have in this group than the other group?"

"Do any of the groups have the same amount?"

"If I give you a new piece, can you tell where it will go?"

"Can you put the pieces into groups in another way?"

As you watch the children work and listen to their conversations, you can learn a great deal about how they're thinking.

Encourage children to determine their own sorting criteria as they work. If you simply ask a student to put all of the same colored objects together, you won't be giving him or her an opportunity to use logical reasoning. Instead, you'll only discover whether the child knows his or her colors and is able to follow directions.

Setting the Stage

Class Meetings

As the school year begins, you'll want to establish order and develop a sense of community in the classroom. One way to do this is to schedule regular class meetings throughout the year, beginning with the first week of school. Class meetings can help you and your students get to know one another. They also encourage collective problem solving, provide a time for you to plan group activities, and give you an opportunity to explain new aspects of school routines. Finally, they can show children that school is a place not only for having fun but for getting work done. Early in the year, as you're establishing routines, you may want to meet as a class more frequently than later in the year.

What do you and your students discuss during class meetings? You'll want to talk with them about the classroom practices you're introducing, as well as help students identify distractions or behaviors that limit their ability to concentrate. But in order for class meetings to be productive, the children must learn to be respectful listeners and to take turns talking. Keep the meetings reasonable in length, and encourage everyone to participate. Typically, a few children will dominate discussions. Consider setting limits on the number of "talking turns" allowed for each individual during a class meeting. You may also wish to use an object, such as a cloth ball, that can be rolled from one speaker to another as the children take turns. Having something tangible to hold onto can help students clearly understand when it is their turn to be "the speaker." A round-robin approach (going around the circle) can also keep things fair.

Start class meetings on a fun, positive note that gets the children's attention. For instance, you might begin a meeting by initiating a clapping pattern, reading a short and lively poem, or leading a movement activity. Use an area of the room where children have space to sit comfortably on the floor. If possible, have everyone sit in a circle so each child can see the others. You might also have a prescribed seating arrangement, such as a boy-girl-boy-girl pattern. Mixing the genders in this way can encourage a respectful tone and attentive listening.

Class meetings enable you to take time to encourage the children to express their thoughts, ideas, concerns, or even fears about school. Once the children begin to build a sense of trust in you and the school setting, they will likely relax. Many children harbor apprehensions that only their family members know about. Look for issues that merit discussion right away—for instance, "What happens if I have trouble learning something?" or "What if I can't get someone to stop bothering me?" Once you and the children start talking about these sorts of concerns, fear or feelings of isolation will likely ease.

Class meetings also provide an opportunity for you to encourage the children to take risks. Remind them that their job is to make sense of their classroom experiences, not to simply mimic behaviors in the hope of getting the "right answer." Explain that you expect the children to work hard and learn, and that you will try to have them work on projects that are just right for their abilities. Invite the students to tell you when they feel that they are working out of their "just-right" range. This kind of exchange can be the prototype for goal-setting conversations you'll have with students throughout the year.

The First Class Meeting

During your first class meeting, mention some topics or units that your first graders will study during the year. You'll establish a sense of context and may tap into concerns that first grade will be "too hard" or "too easy." Also, briefly discuss routines and subjects that will come up every school day. Show the children an enlarged weekly schedule (see page 10 and Blackline Masters) and explain daily or weekly routines. Knowing that they will soon encounter familiar patterns helps children feel a greater sense of control over their lives. Assure your students that parents will also have the same information about the daily and weekly class schedule. (Parents will find it just as comforting as students to have the schedule readily available.) Finally, explain that the children will be getting into the habit of ending each day with some "daily news," and from that you'll decide on the contents of your weekly parent newsletter.

During this initial meeting, consider asking each child to share something that he or she particularly likes to do, or to cite favorite foods, animals, colors, places, etc. You might also ask the children to think about and then discuss what they would like to learn about during the school year. Use a piece of chart paper and list the students' responses. Put a star beside those topics that you'll introduce early in the school year, so the children can get a sense of what to expect. This is also a good opportunity to emphasize that people learn things at different times and in different ways. Ease concerns by assuring students that you expect and accept differences. By addressing the tension that many children feel during this early school experience, you'll help them be more involved and productive as the year unfolds.

Classroom Expectations and Rules

Your initial class meetings let you answer questions about what first grade will be like. They also enable you to establish expectations about behavior in the classroom. One way to start this process is to give the children an accessible assignment with clearly understandable directions. For example,

Weekly Planning Chart

Teacher's Name:	Date:	Curricular Focus or Unit of Study:

Math Priorities:

Monday	Tuesday	Wednesday	Thursday	Friday

Weekly Routines:

Needed Materials and Literature:

in the first or second week of school, invite them to draw a picture or write about something they experienced during these weeks in school (e.g., something they did at recess, something they had for lunch, etc.). During your next class meeting, ask the children to talk about what helped them to complete this assignment, and what made it more difficult for them to focus and get the work finished. Ask, "What is it that helps you work and play in ways that feel good?" Write down responses as children offer them.

If you notice that an important idea—such as "It's hard to work when someone's bothering you"—is not coming up, pose questions such as, "How do you feel when someone is bothering you as you try to work?" or "What can you do to solve the problem?" These questions—and the responses they generate—will steer the discussion toward the characteristics of a positive working climate.

Children seem to naturally think in terms of what *not* to do, and many of their comments may begin with "Don't": "Don't push" or "Don't yell." These sorts of statements don't necessarily help children envision the *right* things to do. For that reason, rephrase them in more positive terminology; for instance, "Keep your hands to yourself" or "Use your quiet voice."

Post the resulting list of classroom rules prominently in the room, and regularly refer to them during the next few days in class. Make a point of mentioning the rules when things are going well. After a week or so, ask the children whether the rules seem appropriate (lots of children will think the rules aren't useful), and encourage them to make any necessary modifications. Use their insights to create a final poster of the agreed-upon rules. Cluster and consolidate ideas to make the list as clear and concise as possible.

Here are some rules one group of first graders came up with:

"We listen to each other and to the teachers."

"We don't bother each other."

"We are nice and help each other."

"We walk instead of run when we're inside."

"We use polite words."

"We try to be quiet, because some of us don't like it too loud."

"We take care of our things and the school's things."

Once the rules poster is complete, each class member can sign his or her name to personalize the list. These student-generated rules will establish the classroom climate for the rest of the year. By defining their own rules, first graders develop their ability to listen to and care about one another. Include the list in a letter to parents, to show them what their children are achieving in school.

Daily Routines

Many routines in first-grade classrooms have emerged out of necessity. Most teachers begin each day with "opening activities" that include taking attendance, determining the lunch count, and tracking the days of the week and months of the year through a calendar. Opening activities provide a wealth of opportunities to explore numerical relationships, and first-grade teachers have a long history of taking advantage of these openings.

Classroom routines create a predictable and reassuring structure. Include them in your plans for each month. During these early weeks, while you're establishing routines, give children plenty of time to master them. You'll likely want to introduce additional—and more complex—routines as the year progresses. For that reason, each chapter in this book offers suggestions for new possibilities within each month.

Attendance and Lunch Count

Consider streamlining morning procedures and details by including your students in the process of taking attendance and managing lunch count. This is also a convenient way to discuss numbers. In addition, you might decide to visually display attendance results, depending on your personal preferences and the classroom's physical space. If you have magnetic chalkboards and name tags, it's fun and easy to display your attendance results or daily lunch count on the boards.

If you don't have magnetic name tags, creating them is quite manageable. Purchase a quantity of the standard small, rectangular name tags (one per student). Then place an adhesive magnet on the back of each tag, with the sticky side attached to the tag, and the magnetic side open to the chalkboard. The children will be able to move the tags around easily. Often you can get these adhesive magnets free from businesses that no longer need them. You can also obtain them from community groups that give out magnetic calendars to advertise their efforts. These calendars often include magnetic inserts that many recipients discard. Ask a friendly insurance or real-estate agent to set these aside for you.

Once you've created magnetic name tags and mounted them on a magnetic board, the children can group them in a variety of different arrangements based on the categories that make sense in your classroom. (See Figure 2–1.)

Lunch circumstances vary in elementary schools. Some lunch programs offer a variety of selections as well as give children the option of bringing

FIGURE 2–1 ▶

Magnetic name tags used to record the lunch count.

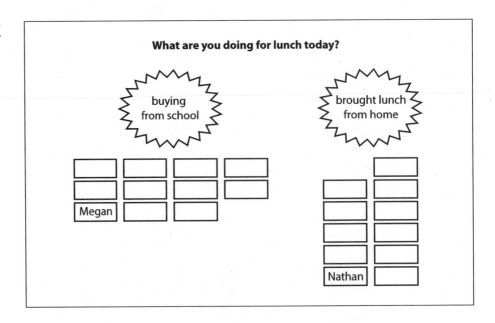

What are you doing for lunch today?

buying from school

brought lunch from home

Megan

Nathan

their lunches from home. Whether you are keeping track of attendance only, or using this routine to determine lunch orders, placing magnetic name tags beneath an identified category can help youngsters begin engaging in sorting and counting. Children can place name tags in groups of twos, threes, or fours. You can then discuss the concepts of even and odd numbers. Name tags can also be configured into rectangles or other shapes that are fun to learn about.

For the first few weeks of school, model the process of placing the name tags beneath the appropriate label on the board. Discuss the various ways you can count and combine the numbers of name tags. When a cluster of name tags is obviously even or odd, discuss this idea. Show the children how to arrange the name tags by twos, so they can easily see if there is an extra name tag left over that would make the total number odd. Mention the number concepts of *more*, *less*, or *same*. Begin asking questions such as, "Which group of name tags has the fewest number?" or "How many more name tags are there in the larger group?" Share strategies for determining the answers to such questions.

Before long, the children will grow comfortable using these same kinds of strategies and will be able to determine the lunch count with minimal support. They'll begin grouping the name tags and counting them in increasingly efficient ways, such as by twos or by tens. After a few weeks, the routine of taking attendance or lunch count can become a "class job"—a task for which a different student takes responsibility every day. Continue to have a daily group discussion about this routine, so the children can observe and listen to one another as they count by twos and combine numbers in various ways.

If magnetic name tags won't work for you, another alternative is to use clothesline rope or thick yarn and clothespins. Write each child's name on both sides of the squeeze end of a clothespin. Write the names so that they'll all read in the same direction when clipped to a length of string or yarn, no matter which way the clothespin is facing. Hang a length of string or yarn for each category you're interested in, and have the children clip their clothespins on the appropriate string. (See Figure 2–2 on the following page.) You can also attach clothespins to laminated construction paper.

Any of these methods will provide a daily opportunity for children to compare and combine quantities as they obtain needed information in a real-life context.

Calendar

Most first-grade classrooms include a calendar display. There are many rich possibilities for calendar work, and calendar activities have been popular for years. These activities introduce the notion that there are patterns to the days of the week and the months of the year. For example, Monday

FIGURE 2–2 ▶

Strings and clothespins used to record attendance.

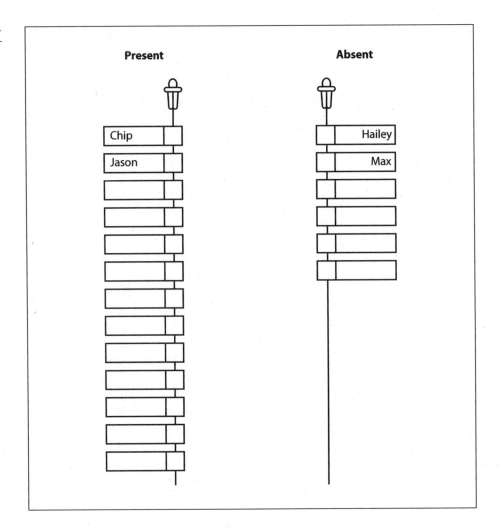

Present   Absent

Chip   Hailey
Jason   Max

rolls around once a week, and there are about four weeks in every month. Children also gain experience with counting numbers in a relatively manageable range (1 through 31). Yet many first graders find weekly and monthly patterns complex and challenging. For that reason, resist any urge to use calendars in which the squares are adorned with complex patterns. Children will more likely focus on the days and weeks if your calendar has plain squares with just the days-of-the-month numbers in them.

Celebrating the 100th day of school has become something of a tradition for many primary classrooms; many teachers include it as an extension of calendar activities. On their first day in the classroom, students begin to keep track of how many days they have been in school. There are several engaging ways to do this:

- Use a counter, such as straws that can be bundled or colored links that can be placed in a chain in groups of ten.

- Add a penny per day to your count. Trade for different coins as needed; for example, when you've compiled five pennies, convert them into a nickel. You can buy commercially made charts perfect for placement of the coins, or you can place the coins in small plastic bags labeled with an enlarged picture of the coins within.

- Add a number each day to a 1–100 pocket chart.

As with the other routines, model these new procedures for your students. Gradually, individual students will feel ready to take on calendar duties as their "class jobs." Encourage children to share these responsibilities with a partner. Calendar activities entail tracking a lot of information, and the resulting discussions between partners can shed valuable light on your students' understandings.

Estimation Jars

Starting the year with an estimation routine can help set the tone for risk-taking during math activities. First graders often have difficulty believing that a good guess, even if it is not an exact answer, is OK. Many children have a deep and generalized fear of being wrong. Helping your students feel safe while expressing their best thinking can have powerful implications for their learning.

You might begin an estimation routine during the first week of school by placing a small, plastic jar in an accessible location in the room. Place just a few objects in the jar; for example, maybe five or ten large gumballs. Tape the jar closed. On a piece of paper, write "How many gumballs do you think are in the jar?" Attach the paper to a clipboard, then place the clipboard next to the jar. Leave a pen nearby. Sooner or later, someone will read and respond to the question. If no one does, you can ask students to do so and jot down a guess or two to get things started. Since the numbers are small and the gumballs are big, chances are that the children will be able to count the jar's contents easily this first time. Their success will give the confidence to take on more challenging estimates.

Sometime during the second week, bring the jar and the clipboard over to the circle area and ask the children what they've noticed about the estimates. Responses may include:

"I know there are seven because I counted."

"Can we eat them?!"

"I think there are six because I'm six."

"I counted too, and I think there are six."

Listen to the children's ideas and ask if anyone can come up with an obviously ridiculous guess. For instance, say, "Is there a number of gumballs that could definitely *not* be in the jar?" Someone may call out, "A million!" Next ask if it is possible that there is only one gumball in the jar. The students will say "No," because they can clearly see that there are more than one. Continue suggesting numbers such as 25, 2, 15, and 3—being sure to include a figure that's fairly close to the actual number in the jar. Explain that it's OK to make a close guess—that estimating is an important mathematical skill and is not really about coming up with the exact answer. Then remove the gumballs and do an exact count. Put the gumballs back in the jar, affix a label telling the number of gumballs in the jar, and set the jar aside for now.

During estimation discussions, use the word *estimate* interchangeably with *guess*. Remind the children that when they make this sort of guess, they will not be expected to get exact answers. The goal is to try to get close and to not make obviously unrealistic estimates.

Tell the children that estimation jars and activities will always be in the same place in the classroom, and to watch that location for a new jar to appear. Sometime in the next couple of days, get another jar that looks just like the first one, and increase the number of gumballs in it. Or, fill the new jar to the same level you did in the first jar, but use marbles instead of gumballs. If possible, present the original jar with its gumball amount, so the children can use it as a comparison in making their next guesses. Place a fresh piece of paper on the clipboard and write a question like, "We know there were five gumballs in the first jar. How many gumballs (or marbles) do you guess now?" Encourage the children to discuss the numbers and to write only reasonable guesses on the clipboard. If more than one person has the same guess, place a checkmark next to that number.

Eventually, you can assign children to take turns managing the daily class job of counting the estimation jar's contents. At the end of the week, the children who counted can report their results to the class during the day's opening activities. If there is any uncertainty or disagreement about a final count, the class can participate in finding a solution. Once the numbers begin to get larger, partners can work together to determine the daily count. This routine will continue to evolve during the year and is featured in the monthly-routine sections of upcoming chapters.

Graphs

Creating graphs or charts is one way to weave mathematical thinking into routines. A graph is a visual, mathematical way to organize and represent information. Different graphs can take different forms. For instance, young children benefit from using real, tangible objects that can be counted and compared. They can also use pictures to represent objects and later will use numbers and symbols to represent ideas. Graphing experiences give children opportunities to use numerical data and can reveal students' latest thoughts and concerns. For instance, on the first day of school, many classes create graphs showing where each child is headed after school. For any first-grader teacher, there is little worse than the fear that a child is unclear about his or her after-school destination. This graph enables you to determine and discuss who will ride which bus, who gets picked up and by whom, or who will be going to a day-care program. Graphing after-school plans is a time-honored activity for the first day of school.

As they create and discuss graphs, children build their mathematical vocabulary and understanding. Words like *more*, *same*, *less*, *column*, and *row* become natural descriptors of what the children notice when looking at graphing results. As you model the use of this language, you encourage your students to articulate their own mathematical thinking.

Offering a variety of graphing experiences on a regular basis will help the children feel more comfortable with interpreting data from graphs and charts. Whenever possible, encourage children to use actual objects—such as sorting sets that are organized by color or shoes organized by whether or not they have laces. These tangible experiences allow children to make sense of graphing with real life connections before we ask them to think in abstractions. Children need to begin counting and comparing amounts with objects they can see and touch. As the graphs become increasingly symbolic, you can use pictures instead to represent ideas and relationships.

Some graphing possibilities for September include:

- today's weather (rainy, sunny, cool, warm).
- ways children will get home (on the bus, walking, getting picked up).
- children's favorite toys from home (teddy bears, bikes, balls).
- the number of letters in students' first names and whether the count is even or odd.

Creating a graph with your class provides remarkably rich learning experiences. Students' responses to and observations about a particular graph can vary widely. For instance, if you're graphing shoes, one child may use counting by ones to determine how many have laces, while another may group quantities of two and compare the graph's categories.

Whole-Group Activities

Your first order of business during first-grade math class will be to develop procedures for children to select, obtain, and work with materials. Begin by providing each child with his or her own sorting and counting sets. That way, students will begin taking responsibility for managing materials and working quietly. During these first weeks, also regularly schedule individual-work time so you can define expectations relating to the use of materials. Individual work encourages one-on-one interactions between your students and you. Through these exchanges, you can glean valuable information about how students count and use language to compare quantities. As the month progresses, your weekly schedule can also include partner and large-group problem-solving situations; for example, two students could sort a set of buttons together or your whole class could participate in making a human graph to show what kind of shoes people are wearing, for example, shoes with laces and shoes without laces.

Thoughts About Math

On the first day of school, gather the students together. Explain that during part of each day, they'll be working on math. Ask them to generate some ideas about the word *math*. Responses might include: some misconceptions about the actual word—children may think it is the word *map*. Often, they volunteer ideas involving counting and numbers. Write the children's thoughts on a piece of chart paper, including numbers, symbols, or pictures that help represent their thinking. As the children work to define the topic of mathematics, you may wish to introduce symbols for ideas such as addition and subtraction. You might also want to mention topics like shapes and measurement. Discuss places that children see math in the world around them. For example, where do they see numbers and shapes in their homes or from the car or the bus? You can send a letter home to parents, to involve families in this activity.

School-Supply Sorting

On Day 1 in school, the children arrive laden with all sorts of exciting supplies. Organizing this initial onslaught of supplies can be a big job in a first-grade classroom. In many classrooms, some items will become "community supplies," while others will be kept in individual desks or cubbies. To ensure a smoothly running classroom, decide which is which, then communicate these decisions to the children. The following list can be used as a guide.

1. After the children have settled in on the first day of school, explain that the initial order of business is to organize all of the new school supplies. Have some extras on hand so you can distribute needed items to individuals who may require essentials. Position signs around the room explaining where the items are to be stored, and demonstrate how materials should be placed next to the signs when they're not in use.

2. Ask the children to bring their backpacks to their desks or tables and remove the supplies they've brought. Anything that is *not* being collected for community use can be placed on top of children's desks or on a tabletop.

3. Collect community supply items.

4. Ask students to think about how their remaining materials could be sorted. Ideas might include "paper versus not paper," "in a box versus not in a box," "things you can make marks with," or "things I like the most."

5. Play a guessing game using attributes of the community-use objects. Have the children listen as you give some clues; for example, "I'm thinking of something that usually has some metal in it, and there are two holes for your fingers. What is it?" Then place a child's scissors in his or her desk. Or say, "I'm thinking of something that is shaped like a tube and you color with it." Then put a youngster's markers or crayons in his or her desk. Have all the students follow your lead, putting their own materials in their desks as the game progresses.

6. After all the materials have been stowed away, ask the children to think about their favorite school supply. List their responses. Later that day or sometime in the next few days, have the children draw a picture of their favorite school supply. Use the pictures to make a graph for display in the classroom. Ask the children to explain what the graph shows. Responses might include "The graph shows our favorite school supplies," and "It shows which things we like the most." Take notes as the children talk.

7. When you have a few minutes, list the children's responses in large print and place the list next to the graph. Read the list to the children. Mention that graphs provide information, so it's a good idea to get in the habit of discussing what we find out from a graph.

8. Discuss any observations that involved comparing amounts or identifying quantities—e.g., "More people like their paints than any other supply," "The same number of people picked folders as markers," or "Four people like their pencils the best." Using a different color marker, write *M* next to these math-related statements. Introduce the phrase *true math statement* and use it during all discussions of graphs and other mathematical observations.

Care of Class Materials

Show the children several sorting sets—for example, the buttons used in *The Button Game* (see page 22) or the beans used in *Shake and Spill* (see page 137). Select one set of objects and explain that even though the materials are fun to feel and use, there is a difference between using the objects to work on math ideas and playing with them.

Take the objects out of one set and carefully place them on the floor in front of you. Ask the children what would have happened if you had held the bag up high and shaken it hard. Explain the importance of using materials responsibly. Talk about and show various sets of objects. Discuss where you got the objects, and show the children that there are plenty of sets for everyone. Tell the children that you want these materials to stay in good shape so that everyone can have opportunities to work with them. Ask if anyone has a friend who is now in kindergarten—then point out that taking good care of the materials will enable next year's first graders to enjoy them.

Next explain that you're going to ask some questions. When the answer to a question is "Yes," the children are to give you a thumbs-up signal. When the answer is "No," they will show thumbs down. Ask a few practice questions, such as:

"Are you a first grader?"
"Do we have lunch every day?"
"Do we get to ride real helicopters at recess?"
"Is there an elephant in our classroom?"

When students have mastered the thumbs-up/thumbs-down signaling system, begin asking questions about care of counting and sorting materials. For instance:

"Is it OK to count the objects in the set?"
"Is it OK to eat the objects?"
"Should materials ever be put in your mouth, nose, or ears?" [If you get a mixed response to this one, take the time clarify the rules!]

Steer the questions toward more subtle but distinct differences between work and play. You can also role-play appropriate activities with the objects, such as putting them into groups, organizing them to make a one-to-one correspondence, counting them, or regrouping them. Contrast these behaviors with demonstrations of inappropriate behaviors, such as zooming an object around in the air while making loud buzzing sounds, piling the objects up and sitting on them, or blowing air into a plastic bag. Mix these examples to increase the level of interest and challenge. At the same time, keep the exchange playful. You'll help students begin to distinguish between work and play. At the end of the discussion, zip up all sorting-set bags, with the objects securely inside, and remind the children to check the tightness of the seal.

Individual Practice with Class Materials

Once you've introduced the materials and students have practiced using them responsibly, the stage is set for productive and independent work time.

During the next scheduled individual math work, invite each child to select a set of counting or sorting objects. As children make their choices, have them look around the room and find a spot with enough space so their things won't get mixed up with a classmate's. Explain that this will be a short work session that will help the students get used to this routine. Keep these first sessions to about ten minutes, to ensure success with the routine and to interest the children in spending more time with the materials during future math sessions.

Let the children know that when they choose a set of materials, they will need to keep the same set of objects for the whole math time. Tell them that the next time, they can choose a different set. Call a few children at a time to make their selections and find quiet workspaces in the room. Once all of the children are settled and have had just enough time to look over their materials, quietly ask them to clean up and carefully return their sets to their designated place. In the beginning of the year especially, you may wish to walk around the room and dismiss children from math time individually as you check returned materials and control traffic.

Then invite each child to tell what set he or she worked with and to share observations about his or her materials. Such sharing encourages children to learn about the variety of materials and to begin digesting math concepts. When children mention mathematical terms such as *more* and *less*, emphasize these ideas by writing them on a *Math Words* poster. Keep this poster on display and add to it throughout the year. Displaying mathematical vocabulary and symbols calls attention to key concepts and encourages the children to use this language.

Over the next few weeks, include this individual work time with sorting sets on a regular basis; i.e., two or three times a week. Gradually extend the period of time that the class is expected to work with the sorting sets to about thirty minutes per session. Use the interest level of the children to gauge how much time to spend each day. Maintain firm expectations of responsible, independent work behavior. Because the children have their own sets of materials, you can reasonably expect them to work silently and to concentrate on their own thinking.

As the weeks unfold, use a record-keeping device—a page for each child, sticky notes, labels, graphic organizers, teacher journal, photos, class composite sheets—to keep track of:

- how far children are able to count independently.
- how they keep track of quantities. (Does the child move the objects as he or she counts them?)
- whether the objects are put into groups based on a consistent criteria.
- whether the child regroups the objects using a second criteria.
- whether the child accurately uses comparison words such as *more*, *same amount*, and *less*.

The Button Game

This lesson introduces students to the notions of *same* and *different*.

Materials

- 30 buttons
- 1 zip-top plastic bag
- 1 plate large enough to display the buttons
- *The Button Box* by Margarette Reid or *Frog and Toad Are Friends* by Arnold Lobel

Instructions

1. Before the lesson, place the buttons in the zip-top bag.

2. Invite the children to join you in the circle area. Read either *The Button Box* by Margarette Reid or the story "The Lost Button" from *Frog and Toad Are Friends* by Arnold Lobel.

3. After reading the story, ask if anyone has some buttons on his or her clothing today. Invite a few children to show their buttons. Encourage the class to discuss the colors, shapes, number of holes, and other attributes of these buttons. Observe that all of these buttons are alike in some ways and different in others.

4. Pour your bag of buttons onto a plate so that everyone can easily see them. Hold up a button and discuss the article of clothing that it might have been attached to.

5. Repeat Step 4 with a couple of other buttons, calling attention to ways in which the buttons are alike and different.

6. Put all the buttons back on the plate, then walk around the circle, asking each child to select a button and place it on the floor in front of him or her.

7. Take a button for yourself and sit down with the children again.

8. Place your button next to that of the child who is sitting to your left or right. Tell the class that you and your partner are going to find one thing about your buttons that is alike and one thing that is different.

9. Ask your partner what he or she notices about the two buttons. Use the responses to identify an attribute that is the same for both buttons, then discuss a way that the buttons are different. (For example, perhaps they are the same because they are both white, and they are different because one is bigger than the other.)

10. Pair each child with a partner and have them spend a few minutes comparing their buttons. Then have the children take turns

sharing their comparisons. On chart paper, keep track of the comparisons.

11. When the students have all shared their comparisons using the language of *same* and *different*, tell them you're going to use their ideas to think about ways to sort the buttons.

12. Ask the children to hold their buttons in the palms of their hands. Explain that you are going to repeat some of the ideas that people have shared. If the sorting idea is true for a particular child's button, that child should place his or her button on the floor in front of him or her.

13. Call out some of the sorting criteria that the students cited when working with partners—for example, round buttons, buttons with two holes, white buttons, etc. As the children begin laying down their buttons, start using comparison words such as *most*, *more*, and *fewer*. For example, "Most of the buttons are round" or "There are fewer buttons with four holes than two holes."

14. Explain to the children that the button set will be available every day during math time, as will many other interesting objects. Remind the children that they sort the buttons by what they have in common, such as color and shape. Mention that these sorting ideas will work for lots of other objects as well.

15. Replace the buttons in the bag while discussing with the children the importance of checking that the bag is secure. Show the children where this and other sorting sets will be kept.

The Name Game

The Name Game helps to create a sense of community and encourages children to build their sorting and comparison vocabulary. First graders generally feel comfortable reading, writing, and recognizing their first names, so using the names is a great way to start the year.

Materials

- 1 sheet of 4 different colors of construction paper
- several different color markers
- 1 scissors
- 1 container for storing completed name tags

Instructions

1. Make a class set of name tags by cutting 3-by-6-inch rectangles out of the four different colors of construction paper. Write each child's

first name on a name tag in large print. The children will be using the tags to get to know one another and to focus on sorting attributes (such as color of the name tag). If you would like to increase the number of ways that the children can sort the name tags, incorporate additional attributes. For example, write half of the names in red, and the other half in blue or black. You could also write some of the names using all capital letters. Include as many or as few sorting possibilities as you wish.

2. Designate a container for storing the completed name tags. You can retrieve the tags whenever you like, to create groups or determine partners for students. You might decide to have children with the same color name tags—or different color ones—to work together. The name-tag container can be helpful for substitute teachers as well.

3. To start the game, explain that different people in the class have names that are alike in some ways. Use an example of two or three children whose first names start with the same letter.

4. Then pick another attribute for sorting names. But don't tell students what it is. Instead, just tell them the names. Ask the children to guess what attribute you were thinking of.

5. Next practice clapping out the syllables of various first names in the class. Ask the children for examples of names that have the same number of claps.

6. Show the children the name tags you have prepared, and ask them if they notice anything right away that is alike or different about the tags. Discuss the varied colors of the name tags.

7. Distribute the name tags. Then ask the children who have, say, red tags to do something like clap, and ask the group with yellow tags to wave to you, and so on—until all four color groups have been identified. Explain that the name tags' different colors make them easy to sort.

8. Remind the children of the other ways they noticed class members' names were alike and different. Ask them if they can think of additional possibilities now, such as number of letters in several names, or same last letter, double letters, etc.

9. Invite the children to compare their name tags with that of the person sitting next to them. What similarities and differences do they notice? If words like *same* and *different* are not already on your *Math Words* poster, mention these ideas and write them down.

   If students have trouble responding, ask if any two partners had the same first letter in their names or the same number of letters in their names. After the children have discussed possible similarities, ask them to move around the room and find two people who have name tags with some attribute similar to theirs. Walk around the room and assist children while you observe and listen to the conversations.

Extensions

Have students create "people" graphs by physically gathering in groups based on a name-tag attribute. For instance, all of the children with the same color name tags could form lines, or children with the same number of letters in their first names could form groups. The children could then represent their sorting on graphs.

People graphs reinforce children's sorting, comparing, and counting skills. Take advantage of the opportunity these graphs provide to add new terms to the *Math Words* poster. After the children have played the game several times and used various attributes, have them make their own new paper name tags and use them on a graph that shows the number of letters in their names. (See Figure 2–3.) Display the graph, and discuss what the children notice about it. Record their ideas and post them next to the graph.

Guess My Rule

Guess My Rule is a versatile game of logical reasoning that your class can play in various ways throughout the year. The game further develops children's understanding of mathematical concepts and counting and sorting

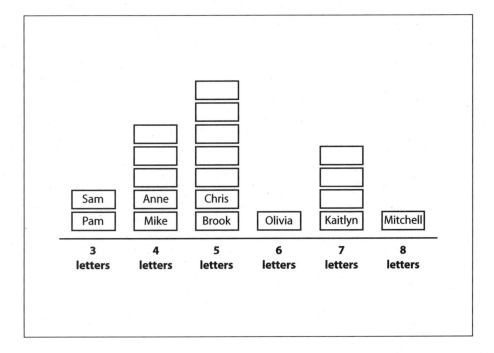

FIGURE 2–3 ◄

How many letters are in your name?

vocabulary. In the version described below, children move to the front of the room to create groups based on a criteria known only to the person who initiates the game. In the beginning, you'll determine the sorting criteria. But once students become familiar with the game, they define the criteria and eventually lead the game independently.

Materials

- Optional: *Bein' with You This Way* by W. Nikola-Lisa

Instructions

1. If you would like to spark discussion of the various ways that people are alike and different, consider using the rhythmic chants provided in the book *Bein' with You This Way* by W. Nikola-Lisa. The children can clap along to the cadence of the text.

2. After reading the story, tell students they're going to play a game called *Guess My Rule*. Begin the game by looking carefully at the children and selecting a sorting rule that enables you to categorize them into two groups. Choose obvious criteria, such as "boys" and "girls." But don't tell students what your rule is.

3. Place a chair in the center of the room at the front of the classroom. Then begin inviting class members to come and stand on one side of the chair or the other based on your sorting rule. Tell the children that as soon as they think they know what the rule is, they should raise their hands and ask you if a particular person who is still sitting can go and stand on one side of the chair or the other. Explain that there is a reason for this system: It keeps the game going so everyone can be thinking about, and trying to guess, the rule.

    Of course, after you've called some children up to the front of the room and asked them to stand in the appropriate place, some students will be ready to test their hypothesis about the rule. Once someone raises his or her hand, guide that student through the process of asking a question like, "Can Anna go over there?" Answer "Yes" or "No, she needs to go on the other side."

Eventually, most of the class will be standing up in front of the classroom. At this point, children may tell one another what they think the rule might be. Play the game enough times so that each child has had a turn to come up to the front at some point during the first few games.

As the children come up to the front of the room, draw attention to the mathematical relationships that you see developing. Highlight amount comparisons involving more-same-fewer, plus one, minus one, how many more, addition and subtraction of the two groups, concepts of even and odd, and ideas of equality between the two sides. As the year progresses, the sorting criteria and the mathematical lessons become more sophisticated. For instance, children will begin choosing subtle criteria such as "collars/no collars" or "designs on clothes/no designs on clothes."

Literature-Based Activities

A number of books lend themselves to counting and sorting activities. The following selections are just a few examples from the many possibilities. Once you begin thinking about books that have a mathematical twist, you'll likely identify additional possibilities and favorites.

Exploring the Word *Math*

If you're interested in using a book to further explore the word *math*, Sara Atherlay's *Math in the Bath* provides relevant connections to daily life experiences and makes math ideas less abstract. The book offers familiar contexts for numbers, shapes, patterns, comparisons, sorting, and part/whole relationships. After reading the book to your class, ask students to think of any new math ideas that should be added to the *Math Words* poster.

Sorting Hats

Margaret Miller uses photography to create interesting sorting challenges for young readers. Her book *Whose Hat?* shows large photographs of a variety of hats, and asks readers to guess who the hats belong to. The answer is revealed on the following page and initiates a discussion about things that belong together.

Sorting Familiar Objects

Another book by Margaret Miller, *Where Does It Go?*, uses humorous pictures and familiar objects to create a playful guessing game about where familiar things belong. When you have a few extra minutes in your schedule, invite your first graders to play a quick guessing game that relates to the book's ideas about things that belong together. You can say the name of a location—for instance, a refrigerator—and ask children to name things that belong in that place.

Use a similar grouping idea, and pick a familiar category, to play a written form of *Guess My Rule*. Draw a large circle on the board, select a category, and write things that belong in that category *inside* the circle. Things that don't belong in that category go *outside* the circle. For instance, if you pick the categories "foods" and "not foods," you can write *pizza*, *bread*, *apples*, and *popcorn* inside the circle and write *car*, *books*, *light bulb*, and *crayons* outside the circle. The children can extend the groupings by making guesses and determining whether their guesses belong inside or outside the circle.

The Important Thing

The Important Book, by Margaret Wise Brown, describes common objects and lists their attributes. The beginning and ending of each description states the most important aspect of that object. For example, the patterned text begins with "The important thing about (an apple) is that it's round." After listing a variety of the objects attributes, each page ends with the sentence: "But the important thing about _____ is _____."

You can easily adapt this pattern for any other objects. For instance, select the word *hat*, and list various things that a hat can do; e.g., "keep people warm," "look pretty," "keep the sun out of your eyes." But the important thing about a hat is that "you wear it on your head." Create a list of simple, everyday objects, such as a pencil, a bed, a book. Invite students to describe the objects and then list their attributes. Once they're familiar and comfortable with the game, the children can create and illustrate a class book using "The Important Thing" pattern.

Another possibility is to have children use this idea to describe themselves. You might initiate the shift from object to people by using a char-

The important thing about _____ is _____. She _____ and _____. **But the important thing about** _____ Is that she _____.	**The important thing about** _____ is _____. He _____ and _____. **But the important thing about** _____ Is that he _____.

acter that is familiar to the children (such as Franklin or Amelia Bedelia). For example, if you chose the character Amelia Bedelia, you might write: "The important thing about Amelia Bedelia is that she is funny. She works hard, she is nice, and she gets confused. But the important thing about Amelia Bedelia is that she is funny." You can also use yourself as an example. For instance, I could say: "The important thing about Mrs. B. is that she enjoys children. She likes to read, she lives in the country, and she loves roses. But the important thing about Mrs. B. is that she enjoys children."

Ask each child to consider three true statements about himself or herself and then decide which one is the most important. Help the children write their ideas and leave plenty of room for a picture. You can have the children create self-portraits, or you can provide a photo to be glued on each child's page. When the pages are complete, compile them into a class book, or place them on the children's desks as a welcome for parents during Back to School Night.

Understanding Number Meaning

From One to One Hundred, by Terri Sloat, is a picture book that helps children develop understandings about the quantities that numbers represent. Elaborate themes illustrate each page. The numbers progress by 1s through the number 10. From 10 to 100, the increase leaps forward by 10s. A key is provided at the bottom of each page so readers know which items have been included on each page. Readers search for the number of items corresponding to the number written on that particular page.

During the first viewing of the book, ask students to identify the theme for each page. Look carefully at the pictures and talk about why the things on the page belong together. Discuss why the author might have decided to include various items on a particular page. Because the illustrations are quite detailed and need to be counted, encourage children to look through the book individually and personally verify the numbers of items in various pictures.

Once students are familiar with the book, introduce the idea of making a class number book that involves themes. Explain that thinking about themes is a way to do some sorting in your mind. You might begin by asking the children to think about a place they particularly enjoy. Have the children talk about favorite places in their neighborhoods, and things that they like to do there. Make a list of potentially relevant theme ideas, such as "a toy store," "outer space," "a park," "a garden," "an amusement park," "a campground," or "a playground." Over the next few days, generate ideas about what kinds of things that you might expect to find in these different places.

You can also play the draw-a-circle-on-the-chalkboard form of *Guess My Rule* (as described in *Where Does It Go?*) to help children think of things that are included within a particular category. For instance, if you were working on ideas for a playground, you could include *swings, a slide, trees*, and *children* inside the circle. *Refrigerator*, *plane*, and *stars* could go outside the circle.

Soon children will be contributing their own ideas, and your list will offer lots of possibilities for the theme pictures. Jot down the ideas inside the *Guess My Rule* circles so you can refer to them over time. This project can be done over a period of weeks, so ideas can accumulate gradually. Once the class has played *Guess My Rule* and generated sorting ideas for about six to ten themes, partners can begin creating the pictures.

Children can sign up for favored themes. If more than one picture is created for a particular topic, you can be sure the illustrations will be unique. After you've assigned the theme topics to partners, determine and control the numbers assigned for illustrations. You've observed your students while they worked with the sorting and counting sets, so you know which children can keep track of larger quantities and which will experience success with smaller numbers.

Write the assignments on a list that can be posted in the classroom. This list will remind children of the theme, the number, and their partner. Before you pass the paper out, give the children time to practice drawing some of the items they will want to include in their pictures. Then ask them to draw their illustrations with pencil first, and use crayons or markers to color them when they are satisfied that they have accurate quantities. Provide partners with a large sheet of white construction paper. (Draw a line two inches from the bottom of each horizontal page, so the children can see where they will draw pictures for their key.)

After the first drawing session, ask the children to explain how they kept track of the number of items drawn in their pictures. As you can imagine, different children will finish their products at different times. Class experts can assist others or create additional pages for the book.

You can also use Scholastic's *I Spy* book to inspire this same type of project.

Chapter 3

October

PATTERNS AND NUMBER SENSE

The Learning Environment

Last month's counting and sorting experiences will help children move on to deeper understandings. In October, math topics include patterns, number sense, and symmetry. In some parts of the country, first-grade classes study the life cycle of butterflies or seasonal changes that occur at this time of year. Such activities can help children see connections between basic math concepts and the real world of nature. ■

Routines

One of the nice things about routines is that once they are in place, they don't require much additional planning or preparation. Here's how to follow up the routines you established in September:

Attendance

This routine can remain virtually unchanged as you move into October. Keep including the "lunch count" in this class job, so each child has a chance to report the numbers—and so *you* can see how students are doing their counting. This quick, easy routine provides a natural opportunity to use vocabulary such as *most*, *fewest*, and *twice as many*. As students give you the lunch count, you might ask a question like, "How did you decide to count?" Responses may range from, "I just counted" to "I counted by twos" or "I did the ones in this row first." Perhaps the child used a counting-on strategy; for example, "I could see that there were four nametags together when I was counting the regular lunches, so then I just kept counting five, six, seven, eight, nine. Nine children need to order a regular lunch." Now that the children are comfortable with this routine, they may be counting in increasingly efficient ways. The attendance and lunch-count routines not only reveal how individual students are thinking about the quantities, but they also give children a chance to see and hear a variety of ways to approach these tasks.

Calendar

In the interest of time, you may wish to feature particular aspects of a daily calendar routine in any given month. Here are examples of the many possibilities for calendar activities:

- Use a colorful or sparkly marker (such as a small, fancy bow) on your calendar display. Have the children move the marker each day and locate the current day and date on the calendar.
- Chant the days of the week or use songs to help the children learn the names and order of the days. (Check out Charlotte Diamond's CD *Diamond in the Rough*, "The Days of the Week," or the Dr. Jean and Friends CD, *Days of the Week*.
- Use a 1–100 pocket chart whose pockets are empty, and add a number card for each day you're in school.
- Place colored transparent squares over particular numbers on a number chart to accentuate patterns (for example, even/odd, or counting by 5s).

- Add a penny for each new day, and convert them to appropriate coins.

- Gather a straw with each new day and bundle them in 10s with a rubber band. Display the bundles so students can easily see them.

- Connect colored plastic links each day and change to a new color every time you get to ten.

- Use a smaller conventional calendar for the children to note special days, or draw a picture of the day's weather conditions (which you can graph at the end of the month).

Estimation Jar

As the school year continues, counting remains a valuable way for first graders to make sense of quantities and see relationships between numbers. The estimation jar gives children lots of opportunities to count. It also requires them to use what they know and make predictions. Here are a few ideas to spice up this routine so the children remain engaged:

- Put particularly interesting items—such as polished stones, toy dinosaurs, or plastic charms—in the jar.

- Ask the children to check the actual count with a partner and record their findings in a secret place in their math notebooks. They can do this recording quietly and quickly in a special area of the room or in the hallway during opening activities.

- Begin recording the estimation-jar guesses on the chalkboard at the beginning of each week, and list the guesses in order by amount. Leave gaps for missing numbers. Last month, you invited children to write their guesses on a clipboard placed next to the estimation jar. This month, you can transfer the ordered list of guesses from the chalkboard onto the clipboard and place it next to the jar. This will give the children time to review the estimates, view the jar's contents, and perhaps revise their thinking.

- Provide two estimation jars that are the same size but hold different contents.

- Provide two jars of different sizes with the same number of objects inside.

At the end of each week, take time to discuss the predictions and actual counts that the children made during the week. Go through the exercise of counting the jar's objects with the whole class. There are many ways to approach this final counting process. Here are some ideas:

- Have the children who have counted the contents of the jar during the week make a report of their findings.

- Use the overhead projector to count, so you can organize the jar's contents on a ten-frame transparency. (See more on ten-frame transparencies on page 85.)
- Encourage continued estimation by counting half of the jar and asking the children to reconsider their original predictions.

No matter how you choose to count the objects, this is another good time to talk with your class about what it means to make a prediction. Children get so caught up in getting the "right" answer that estimation can easily become a competition or a quest to "win" by guessing the exact number of objects in the jar. The problem is that when we see estimation jars in real life—for example, in a business contest—it's often only the exact guess that wins the prize. Remind students that the point of the estimation-jar exercise is to use what you know to make a reasonable guess. Describe some real-life circumstances in which you, as an adult, use estimation rather than try to arrive at an actual number. For instance, if you are feeding coins into a parking meter, you may not know exactly how long you'll need the parking space—and therefore how much money you should put into the meter. Or, if you are bringing popcorn into school for your class, you want to be sure you have enough, but you don't need to know exactly how many kernels of popcorn to bring in.

Math Notebooks

As you saw in Chapter 2, students can use a simple spiral notebook labeled *Math* to record their understanding of numbers, patterns, operations, geometry, or any other mathematical ideas they learn about in class. They can practice writing symbols and extending their thinking in their notebooks as you discuss various topics in class. The notebooks provide a place for children to get in the habit of keeping track of ideas on paper.

For the first month or so, encourage the children to turn to the next blank page each time they write something new in their notebooks, and to put the date at the top of the page. These things seem obvious, but you can't assume that young learners will be attuned to practical details. By helping children to organize their work in these ways, you'll ensure that the math notebooks will remain useful tools for the children and you.

The 1–100 Chart

You're probably already using the 1–100 pocket chart to help students track the number of days they've been in school—with the major goal of marking that all-important Day 100. Consider placing *all* of the cards for the numbers 1–100 in the chart. Most of the time, the only numbers that will face forward and reveal a numeral will be those indicating how many days have passed in the school year. The other cards will show only their blank sides. But by putting all the cards in the pockets, you'll find it easier to retrieve and turn them over whenever you want to explore additional number patterns. To get students thinking more about the numbers 1–100, consider these activities:

- Gather the class around the pocket chart so all can see and participate. Ask if anyone has an idea about how far the numbers in the chart actually go. Find out the thinking behind the children's responses by asking them how they arrived at their guesses. Once children have made predictions, have the class count out loud as you turn the numbers over, one by one. Discuss any patterns that the children may notice, such as:

1	2	3	4	5	6	7	8	9	10
11	12	13	14	15	16	17	18	19	20

  Then take the numbers that go beyond the days-in-school count and turn them back to their blank side.

- When you have some extra time in your schedule, reveal a series of numbers, while leaving some numbers in the pattern face down, with the blank side up. For example, turn over the 10, 20, 30, 40, 60, 70, 80, and 100—and leave 50 and 90 blank. Ask the children what numbers they think they'll see when you turn over the blank cards. Discuss how they knew what to expect. You can do this type of "What's Missing?" activity with a variety of number sequences. All of them will help children identify and articulate number patterns.

- Once you've passed the twentieth day in school, ask the children to close their eyes. Then remove one of the numbered cards from 1 to 20 from the pocket chart and conceal it in your hand. Ask the children to reopen their eyes, examine the chart, and tell you what is missing from the chart. Reveal the missing number, then ask how the children figured out the missing number without seeing it. This exercise typically initiates intense conversation about counting and number patterns.

- Turn over all 100 cards in the pocket chart so that their number sides are facing up. Invite the children up to view the chart again. Now remove the cards for the numbers 20 through 30. Shuffle the cards and invite a child sitting near you to pull one of them from your hand. Ask him or her to decide where the number on that card belongs on the chart. Then have another child do the same thing—and so on—until all the number cards have been put back in the chart.

  If the children seem unsure about where the numbers go, remind them that in an earlier activity they were able to tell you what number was missing without even seeing it! Discuss number patterns and ask the class if they think a number could be placed correctly even if a person didn't know the name of that number. Ideally, this conversation will ease the minds of students who may be feeling worried or self-conscious about not knowing all of the numbers' names.

You may also want to select one of your more confident students to come up, take one of the missing numbers, and place it in the chart—to model the process. As the children place the numbers, ask questions about how they selected particular slots. Ask if any of the numbers could go in another spot. "If so, why?" "If not, why not?" Once again, discuss the clues that can help the children put the numbers in the correct sequence.

- When the number chart is back in order, pull out two related numbers—such as 24 and 42—and talk about how they are alike and how they are different. Many first graders easily confuse two numbers that are reversals of one another. Talk about this tendency openly. Explain that even though the two numbers look just a little bit different, they actually mean two *very* different things. You might ask questions like, "When you go trick or treating, would you rather have twenty-four pieces of candy or forty-two? How about when you need to wait for something that you really want—would you rather wait twenty-four minutes (or days), or forty-two?"

Children quickly learn to mask their confusion or misunderstanding. To cultivate a supportive classroom atmosphere, periodically revisit the fact that it is OK not to know everything. Remind students that making sense of new ideas can be challenging. Sometimes I ask my students whether they would get mad at me or make fun of me if I made a mistake because I got mixed up. At this age, they (fortunately!) have always assured me that they would not get mad or upset. So I encourage them to extend that same acceptance and generosity to one another.

The key is to let children know that even when things aren't clear, you want them to keep trying to make sense of their work, to ask questions, and to not worry about what other people think of their efforts. Explain that although confusion over reversed numbers is natural, the numbers do mean different things—so it's important to get used to them. And don't forget to mention that these things *will* get easier with practice.

Through these kinds of discussions, children become aware of the counting sequence that gets them to 100. They also begin discerning predictable patterns within the number system. Conversations about comparisons of numbers such as 24 and 42 can help establish the idea that numbers have magnitude. Using the 1–100 chart is an excellent means of encouraging students to talk about math concepts. As children listen to one another and express their own ideas, the numbers from the chart visually support their thinking.

After your students have taken time to explore numbers 1–100 using the pocket chart, consider giving them their own copies of the chart to tape into their math notebooks. (See Blackline Masters.) Explain that having their own chart will enable them to look at the numbers at their leisure.

1	2	3	4	5	6	7	8	9	10
11	12	13	14	15	16	17	18	19	20
21	22	23	24	25	26	27	28	29	30
31	32	33	34	35	36	37	38	39	40
41	42	43	44	45	46	47	48	49	50
51	52	53	54	55	56	57	58	59	60
61	62	63	64	65	66	67	68	69	70
71	72	73	74	75	76	77	78	79	80
81	82	83	84	85	86	87	88	89	90
91	92	93	94	95	96	97	98	99	100

Moreover, the chart can come in handy if they want to remember a particular number or need to check which number is 12 and which is 21.

Provide the children with paper 1–100 charts. Trim the edges of the charts so students can easily tape them into the next blank page in their math notebooks. Demonstrate taping a chart onto a blank page of a student's notebook. Suggest that if the children have some free time, they pair up and play a quick round of *Guess My Number*. For instance, one partner could say to another:

"I'm thinking of a number that is one more than twenty."

"I'm thinking of a number that is one less than twenty-one."

"I'm thinking of a number that is ten more than twenty."

The Mathematics

At this point in the year, your students have had practice using math materials and working independently. If you feel that the time is right, considering offering the children some choices that will allow them to work with partners. Take things slowly, and make sure the children clearly understand their tasks. That way, they'll be better able to adapt as these tasks' complexity increases.

October's activities center on patterns, number sense, and symmetry. You'll be offering your students a selection of activities that engage them in these concepts. The idea of offering choices is a comfortable one for many early-childhood educators. "Menu" closely resembles the concept of "centers"—classroom areas where small groups of children work independently or with partners while the teacher meets with other small groups at the reading table.

Below, we take a closer look at math menu.

Introducing Math Menu

Math menu differs from centers in one important way: It's designed to engage both students and teacher in the selected activities. While centers free the teacher to pull students out (for guided reading groups, for example), menus invite the teacher to go from group to group. Math menu provides a time

---

Pattern Menu

T Shirt Patterns　　_____ date

_____ date

Paper Tube Patterns　　_____ date

_____ date

Pattern Block Caterpillars　_____ date

_____ date

Code Patterns　　_____ date

_____ date

Roll and Extend　　_____ date

_____ date

for the teacher to visit with children, observe what they do and how they work, ask questions, facilitate discussions between students, and model mathematical language. These observations and conversations help you determine how to select and design whole-class discussions and lessons.

So how do first graders learn to work independently on a variety of activities of their choice? Introduce menu activities as whole-group lessons first. Select or design menu activities that are accessible to everyone and that focus children's attention on the math concepts you're introducing that month. Once you've gathered the materials for the menu choices, you can keep them organized and accessible so menu-time preparation is minimal.

Begin with just a few menu choices. Once you have selected a number of activities, decide how you'll keep track of students' choices and work. Some children may repeatedly select the same menu choices. To monitor this and encourage them to branch out, create a sheet of menu choices that the children can place in their math notebooks. Explain that you expect students to try all of the choices eventually. Design the recording sheet in a way that helps children see what choices are available and make responsible selections. The recording sheet includes the names of the activities, with two lines next to each choice. (See the Pattern Menu at left.) Each time a child selects a menu activity, he or she will write the date on one of the two lines next to that choice. When both lines have been used, the student needs to make a new selection.

Consider also listing the menu choices on a piece of poster board, in the same order as on the math-notebook sheets. That way, the children can easily follow along as you remind them of the menu possibilities, and you can quickly jot down their names when they make choices.

Pattern Activities

By learning to notice patterns, children can begin seeing relationships in our number system and make predictions. Pattern activities help children make sense of our number system and, later, master more advanced mathematical areas such as algebra. Patterns can take a wide variety of interesting forms—from visual and auditory, to movement and numerical. The pattern activities described below focus first graders' attention on these mathematical ideas:

- Patterns can repeat.
- Patterns can grow.
- Patterns can be named.
- Patterns are sometimes similar to one another.

- Patterns can be used to make predictions.
- Patterns appear in many forms.
- Patterns can be identified, extended, created, described, and also interpreted.

As you read through the following lessons, brainstorm additional ideas that will be useful in your classroom.

Literature-Based Activities

How Many Letters in Your Name?

Based on Kevin Henkes's *Chrysanthemum*, this activity focuses on the patterns found in the letters of names. The description below is from lessons taught with a "buddy" class, in which fifth- and sixth-grade students worked together with first graders on the activity. You may choose to modify the activity if this kind of collaboration doesn't suit your circumstances.

In his book, author Kevin Henkes introduces a delightful young character named Chrysanthemum. Chrysanthemum has the great confidence of a cherished child. Knowing that her parents consider her absolutely perfect, she enthusiastically skips off to her first day of school. Reality quickly sets in as Chrysanthemum's classmates immediately begin teasing her about her long name. An engaging music teacher, Ms. Delphinium Twinkle, arrives on the scene and helps to set things right. This story provides a wonderful opportunity for you to discuss name patterns as well as issues of acceptance and kindness.

Materials

- about 13 Snap Cubes per child
- *Chrysanthemum* by Kevin Henkes

Instructions

1. Read the story to the class. Note that the name "Chrysanthemum" contains thirteen letters.

2. After reading the book, ask questions like: "Does anyone in our room have a first name with thirteen letters?" "How many letters do you think a very short name might have?" "What is a name that has two letters?" "How many letters are in your name?" "Who do you think has the longest name in your family?" "Which has more letters—your first name or your last name?"

3. The next day, ask the children to use Snap Cubes to show the length of their names. Every child uses one cube to correspond with each letter in his or her name. To make this connection more explicit, you could also provide small, round stickers on which the children can

put the letters of their names and then attach the stickers to a cube. The children can put the cubes together to make a "name train," and compare their trains with those of their classmates.

4. Ask questions like: "Which name has the fewest letters?" "Which name has the most letters?"

5. You can also compare the class's findings with those from another class. If you do this, have the other class "buddies" compare their name trains and record their observations in their math notebooks. When the children return to their classroom, ask your students to discuss their observations about the name comparisons. Mention the idea of a range of numbers and point out the greatest and least number of letters from the other class's names. Talk about whether the other class had any names with more letters than your class, or fewer letters. Write the different numbers of letters in your students' names across the bottom of the chalkboard.

6. Give each child a sticky note and ask them to write their first names on the note. Call out the various numbers of letters, and have the children come up to place their notes above the number of letters in their names.

7. Once all the sticky notes are displayed, ask what the children notice. Point out that what they are looking at on the board is a graph. Ask them to make "true math statements" about the graph. Responses might include:

- The number 5 has the most names above it.
- No one in our class has nine letters.
- Two people have three letters and two people have eight letters—that's the same amount.

Record the students' ideas on a large piece of paper and identify which observations are mathematical in nature. Discuss the ideas of *most*, *least/fewest*, and *same amount*, and talk about the act of combining quantities. For example, students may choose a category such as "names that have three letters" and then make a statement like, "Three children have names with three letters, so there are nine letters altogether."

Asking for true statements about a graph is a good way to elicit thoughtful responses from children and generates a greater variety of responses than do specific questions such as "Which column has the fewest names?" It also gets the children using math vocabulary themselves. Initially, the children's responses may not be mathematical in nature. Rather, they may take the form of "I like Shatani's name" or "My aunt's name is Anne, too." Accept these comments with mild interest. When a child *does* make a mathematical observation, accentuate the fact that it is "a true math statement" and explain what constitutes such statements. For instance:

- Five-letter names have the most. We have nine people with five letters in their names.

- T. J. is the only person with two letters in his name, so that's the least.

- If you add together all of the names there are twenty-three.

Gradually, this kind of thinking will become a habit.

8. Now expand the conversation to include questions about "How many letters altogether?" For example: "How many letters are there in all of our names?" "How many letters are in all of the names that have eight letters?" By suggesting that children use cubes to count, you can plant the seeds for thinking about multiples.

9. During another math time, ask the children to observe as you use the overhead projector to model printing your name repeatedly on 8-by-10-inch grid paper. Point out to the children that no squares can be left empty.

10. After the name chart is complete, select a separate color for each letter in your name—for example, red for *A*, green for *S*, etc. Color in all the letters on the grid. Then point out patterns. Ask students to fill out grids for their own names. (See Figure 3–1.)

     Coloring in the grid requires concentration, and inevitably mistakes are made. If you have white Reading Recovery tape, you might let children use it if they've made an error and are unduly upset by the mistake. But most children will be comfortable simply coloring over any inaccuracy. You can also suggest that the children place just a dot of color on each square when they start out. After they feel they've accurately marked the squares, they can color them in more thoroughly.

11. Once the children finish coloring in their name patterns, use the same format of posting the number of letters in the names and then display the name patterns above the corresponding number (see below). This will become a big enough display that you may want to put the final product in a hallway.

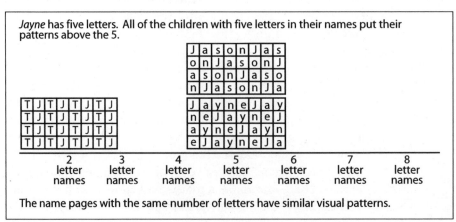

The name pages with the same number of letters have similar visual patterns.

FIGURE 3–1 ◀

Jayne's name creates an interesting pattern.

12. Once all of the pattern pages are completed and posted, ask the children to describe the geometric designs they see in the colored grids. The patterns will range from stripes and diagonals to checker-board shapes. As the class discusses the patterns, weave in terms such as *diagonal*, *column*, *repeating*, *over*, *under*, *left*, and *right*.

Extensions

Consider having your students make name patterns with buddies. This activity offers several benefits. First, each child has a personal helper and will likely complete the task more quickly. Second, more data is produced.

After you've displayed and discussed the new name patterns, students a second grid—this one 10-by-10 inches. This grid will have more squares than the last ones the children used. Ask the children to make predictions about how their name patterns would look on this new grid. Responses might include: "I think mine will be stripes, because it was the last time" or "Mine could look like a checker board" or "Mine will probably make slant lines."

When the second "buddy" page is complete, compare it to the first page done by the class. You can then make two class books of name patterns. Organize each book by fewest number of letters to greatest number.

Eric Carle

Eric Carle has been a prolific writer and has provided us with a wealth of books that have math connections. At our school, Mr. Carle's books are regularly featured in an author study. Weaving together language arts and mathematics can be a very natural process when using these books. Here is a list of titles that I have used successfully in this way.

Growth Patterns

The Very Hungry Caterpillar
Rooster's Off to See the World
The Tiny Seed—life cycle
The Grouchy Ladybug—time

Repeating Patterns

From Head to Toe—language arts; could make similar book, "Can you do it? I can do it."
The Very Quiet Cricket—repeating text
The Very Busy Spider—repeating text
Today Is Monday—days of the week
A House for Hermit Crab—months of the year

After enjoying the books together, we discuss our favorites, narrow the list to four or five books and create a bar graph to indicate each child's very favorite. Since other classrooms are also featuring Eric Carle books, we compare the graphs from one classroom to another.

Patterns in Nature

Nature offers numerous opportunities to spot patterns and symmetry. This activity involves exploring the visual patterns of caterpillars and butterflies.

Materials

- 1 book about caterpillars and butterflies; consider Bobbie Kalman's *The Life Cycle of a Butterfly*, Gail Gibbons's *Monarch Butterfly*, or Emily Neye's *Butterflies*

Instructions

1. Read the book with the class and look at the photographs of caterpillars. Monarch caterpillars are particularly vivid in their pattern distinctions (black, white, and yellow repeating patterns). Call attention to the repeating patterns and ask a volunteer to identify the caterpillar's pattern. Then, together with the class, chant the names of the colors that make up that pattern.

2. On a piece of chart paper, draw the outline of a large caterpillar and re-create the pattern using the appropriate colored markers. Ask the children how this pattern could be expressed with words or letters if colors weren't available. They might suggest writing the names of the colors: *yellow, white, black*; *yellow, white, black*. Someone will likely then come up with the idea of using letters to shorten the process of writing out the words. Show this pattern by writing *y, w, b, y, w, b*, and so on.

3. Ask the children to think of other possible patterns for coloring imaginary caterpillars, then demonstrate some of those ideas as well. Discuss the fact that the imaginary caterpillars could have many different colors that create a repeating pattern.

Whole-Class/Menu Activities

T-Shirt Patterns (Menu Possibility)

This is a whole-class lesson that you can also offer as a menu choice. Before using it as a whole-class lesson, ask the children to look around the room to see if they notice any patterns. Call their attention to the room itself, the walls, ceiling, and bulletin boards. Identify some patterns that you notice in other things, such as the children's clothing, and invite the children to guess what you're seeing. This turns into a kind of *I Spy* game.

On a piece of chart paper, list about ten examples of patterns that the children have generated, and then stand back to look at the list together. Patterns might include clothing, days of the week, bricks, ceiling tiles, rhyming words. Ask students, "What makes a pattern a pattern?" "How can you tell if something is a pattern?" Give the youngsters a few minutes to discuss these questions with a partner or in a small group before sharing the ideas as a class. By providing this bit of "think time," you'll help the children to organize their thoughts and get them engaged in the discussion. At the bottom of the list, write words that emerge from the conversations; e.g., *repeating, predictable, happens over and over*, and so forth.

Now you're ready to introduce the *T-Shirt Patterns* activity:

Instructions

1. Begin with a round of *Guess My Rule*. Invite children with patterned T-shirts to come up to the front of the room and stand on one side

of a chair. Then ask the children with plain shirts to stand on the other side. (See Chapter 2 for a detailed description of *Guess My Rule*.)

2. Now invite the students to guess the rule you've used to organize them into the two groups.

3. Explain that the children will be designing T-shirts and drawing their designs on pages you provide. Suggest that the children pretend to be designers whose job is to create T-shirt designs for a clothing-company.

4. Show the children a picture of a T-shirt with horizontal stripes, and ask them to help you think of a pattern that you might use on the shirt. Responses might include something like "Color the stripes red and blue and red and blue. Draw the pattern on the shirt and ask for some additional ideas. Suggest that the students can use more colors, as long as they form a pattern—a predictable form. Ask whether the shirt would show a pattern if you colored each stripe a different color. Discuss the children's comments.

5. Next, show the children a picture of a blank T-shirt. Ask whether they think that it would be possible to make a pattern on the shirt. Discuss their reasoning, then demonstrate an example of a possible pattern. For instance, you might draw half of a heart-shaped symbol or butterfly—anything that's symmetrical. (See Figure 3–2.) Then fill in the other half of the drawing.

6. During your and the children's conversation, add any new terms—such as *pattern, predictable, symmetrical, repeating, before, after, in between, left, right, above,* and *below*—to the *Math Words* poster.

7. If you want to provide this exercise as a menu choice, give children pictures of striped and blank T-shirts on which they can create their own patterns. (See Blackline Masters.)

Extensions

- Have students work in pairs to design their T-shirts. One partner begins the design; the second partner completes it based on the established pattern.

- Have the children create paper dolls or paper puppets of characters from familiar stories and then make patterned clothes for them. Encourage them to think about how to create the right size clothing, with the right proportions, to fit the dolls or puppets.

Cube Caterpillars

This activity enables children to practice using cubes to create visual patterns and then compare them.

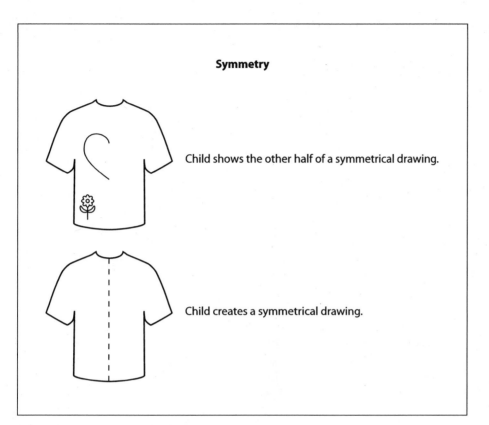

Symmetry

Child shows the other half of a symmetrical drawing.

Child creates a symmetrical drawing.

FIGURE 3–2 ◀

T-shirt symmetry and patterns.

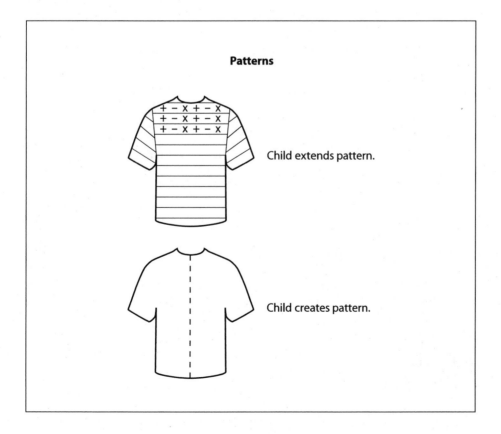

Patterns

Child extends pattern.

Child creates pattern.

Materials

- 1 set of Snap Cubes
- several sheets of newsprint
- sheets of white construction paper with the outline of a large caterpillar drawn on them; several per student

Instructions

1. Use Snap Cubes to create two different *a*, *b* pattern trains. (Make each train about twenty cubes long.) For example, one pattern train might be blue/red; the other, yellow/green.

2. Roll the pattern trains in newsprint to create two tubes.

3. Make a third pattern tube using *three* colors in an *a*, *b*, *c* repeating pattern.

4. Gather the children, and show them one of the wrapped *a*, *b* pattern tubes without revealing the tube's contents. Ask if anyone has a guess about what might be in the tube. After the children make a few guesses, tell them that you have made some pretend caterpillars out of cubes and that you'd like them to speculate about what the caterpillar patterns might look like.

5. Push just the first cube out, and ask for predictions about what will come next. Then push out the second cube, then the third—until the children discern the pattern. Once the pattern has been revealed, have the class chant the names of the colors in the pattern.

6. Now connect physical motions to the visual pattern. For instance, the students could alternate a clap for the first color with a knee pat for the second. For instance, if the colors are blue/red, blue/red, then the children would clap/pat knees, clap/pat knees.

7. Once the class is comfortable with this movement pattern, reveal the pattern tube that contains the *a*, *b*, *c* pattern. Add a third motion—such as "Put your hands on your head." So, using the same example, the pattern becomes clap/pat knees/put hand on head, clap/pat knees/put hands on head.

8. Finally, reveal the second *a, b* pattern. Use the same motions (clap/pat knees) with this pattern that you used for the first *a, b* pattern. As the children are acting out this pattern, ask them which of the other patterns is like this one. The physical actions call attention to the fact that even though the patterns look different because of the varied colors, they are in fact similar.

9. Using large chart paper, draw the patterns that have been shown in the tubes and post them somewhere in the room.

10. Now give each child several of the pieces of white construction paper with the caterpillar outline drawn on them. Invite them to create their own caterpillar patterns on the paper. Suggest that they use two, three, four, or five markers to create their patterns. Once again, ask the class, "How will you know it's a pattern?"

11. As the children begin their work, walk around to visit with individuals and ask them to tell you about their patterns. If a student is having difficulty creating a pattern, ask the child to pick his or her two favorite colors. Talk about how these colors could be used again and again in the same way. Together, chant the identified pattern, such as "red, yellow, red, yellow . . . ." Ask the child if he or she thinks that pattern could be shown on the caterpillar picture with markers.

12. The next day, look at each of the patterns that the youngsters have drawn. Discuss how these pictures are alike and how they are different.

    Remind the students of the fun they had yesterday when everyone clapped out the patterns. Select a child who created a pattern with two attributes and invite the class to clap that pattern. Ask anyone else who has a pattern with two colors to stand and show their pattern through motion. Have the class clap a few of these patterns, chanting the color names as you go along. Again, point out that even though the patterns look different because they have different colors or shapes, they are alike when put to motion.

13. Have the children cut out their caterpillars. Then mount and display similar caterpillar patterns (e.g., *a, b* or *a, b, c*) together on one large piece of black construction paper. Label the display *Guess Our Rule: Why Are These Caterpillars Together?*

Paper-Tube Patterns (Menu Possibility)

This activity can be done in conjunction with, or instead of, the preceding activity.

Materials

- 1 set of Unifix cubes for you, and 1 set for each student
- several sheets of newsprint, or several cardboard tubes from paper towels

Instructions

1. Create an *a, b* pattern train of Unifix cubes (e.g., red/blue, red/blue) and hide it in rolled-up newspaper or a paper-towel tube. Then create an *abc abc abc* pattern, and conceal it similarly. Finally, prepare a growth pattern, such as *ab, abb, abbb, abbbb.*

2. Gather students together and hold up the paper tube with the *a*, *b* train. Make sure the cubes are completely hidden from view inside the tube. Ask the children what might be inside the tube. Students will use some mental classification to think about objects that could fit into such a tube. They'll probably make guesses like "a snake," "markers," or "candy."

3. After the class has generated some possibilities, squeeze the first cube out of the tube. Tell the children you have additional cubes in the tube, and ask them if they know what color the next cube will be. Some of the children are likely to be extremely confident and enthusiastic about their guesses. Other first graders will realize that there is really no way to know what color the next cube might be.

4. Squeeze out the second cube. The children who happened to guess the correct color will be delighted and more confident than ever.

5. Continue revealing cubes one at a time and inviting predictions.

6. Once the pattern has clearly emerged, ask the children to explain exactly *when* they were able to tell for sure what the pattern was going to be. Discuss the idea of patterns being predictable, and identify the segments of the pattern that are repeated; e.g., red/blue, red/blue.

7. Follow a similar process in revealing the other tubes.

8. Now have the students create their own pattern trains. If you have enough materials, ask the children to work in pairs in which each partner builds a similar, but not identical pattern. For example, one partner could build a red/red/blue/blue, red/red/blue/blue train, while his or her partner could build an orange/orange/yellow/yellow, orange/orange/yellow/yellow train.

9. If supplies are limited, ask the children to help you decide what kinds of similar patterns you could build next. Create several pattern trains and have the class discuss how the patterns are alike and how they are different.

10. After the class has generated several repeating patterns in this way, remind students of the growth-pattern example (red/blue, red/blue/blue, red/blue/blue/blue). Ask them how you might make a similar pattern but using different colors. An example might be orange/yellow, orange/yellow/yellow, orange/yellow/yellow/yellow, and so on. During the resulting discussion, ask the children whether this is a pattern; i.e., whether it's predictable. Ask questions like, "Is there a way we can know what color will come next? Is there a special plan?" Help the children articulate the idea that even though the pattern does not simply repeat, the "plus-one" structure does make it predictable.

11. Consider having the children create and demonstrate growth patterns of their own. They can continue to explore repeating and growth patterns using cubes as well as other materials, such as pattern blocks or cut-up colored straws that can be strung onto yarn. Display their creations in the room, grouping similar patterns together and articulating what makes them similar.

Pattern-Block Caterpillars (Menu Possibility)

Pattern blocks are so inviting that children typically need some time to explore them before performing specific tasks with the materials. Open exploration of the blocks enables them to learn new vocabulary terms for the blocks' various shapes. As you and the children explore the blocks, use color names *and* geometric words to refer to the blocks' characteristics. This kind of casual introduction will help to prepare students for later work geared to geometry.

Materials

- 1 overhead projector
- several blank transparencies
- 1 set of overhead pattern blocks
- pieces of black construction paper, with the outline of a large caterpillar drawn in white on them; 1 per child

Instructions

1. Draw the outline of a large caterpillar on a blank transparency.

2. Add one pattern block at a time to create the beginnings of a simple pattern in the caterpillar outline; for example, green triangle/red square, green triangle/red square. Ask for volunteers to raise their hands and name the pattern as soon as they think they know what it is.

3. Once someone guesses the pattern, ask another person to come up and extend it. Repeat these steps several times, using simple patterns.

4. Now introduce a growth pattern, such as orange triangle/green square, orange triangle/green square/green square, orange triangle/ green square/green square/green square, etc. (See Figure 3–3 for examples of pattern-block caterpillars.)

5. Once the youngsters identify the pattern, explain that it's another example of a growth pattern. Point out that even though such a pattern may seem unusual, the question to keep in mind is whether it is predictable.

FIGURE 3–3   ▶

Caterpillars with pattern blocks.

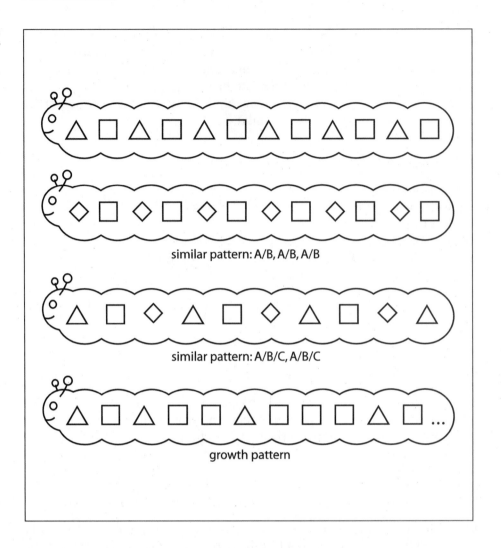

A note to you: Growth patterns are mathematically significant and have many practical applications. For instance, the study of growth patterns allows us to make decisions about the number of schools and fire stations that a community might need as it grows and to figure out how much money will be needed for Social Security as the population reaches retirement age. Such issues exert a huge impact on our lives. Your first graders will benefit from developing an awareness of the predictable nature of growth patterns as well as repeating patterns.

6. Once the students feel comfortable creating pattern-block caterpillars as a group, give each child a piece of the black construction paper with the outline of the caterpillar drawn on it. Have the children use pattern blocks to create patterns inside the outline. Once each child has had a chance to experiment, let them get up and walk around the room to see what their classmates have created.

7. The next time you use this activity, ask the children to work in pairs and to take turns completing each other's patterns. At some point, let the children select their favorite pattern and have them use paper pattern block shapes to glue it onto the paper. On a recording sheet, list the children's names and indicate which pieces they used and how many they used.

Patterns and Movement (Menu Possibility)

This movement-pattern activity lends itself to the menu format once students have mastered the physical motions required and the rule, or code, for performing the motions.

Instructions

1. Have students sit in a circle so they can all see each other.

2. Going around the circle, ask each child to say his or her name and use a different motion to indicate each syllable. For instance, a child named Shatani might clap for *Sha*, raise both hands *tan*, and stretch both hands forward for *ni*.

3. When everyone has had a turn, invite the class to discuss the various kinds of movements that were used. Challenge the students to practice and memorize the movements each person used for his or her name.

4. Now make up some written symbols to indicate those movements. Explain that these symbols create a *code* or set of rules. For example, "|" could mean "clap," "||" could mean "clap twice," "=" could mean "two hands clapping knees," and "^" could mean jump.

5. Document the code on chart paper.

6. Ask the children to suggest a pattern, using the code, for the class to try. For example, "||, =, ^^, ||, =, ^^, ||, =, ^^" could mean "clap twice, hands on knees, jump, jump—then repeat twice."

7. Practice acting out the code. Ask students how many times the pattern needs to be repeated the code in order for them to master it. (My students answered, "at least three times.")

8. Have the children use their math notebooks to create additional patterns out of the agreed-upon code. Select an interesting-looking pattern, write it on a sentence strip, and encourage the children to practice the code as a group during daily transition times, such as right before lunch or recess. The children can just stand by their desks and act out a particular code.

   Yes, chaos will reign as the children laugh, make mistakes, and hold onto their chairs for support as they act out codes—but this exercise encourages them to pay close attention to the patterns.

9. Consider making code creation a menu item for up to three students. Children can use their math notebooks and take turns creating and recording the patterns that they and the other players will act out. You might also want to ask the class to set a limit for the number of times someone can include a particular move (e.g., jumping) in a code. (My class settled on a limit of ten for jumping.)

Pattern Rolling and Extending (Menu Possibility)

You can use a variety of materials—pattern blocks, colored tiles, paper shapes—for this activity. The activity is most appropriate for three participants. A trio gives the children a chance to extend their cooperative efforts beyond the usual partner work.

Materials

- 1 overhead projector
- transparent color tiles, paper pattern blocks, or simple paper shapes
- 1 die

Instructions

1. Invite three children to come up to the projector.

2. Using your color tiles, pattern blocks, or paper shapes, create at least two repetitions of a pattern. Have the class discuss, and perhaps chant, your plan.

3. Have one of the three children roll the die and read the resulting number. That player then adds exactly that number of pieces to the pattern.

4. The second student repeats this process.

5. Continue the game until each of the three players has had another turn.

6. Now, as a class, put limits on how far a pattern should be repeated. For example, the class might decide on a total number of pieces to be added, or a total number of times that the die can be rolled.

7. Demonstrate the game again, this time with Player 2 creating a new pattern.

8. Now the children can break into groups of three and play the game themselves.

    Note: It's always helpful to give children criteria for deciding who will go first, second, and so on in any game. Examples might include roll of a die from highest number to lowest, the first letter of a person's first name in the alphabet (for example, Ann would go first, then Barry, then Charlie, etc.), age order from youngest to oldest, or the other way around.

Number-Sense Activities

While they've been counting, sorting, and developing an awareness of patterns, your students have also been learning how to combine and separate quantities, as well as to begin learning about addition and subtraction. The following activities will help them gain several key understandings about number sense:

- Numbers have magnitude.
- Numbers have relationships with other numbers.
- Numbers can be represented with symbols.
- Numbers can be put together and taken apart.
- Numbers are useful because they help us make sense of our world.

Butterfly Combinations

This activity entails using construction-paper butterflies and storyboards—rectangular pieces of cardstock about the size of large index cards—to teach your first graders about combining and separating numbers. Draw an identical picture of a flower on a series of eight storyboard cards to create a background context for the combining and separating activity.

Materials

- 8 storyboard cards with an identical picture of a flower drawn on each card
- 2 sets of 20–30 construction-paper butterflies; each set should be a different color (e.g., yellow and orange); butterflies must be large enough to be seen by students as they sit in the circle area

Instructions

1. Gather your students together and explain that you're going to act out some butterfly number stories. Show the children the yellow and

orange butterflies. Put a piece of tape on the back of a yellow butterfly, then hold the butterfly up and pretend it's flying around and landing on one of the storyboard flowers. Explain that the students will be working to put the same number of butterflies on each flower.

2. Tell the children that you are thinking of the number that comes between 2 and 4. Write the number 3 on a small sticky note and place it in a corner of the storyboard. Remind the children that you have yellow and orange butterflies. Ask them to help you find different combinations of the butterflies to make 3. Responses might include "three yellow butterflies and no orange butterflies," "two yellow butterflies and one orange butterfly," etc. Show the children's ideas by attaching the corresponding butterfly configurations to the storyboard.

3. Continue the conversation until the children have generated all of the possibilities: 3 yellows/0 oranges, 2 yellows/1 orange, 1 yellow/2 oranges, and 3 oranges/0 yellows. Have the children revisit the idea that there are three butterflies on each flower.

4. Now act out some stories. For example, you or a student could offer something like, "Once upon a time, there were three butterflies on a flower. The two yellow butterflies flew away to find another garden and one orange butterfly was still on the flower." Remove the yellow butterflies to show the events in the story.

5. On a large piece of chart paper, write the story exactly as it was told. Reread the story to the children, then point out how long it took you to write down that whole idea.

6. Explain that math has a great way to write ideas much faster. Write the equation $3 - 2 = 1$ on the chalkboard and discuss what each of the symbols (the "$-$" and the "$=$") means. If these symbols are not yet on the *Math Words* poster, add them.

7. Next go through the process of bringing the two butterflies back. This time, talk about the addition (plus) symbol, showing the equation $2 + 1 = 3$.

8. Revisit this activity over the next couple of weeks, each time altering the total number of butterflies.

Butterfly Attributes

This lesson teaches children to count and aggregate butterflies' physical attributes.

Materials

- 1 picture of a large butterfly that clearly shows its 2 antennae, 4 wings, and 6 legs

- several colored butterflies from the previous activity
- sticky notes

Instructions

1. Show the class the picture of the large butterfly. Have them count the butterfly's antennae (two), wings (four), and legs (six).

2. Show the children a chart with the following sentences, or write the sentences on the chalkboard:

   - *There are __ butterflies, and together they have __ antennae.*
   - *There are __ butterflies, and together they have __ wings.*
   - *There are __ butterflies, and together they have __ legs.*

3. Hold up one colored butterfly. Ask the children how they would fill in the blanks in the sentences you've shown them. Write their responses on the sticky notes, and place the notes onto the appropriate blank spaces.

4. Extend this discussion by asking the children to propose any number of butterflies they want, and to count total antennae, wings, and legs. Invite them to keep track of their work in their math notebooks. I use the chalkboard or overhead to model this process and then the children record as it makes sense to them. Offer the use of any math manipulative that the children might find helpful.

5. While the children are working, walk around and see how individual students are approaching the problem. This is a time to observe, ask questions, make subtle suggestions, and assist anyone who is having difficulty conceptualizing the problem. (See Figure 3–4 and Figure 3–5.)

6. After the children have worked for a while, ask if anyone has an example that he or she would like to share. Once a few students respond, others usually become eager to show their own thinking. This "processing time" highlights the variety of ways the different individuals approached the problem, helps children clarify their own thinking as they communicate, and increases numerical flexibility as the children listen to each other's solutions.

Your listening and encouragement help them to further articulate their thoughts. Many first graders find it challenging to listen and engage in mathematical discussions, and these skills develop gradually. Familiar objects such as butterflies, as well as tangible items, help children focus and engage with mathematical questions. Even on days when it feels difficult to facilitate mathematical conversations, it is well worth your effort, time, and patience.

FIGURE 3–4 ▶

This student counted the attributes of four butterflies.

16 wings
8 antenna
24 legs

FIGURE 3–5 ▶

This student counted five butterflies' attributes.

wings 20
antenna 10
legs 30

Symmetry Activities

The topic of human symmetry can take the class in a couple of different mathematical directions.

Are We Symmetrical?

This activity is similar to the butterfly-attribute activity.

Materials

- any book that clearly depicts faces in the illustrations (e.g., Roberta Interater's *Two Eyes, a Nose, and a Mouth*)
- 1 large piece of graph paper
- 1 ruler

Instructions

1. Show the class the pictures in the book.

2. Create a graph with two columns labeled *number of people* and *number of eyes*.

3. Ask the children how many total eyes one person has, two people, three people—and so on up to 10 people. Record their responses on the graph.

Number of people	Number of eyes
1	2
2	4
3	6
4	8
5	10
6	12
7	14
8	16
9	18
10	20

Ask them if they notice any patterns. Their responses might include:

- It's just counting numbers going down in that first line (column).
- It's a pattern going down on the other side—by twos—all of the even numbers.
- From one side to the other—it's the doubles!

Extensions

- To introduce the idea of symmetry, divide a picture of a face down the center using a ruler. Ask the children to describe what they see. Encourage or introduce use of terms such as *divide*, *whole*, and *half*. Explain the word *symmetry* by asking the children to find a match or counterpart for an eye, an ear, etc.

- Next, draw half a face on the chalkboard or on a piece of chart paper. Invite a child to come up and draw corresponding parts of the other side of the face. You can further adapt this activity easily by having the children carve symmetrical jack-o-lantern faces.

Butterfly Symmetry

Having looked closely at butterflies and human faces in some of the preceding activities, students should be able to now establish the fact that many living things are symmetrical. This activity helps them engage actively with this concept.

Materials

- 1 set of pattern blocks per child, drawing or painting materials, several pieces of 8-by-11-inch paper per child

Instructions

1. Have each child practice making examples of symmetrical butterflies. If you want the students to draw or paint the butterflies, ask them to fold a piece of paper in half to create a center line. Discuss the idea of a *line of symmetry*. Explain that this line shows the middle, or center, of the design, with the two halves on either side. Using the center line as their guide, the children draw first one half of the butterfly and then the other half—making the two sides identical to create a symmetrical butterfly.

2. Now ask the children to work in pairs. Each partner draws half a butterfly on his or her paper. Then the partners trade pictures and complete each other's work. The goal is to practice matching someone else's design.

Extensions

Children can create symmetrical drawings of everything from spiders to hearts. This is also a fun activity for parent night. Have the children and parents partner up and trade papers. (If some children do not attend with their parents, have them leave their half butterfly, or other drawing on their desks for their parents to complete when it's convenient.)

Mirror Movement

After the children have learned the word *symmetry* and have some understanding of the concept, you can expand on the idea by introducing some movement.

Materials

- a tape or CD player for playing music

Instructions

1. Explain that the class is going to do a "mirror partner dance," then start playing an upbeat music tape or CD.

2. Initiate movements to the music, emphasizing using one side of your body. For instance, put you head to the left side and do some movement with your left arm and left leg. The children must "mirror" your movement.

3. After a bit of practice, have the children partner up to do the dance. You can stop and restart the music to indicate that partners should switch roles of leader and mirror. Discuss the fact that, like butterflies, people also have symmetrical bodies.

Chapter 4

November

NUMBER AND OPERATION

The Learning Environment

Now that your students have had experience with sorting, counting, and patterning, and have been introduced to the ideas of addition and subtraction, you can build on their new knowledge during November. This month, continue to explore number combinations, up to those that create 10. Combinations of numbers that create 10 serve as the foundation for much elementary arithmetic work, so revisit them regularly and in a variety of ways.

As in previous months, some of the activities offered for November connect math ideas with real-life contexts. Holidays and other events, such as Thanksgiving, offer some natural contextual opportunities. Other interdisciplinary links depend on your curriculum. The contextual activities offered in this chapter are designed to connect with the topics of Thanksgiving, traditions, and families. ∎

Routines

Calendar

Reinforce the days-of-the-week sequence by chanting, reading poems, and singing songs. (I like to play "The Days of the Week," from Charlotte Diamond's *Ten Carrot Diamond* CD.) Repetition is a key to success in this area. Consider typing up song lyrics (use bold print for the days of the week) and handing them out to the children, then asking them to follow along with the text while the class sings. The children can collect the lyrics for a variety of songs in a "songs" folder and keep it in their desks. You can also write the lyrics on large posters and point to the words as they are sung. You might have the children who have the calendar job (responsibility) point to the word for each day of the week as it's being featured on the song.

Young children have a hard time remembering the order of the days of the week, as well as the sequence of the months (especially because so much time passes before a new month arrives). Special events, like birthdays, can heighten awareness of this yearly pattern. Here are some other ideas:

- Every month, introduce a new poem, such as those in Maurice Sendak's *Chicken Soup with Rice*.
- In addition to changing the calendar, make a big deal of the new month by changing student art work on a bulletin board.
- Put a slash though the completed day on the lunch calendar, to help the children keep track of where to find current lunch information.
- Move the desks into new arrangements on the first school day of every month.
- If children use personal writing journals each month for writer's workshop, put decorative covers on the journals indicating something special about that month (e.g., a picture of a turkey for November's journal).
- Use a conventional flip calendar to write special school and class events. Place this calendar next to the bulletin-board calendar for easy comparison.
- Hold a class meeting to list accomplishments of the previous month and set goals for the upcoming month.
- Have the children plan special events for the first school day of the month. Examples include bringing a snack for sustained silent reading (SSR) time, keeping a stuffed animal at one's desk for the day, and wearing a hat during class.
- Discuss ways that parents use calendars at home.

One more calendar recommendation this month involves counting down to Thanksgiving by "subtracting" the days. Since Thanksgiving is an event of historical significance in the United States, many families celebrate it. Create a paper chain to show the number of days from November 1 to Thanksgiving. Remove one link each day, being sure to discuss the concept of the *weekend* as you maintain an accurate count. You may wish to build the chain by using ten yellow links, ten orange links, and the remaining links in a third color. As you check the remaining number each day, discuss the groups of ten and how they can help with counting.

Estimation Jar

This month, the estimation jar can have a dual purpose. In addition to making guesses about quantities, the children will have ongoing practice recognizing and naming coins. Children need repeated opportunities to look closely at coins. Even though many first-grade students won't yet be able to read the words *penny*, *nickel*, *dime*, or *quarter*, use these words while showing pictures of the coins, and label the estimation container with the words each week. If the children have some familiarity with coins, they will be cued by the sound of a word's first letter as they look at a label. This is an opportunity to show the coins' worth as well; for instance, you can represent a penny with "1 cent" or "1 ¢".

During each of November's four weeks, feature a particular coin in the estimation jar. It's perfectly reasonable to use the same estimation jar over time—by doing so, you'll gives students a familiar frame of reference. They'll be more likely to focus on the size and number of the objects and the amount of space the items are taking up in the jar. Students may even mentally compare the jar's current items with objects they have counted previously. If you wish to make a point of the significance of a coin's size, place the same *number* of coins in the jar each week.

In September and October, students wrote estimation-jar guesses on a clipboard located next to the estimation jar. It might be time to vary that routine. This month, place the jar in its usual location—but withhold the clipboard for now. Ask the children to look carefully at the coins and make some mental guesses. After the jar has been on display for a couple of days, have a class discussion in which you ask for volunteers to offer their guesses. Write the guesses on the board. Organize the guesses in a column (so the numbers don't look like one long number), with the lowest count at the bottom and the highest at the top. Leave spaces for missing numbers in the sequence.

When you've recorded all of the guesses, put the clipboard next to the estimation jar again. Ask a student to transfer the information from the chalkboard onto the clipboard. As the children look closely at the jar once again, they may wish to revise their estimates. They may do so by placing a check mark next to the number that seems most reasonable, or by inserting additional numbers in the open spaces.

Guess My Rule

Variations of the game *Guess My Rule* can make excellent routines. This month, use a version that reinforces understandings of the quantities that coins represent. As in past months, play the game by removing specific numbers from the 1–100 chart. For the purposes of this game, you may wish to mark the day of school that the class has reached (which will now be getting closer to that all-important Day 100, usually in February), and insert all of the numerals up to 100 in the chart. If you are featuring nickels in the estimation jar this week, remove the pattern of counting by 5s in the pocket chart. Ask the children to help remove selected numbers—5, 10, 15, 20, up to 100, and have students replace in appropriate sequence while discussing the counting-by-five sequence.

The following week, repeat the process, this time drawing attention to dimes and counting by 10s. When you get to quarters, discuss the visual pattern to 100 after removing the numbers 25, 50, 75, and 100 from the chart. Ask the children what patterns they notice and what they would expect to see if this pattern were continued *beyond* 100.

Math Notebooks

Students can use their math notebooks to write equation ideas about particular numbers that you present each day. Now that you've introduced the concepts of addition and subtraction, have the children generate examples of these for a number that is being discussed. Use numbers of a manageable size, such as numbers 6 through 16. For example, if you've suggested the number 7, get things started by writing some "number sentences" involving addition on the board—such as 6 + __ = 7, or 3 + 4 = __. Show subtraction with equations like 7 − 1 = __ or 7 − 4 = __. If you wish to increase the level of difficulty, subtract 7 from a larger number; e.g., 10 − 7 = __ , or 14 − 7 = __. Ask the children if the following statements are true: 6 + 1 = 3 + 4; 8 − 1 = 7 − 0.

Modeling the use of addition, subtraction, and the equals sign by writing equations helps reinforce the children's understandings about symbols. To further strengthen their learning, remind students that they should write about addition and subtraction ideas that make sense to *them*. Encourage them to ask questions and discuss unclear ideas. Reassure them that learning takes time. It is perfectly natural for learners to have partial understandings as they encounter new ideas.

Many teachers also like to see students work on a "problem of the week" in their math notebooks. For example, "Lauren put six beads on a string. Her brother put six more. How many beads does Lauren now have on her string?" When children record their thinking about these word problems in their notebooks, they document their problem-solving efforts—a process that's valuable for them *and* you.

Introduce a new problem by writing it on the chalkboard so everyone can see it clearly. Check for comprehension by having several children restate the problem in their own words. Offer free access of materials and let the children use manipulatives such as cubes, Popsicle sticks, and other tangible objects to work out the problem. Remind the children of the availability of these items as you're introducing a new problem.

Here are some additional examples of problems:

"Alex had fifteen pennies. He gave his brother seven cents. How much money did Alex keep?"

"Chris's mother made twelve cupcakes for his birthday. Nine children ate cupcakes at the party. How many cupcakes did Chris's mother have left?"

"There were three children and two dogs at the park. How many feet do they have altogether? How many tails?"

After the children have worked on the problem by themselves, have a second class discussion to explore the various ways the students chose to demonstrate their thinking. Also, build their skills by altering the problem slightly; for example, "There were two farmers and four horses in the barn. How many feet did they have? How many tails?"

Math notebooks encourage children to practice recording their thinking and working through ideas—an essential life skill. But at this age, their notebook recordings may be limited. In addition to the math notebooks, you may wish to keep a small portfolio that includes examples of each student's word-problem work. Periodically collecting sample work can be less cumbersome than sifting through math notebooks. Collected samples can also be sent home or viewed and discussed at parent/teacher conferences.

Perceptual Number

You can also use routines involving dice, dominoes, or card configurations to help children quickly recognize and visualize small quantities. Here's one idea:

Arrange three or four small counters on the overhead projector. Turn the projector on for several seconds, then turn it off. Ask the children to show the number of objects they saw by holding up that number of fingers. Have them draw what they saw in their notebooks. Change the arrangement or the quantity of the objects and repeat.

Gradually the numbers can be clustered in combinations including single dots, and groups of twos or threes. The children can use their math notebooks to record what they have seen. This visual clustering of combinations of numbers can build the capacity for combining and separating quantities. The exercise takes very little time, and the children enjoy it as well as benefit from it.

The Mathematics

This month's activities are designed to develop the following mathematical capacities:

- combining and decomposing numbers to 10
- adding and subtracting numbers to 10
- becoming aware of doubles
- keeping track of quantities beyond 10
- using patterns of 2s, 5s, and 10s

Much of classroom work in first grade asks children to determine "How many?" or "How many now?" These seem like simple questions, but the level of difficulty changes depending the numbers involved and the problem's context (such as "How many people in your family?" vs. "How many fingers for the people in your family?"). Observing the children as they work can shed light on how they are approaching problems. By finding out how your students are thinking, you can adjust your teaching so as to challenge but not overwhelm students.

The lessons and games described below provide many opportunities for you to watch children approach a range of problems. Student responses and class discussions will help you understand where the children have gaps in their abilities. You'll see how children keep track as they count, record their thinking, combine and decompose numbers, and use strategies such as grouping numbers in meaningful ways.

Literature-Based Activities

How Many People in Your Family?

Asking the question, "How many people in your family?" usually yields numbers with magnitudes that most first graders find manageable. This activity sets the stage for many discussions about numbers and families.

Materials

- a book about families—such as Mark Brown's Arthur series, Laura Kvasnosky's Zelda and Ivy books, Beverly Cleary's Ramona titles, or Barbara Park's Junie B. Jones series

Instructions

Day 1

1. Read the book about families to the class, then discuss the story.

2. Ask the children to think about how many people there are in their own family. Remind them that *they* are important members of their families and that they should make sure to include themselves in their count.

   The topics of home and family are very familiar to first-grade students, and they usually enjoy sharing their ideas.

3. Encourage the children to describe siblings in comparative terms as older or younger than themselves. There's no need to distinguish between step-siblings and biological siblings. If a child has a sibling of any kind, that relationship will be described simply as a brother or a sister.

4. Introduce the notion of immediate family. Explain that the class is going to participate in an activity about immediate family members, and that pets will not be included—for now.

5. Ask the children to draw a picture of their family on a 3-by-5-inch index card. Those who finish early can use some of the pattern ideas from last month to create a frame around their picture, or label the family members. (See Figures 4–1 and 4–2.)

6. When all of the children are finished, ask if anyone in the class could have just one person in his or her family. (Remind them to include themselves.) Ask if it would be possible to have two people in a family.

FIGURE 4–1 ▶

Harry drew the five members of his family.

FIGURE 4–2   ◀

Sasha drew a family of four.

7. Once students agree that a family of two is possible, write a 2 on the lower *left* side of the chalkboard. Ask the children to think of the largest family that they believe will be in the class, and write that number on the lower *right* side of the chalkboard.

8. Ask the children what other sized families should go between those lowest and highest numbers, and write them on the board. Draw a horizontal line above the numbers. Ask the children to record those same numbers in their math notebooks. Explain that this will help everyone to remember the information for the next discussion about families.

9. Collect the family pictures for use the next day.

Day 2

1. In preparation for the next portion of the lesson, write the numbers that show the range of family members on small index cards. For example, on one index card, you'll write "2 people in my family," on another "3 people in my family," and so on.

2. Post the cards in a row to create a baseline starting point on the classroom wall, chalkboard, or bulletin board, and ask children to tape their family pictures in columns above the corresponding number. The children have created a graph. (See Figure 4–3.)

FIGURE 4–3　　▶

How many people are in your family?

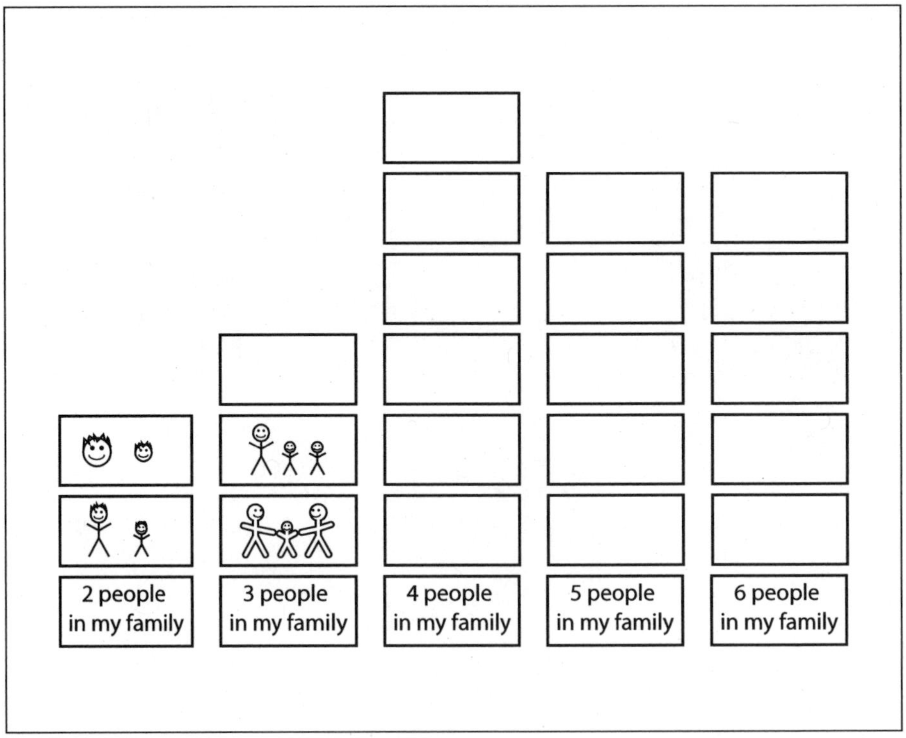

3. After the graph is complete, invite students to tell you what they notice about it. Introduce the word *column* by pointing to the vertical arrangements.

4. Ask the children to record *true math statements* about the graph in their math notebooks. Listen for accurate comparative terms such as *most* and *least*. Have the children locate their notebook pages that show the range of possible numbers in families that they wrote earlier. Ask them if they can think of ways to record the graph information on this page in their notebooks. As children make suggestions, such as "put an X above the number for each family" or "draw a picture frame," discuss the various possibilities. Encourage the children to use ideas that make sense to them to re-create the graph in their notebooks. At the same time, gently rule out time-consuming endeavors such as drawing each family picture.

Recording their thoughts in the math notebooks will give students practice organizing data and representing mathematical information. Some of these efforts will look confusing and even inaccurate. The point of the experience is to give the children an opportunity to make an attempt. Observe the children to see who is struggling, who has number-reversal problems, and assist and support individual children in these attempts. Though this activity provides observational information, it is not designed to be a formal assessment of the children' skills. Rather, it's intended to give the children a sense of accomplishment, making them more willing to record their ideas in the future. Inevitably, some children will finish earlier than others; these girls and boys can compare one another's graphs while the rest of the students finish up.

How Many People in *All* Our Families?

This activity builds on the previous one, enabling you to shift the investigation to larger numbers.

Materials

- Snap Cubes or Unifix cubes, enough for counting the class's total number of family members
- several index cards, or a 1–100 pocket chart

Instructions

1. Ponder aloud, "I wonder how many people are in *all* our families?" Give the children time to discuss how they might approach this problem.

2. Explain that the class will first try solving the problem through counting and keeping track.

3. Ask each child to gather one cube for each person in his or her family (including himself or herself).

4. Have the children help you connect all the cubes while, together, you count the cubes by 1s. Children enjoy chanting counting words aloud. In fact, they will often tell adults how far they can count, and eagerly offer to demonstrate.

5. Ask the children why it's harder to count the cubes than it is to just count out loud. Discuss the importance of counting each cube only once. Mention that it's easy to lose track as the counting goes along.

6. When you have counted all the cubes, write the number on an index card and show it to the class. If you have a number pocket chart, you can simply remove the number that represents the total and have the children read the number.

7. Explain that there are other ways to solve this big number problem. Tell the children that they will use the cubes again—but this time they will be snapping cubes together to make sticks of ten cubes. Ask for predictions about how many people the children think will be in all the families when you count the cubes using sticks of ten.

8. Have each child snap together the number of cubes representing his or her family. Write *10s* on the left side of the chalkboard and *1s* on the right side. Draw a vertical line between the words.

9. Look at the graph that you've already posted in the room, and ask the children if anyone has exactly ten people in his or her family. If they do, have them bring those sticks of ten to the front and stand them on the chalk tray (or display them in some way that will be visible to the class).

10. Next ask children with nine people in their families to stand up. Tell them that you are working to make sticks of ten, and ask them what number goes with 9 to make 10. Explain that since no one has just one person in his or her family, we'll have to wait to add 1 to the 9s.

11. Next have children with eight family members stand. Match them up with any students who have two. Attach the sticks of two cubes to the sticks of eight cubes, to make sticks of ten cubes.

12. Now have "7s" stand and put their cubes together with "3s." Continue connecting sticks to make "10s" until you have only extras, or "1s" left. If you have any sticks of 9, add the 1s to create a 10.

13. Ask the children to remind you how many cubes each stick has. Then determine with the class how many sticks of ten cubes there are. Record that number under the *10s* on the board.

14. Have the class count the 1s and place that number beneath the label on the board. Count the sticks together by chanting the pattern count of tens, and counting on for the extras. Write the double-digit (or triple-digit) number beneath the vertical line you drew on the board.

15. Discuss the connection between the tens and ones and the double-digit number.

Also discuss the importance of writing numbers carefully so they don't get reversed. (Reverse the digits and discuss the difference; e.g., 92 and 29.) The children can record information about the total in their math notebooks to gain some practice writing double-digit numbers. To make things easier, you could provide framed sentences such as, "I have __ people in my family. There are __ people in all of our families."

Extensions

In *Math and Literature (K–3): Book Two* (1995), Stephanie Sheffield describes a wonderful lesson through which each child makes a house of folded paper and draws his or her family inside the house. Incorporating this geometric link makes thinking about families even more fun. You could also have the children include pets in their pictures.

How Many Feet?

If you'd like to offer another learning experience involving large numbers, consider using the book *How Many Feet in the Bed*, by Diane Johnson Han.

Instructions

1. Read the book out loud to the class.

2. Ask students to remind you how many people are in their families.

3. Now ask them how many feet are in their houses. Offer cubes or any other manipulatives they may choose. They can also use pictures, numbers, and words in their math notebooks to show how many feet are in their houses.

4. While the children are working, walk around and observe how they are tackling the problem. Are they relying on pictures? Do they use numbers? Are they seeing patterns? How are they organizing the information? These informal work sessions can give you a lot of valuable information about how the children are thinking. (See Figures 4–4 and 4–5.)

CGI - grouping problem

FIGURE 4–4 ◀

Marc calculated the number of feet in his house by drawing them on a bed.

FIGURE 4–5 ▶

Sally calculated the number of feet by counting up, family member by family member.

5. After most of the children have completed the problem, have several of them share their solutions. (Someone will likely have included pets' feet in their calculations. This adds a new level of challenge to the problem and invites extension possibilities.) Discuss the least sophisticated solutions first, so the children feel increasingly confident as they explain their thinking, and the logic builds gradually. Some children's solutions will very likely elude some of their classmates. However, children often adopt new problem-solving strategies from this kind of discussion

6. As you discuss the problem, ask the children if they notice anything about the numbers that are cropping up in the various solutions. You might remove those numbers from the 1–100 pocket chart or ask the children to place a cube on the corresponding numbers in their notebook copies of the chart.

Number of people	Number of feet
1 person	2 feet
2 people	4 feet
3 people	6 feet

FIGURE 4–6   ◀

T-chart with the number of people and the number of feet.

7. See if anyone points out that the solutions to the problem are all even numbers. If no one sees this relationship, draw a large circle on the board and play a game of *Guess My Rule*. Tell the children that the numbers inside the circle (for example, 2, 4, 6, 8) are alike in a special way. Then ask them to tell you some numbers that would not go in the circle. Use the words *even* and *odd*.

8. To give the children more practice counting by twos, have them pattern count the number of feet in the class. They can approach this almost like a dance: While they tap one foot and stomp the other, they can whisper the odd numbers and call out the even numbers. You can also use a T-chart to show examples of how to count feet. Seeing this method of organizing data may help some children apply a similar approach to other number problems that involve patterns. At the very least, T-charts help children to visually discern patterns. (See Figure 4–6.)

Age Comparisons

The book *Zelda and Ivy*, by Laura Zoltowsky, features sisters who are two years apart in age. During the girls' many adventures, Zelda's status as the older sibling is significant. The story offers opportunities for students to think about number comparison.

Instructions

1. Read the story to the class.

2. Ask questions such as "When Zelda is six years old, Ivy is four. How old was Zelda when Ivy was born?" Students can also make up their own questions for the rest of the class to solve.

3. As the children work on the various problems, discuss the different methods they're using to keep track of the sisters' ages.

4. Encourage the children to think about the age differences among people in their own families and to solve similar problems with that information. Create a graph indicating the relationships of the siblings of class members. (See Figure 4–7.)

5. As always, have the children interpret the graph by offering a list of *true statements* about it. They can then write their ideas in their math notebooks.

FIGURE 4–7   ▶

After reading *Zelda and Ivy,* children made a graph to show older/ younger siblings.

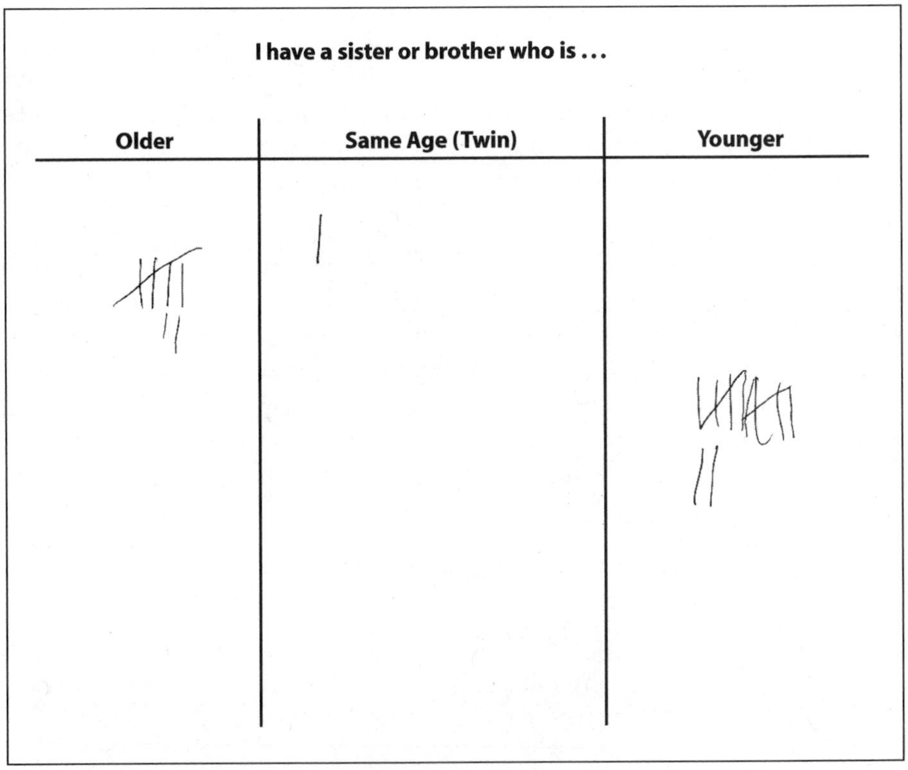

I have a sister or brother who is . . .		
Older	Same Age (Twin)	Younger

Sisters and Brothers

This activity builds on the last in a way that lets you introduce Venn diagrams.

Materials

- 3 lengths of yarn, each a different color; each length should be long enough to make a circle in which 10–20 children can stand
- 3 pieces of $8\frac{1}{2}$-by-11-inch construction paper
- 1 standard 24-by-18-inch piece of poster paper

Instructions

1. After discussing *Zelda and Ivy* (or any other book featuring siblings), look at the information you've gathered about your students' families. Ask the children if it's possible to tell from our graphs *who* has sisters or brothers.

2. Discuss what the graphs tell you about families, and what they don't tell you.

3. Ask your students who are the only children in their families to help you out. Invite them to talk about the best aspects of being an only child, so they will feel more comfortable during sibling discussions.

4. Then ask who has sisters, who has brothers, and who has sisters *and* brothers. Again, discuss the best aspects of these situations.

5. Explain that you plan to organize this information about sisters and brothers in a special way. Next, use two lengths of the yarn to create two large overlapping circles on the floor.

6. Write the word *Sisters* on a piece of construction paper and place it in one of the circles. Write the word *Brothers* on another piece of construction paper and put it in the other circle.

7. Use the third length of yarn to form a large rectangular area above the overlapping circles. Write *No sisters or brothers* on another piece of paper and place it in the rectangle.

8. Ask the class to point to the circle that is for children with sisters. Then repeat the question for brothers and for only children. Discuss the area where the circles overlap. Explain that it's for children who have both sisters *and* brothers. Point out that both yarn colors are included in this area.

9. Ask students to stand in the appropriate places. Then count how many children are in the various locations and compare the amounts.

10. The following day, display a large piece of poster paper with two overlapping circles. Use colors that correspond to those that you used in

the yarn circles. If you have small photos of the children, have each child place his or her picture in the appropriate area of the diagram. If not, the children can write their names or initials, or place an X on the diagram. (See Figure 4–8.)

11. When the diagram has been completed, compare amounts and discuss what the diagram shows. Generate and record a list of true statements about the diagram. Ask the children to talk about how they counted each category. Note their clustering, combining, and pattern-counting strategies. Pose some questions about the diagram that prompt children to combine categories, or subtract a category from the whole. For example:

   ■ How many children have only sisters or only brothers?
   ■ Which part of our graph has more people than other parts of the graph?
   ■ How many people have at least one sister and one brother?

   If you wish to continue this conversation, you might suggest that the children invite another class to create a similar diagram and then compare the results.

FIGURE 4–8 ▶

Classmates wrote their initials in this Venn diagram.

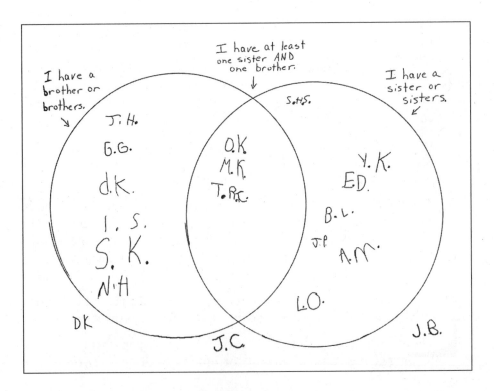

Counting and Money

This activity is drawn from the story *A Chair for My Mother*, by Vera Williams. The book tells the tale of a little girl, her mother, and her grandmother, all of whom lose their possessions in a fire. Neighbors and caring members of the girl's extended family provide replacements for many of the things that were destroyed. Once they are settled again, the family decides that what they need most of all is a really comfortable chair. The little girl, her mother, and grandmother save all of their change in a huge glass jar until they have enough money to purchase a fine new chair.

This story provides an opening for discussing all of the places that families collect coins.

Materials

- 1 jar or small plastic bag per pair of students or per student
- 1 set of plastic coins for pair or individual

Instructions

1. Give each child or pair of students a jar or small bag and a set of plastic coins.

2. Ask the children to identify the coins, compare them, and discuss their worth. Students can determine which coins have the most and the least. The class can discuss the value of the coins and do some pattern counting. Dollar and cent symbols can be reinforced as well. Use this month's estimation-jar routines to build additional understandings of particular coins. This is a good opportunity to observe and assess student understanding.

Whole-Class/Menu Activities

Storyboards

You introduced storyboards last month when you showed butterflies of two colors settling on a background of flowering plants. The class counted the yellow and orange butterflies. They learned that each plant had the same number of butterflies, but different numbers of the two colors. The children created and enacted stories about butterflies flying way and counted how many butterflies remained on the plants.

First graders need to practice working with part/whole relationships, addition and subtraction, and number-family relationships on an ongoing basis and in a variety of ways. This menu possibility enables you to strengthen your students' learning by creating a simple contextual storyboard: a turkey.

Materials

- 5 pieces of $8\frac{1}{2}$-by-11-inch brown construction paper
- several pieces of $8\frac{1}{2}$-by-11-inch red construction paper
- several pieces of $8\frac{1}{2}$-by-11-inch black construction paper
- 1 small, clear plastic bag
- 1 glue stick
- 1 red marker; 1 black marker

Instructions

1. On each piece of brown construction paper, draw an outline of a turkey with no tail. Tape the tail-less turkeys on the chalkboard or bulletin board.

2. From the red and black construction paper, cut out an equal number of long, thin pieces that look like tail feathers. Put all the feathers into the bag.

3. Remind the children of last month's butterfly problem that involved combinations for the number 3.

4. Explain that the students will now generate combinations for turkeys with four tail feathers each. Hold up the bag of tail feathers and point out that feathers are either black or red. Remind the class that no two turkeys can have exactly the same number of red and black tail feathers—but that they all must end up with four.

5. Point out the five tail-less turkeys on the board. Ask the children to tell you the greatest number of black feathers a turkey could have. Most likely, someone will answer "four." Write *4b* (for black) + *0r* (for red) = *4f* (for feathers) on the board under that first turkey. Use a glue stick to glue the black feathers on to one of the turkeys. (You may wish to write the equations using black and red markers, to visually reinforce the connection with the feather colors.)

6. Explain that you still want to use as many black feathers as possible on the next turkey, but that you know you can't have two turkeys look alike. Ask the children how many of each color feather you can use. Record the appropriate response—*3b + 1r = 4f*—on the board under the second turkey.

7. Continue this process through the various remaining combinations (*2b + 2r = 4f*, *1b + 3r = 4f*, and *0b + 4r = 4f*).

8. When the children feel that they have generated all of the combinations, ask them if any two turkeys have exactly the same combinations of feathers. Check that the written equations correspond accurately with the pictures.

This exercise can help demonstrate that 3 + 1 and 1 + 3 are two different pictures. In the next few days, try various numbers instead of 4—each time asking the children if they think they have generated all of the combinations. During one of these discussions, a child may notice a pattern and order the combinations; e.g., 0 + 4, 1 + 3, 2 + 2, 3 + 1, 4 + 0. If this happens, physically rearrange the storyboards to show this idea as clearly as possible. This ordered display will create a visual representation that can help children see the patterns of red and black feathers.

Extensions

After the children have worked on this problem several times, give them an opportunity to select a number from a range (5 through 8, for instance) and to show turkey-feather combinations for that number. This time, they can work out the problem on their own, with paper and markers. If the children aren't comfortable drawing the turkeys and their uncertainty would create a distraction, provide copies of small turkeys without feathers so students can simply draw the feather combinations on them.

If you use turkey storyboards as a menu option, designate a range of appropriate numbers from which the child can choose. Use your observations from the previous individual work to determine the appropriate range for particular students. As the children gather their materials, quietly tell each his or her number range. The children can make small booklets of turkey pictures and number combinations during the menu activity. You can then compile their booklets to create a class book, or create a smaller version of a class book that the youngsters can take home after menu time.

Build a Number

Like the storyboard work the children have been doing, this activity emphasizes number combinations.

Materials

- 1 set of Snap Cubes or Unifix cubes per 3–4 students (borrow some from other classrooms if needed)
- 1 set of cubes for you

Instructions

1. Conduct a whole-class lesson in which you have small groups of students (perhaps three or four) build sticks of five cubes, using two different colors of cubes. Remind the children about the storyboard work they have already done involving combinations of butterflies and turkey feathers. Explain that the idea of using two different colors

to show combinations of five is like using red and black tail feathers to show various combinations, or orange and yellow butterflies to show combinations of three.

2. After the children have had some time to explore combinations, invite them to demonstrate their results.

3. Reinforce their learning by demonstrating combinations using your own set of cubes. Suppose your set has red and blue cubes. Write the number 5 on a large piece of chart paper or on the board, and ask the children to help you build the various combinations with your set.

4. Using the red and blue cubes, build the various models of the number 5. Introduce the term *number family*, and point out that the children investigated other number families (such as 3 and 4) in the butterfly and turkey activities. You may wish to ask some questions to help the children order the combinations of five; for example, "What would we need first if we wanted to use lots of blue cubes and have a total of 5?"

5. Prop your sticks in random order on the chalkboard tray to display them, and ask which stick has the most red cubes. Write *5 red plus 0 blue equals 5 cubes* on the chart paper or chalkboard.

6. Next ask, "If we don't count the stick with the five red cubes, which of the remaining sticks has the most red?" Write *4 red + 1 blue = 5 cubes* on the board. Position this stick next to the one with five red cubes.

7. Continue this process until you've placed all the sticks in order. (See Figure 4–9.)

8. This arrangement of the sticks reveals obvious color and geometric patterns, such as stair-step growth and triangles within a rectangle. This visual is very powerful for some children, and brings a new dimension to the study of number families.

As with the storyboards, children need many experiences with these number-family combinations. If you offer this activity as a menu choice, students can use their math notebooks or some other form of recording sheets to practice writing symbolic representations of number combinations in the form of simple equations. Observe the children while they work, to find out if they're seeing patterns. Additionally, you can play a game with the cubes as you walk around and visit various children during menu time. Select a stick that a child has made, snap off all the cubes of one color, and conceal those cubes behind your back. For instance, if the child has made a combination of five by using three red cubes and two blue cubes, snap off and hide the segment of three reds. Show the child the remaining segment of two blues and ask how many cubes are

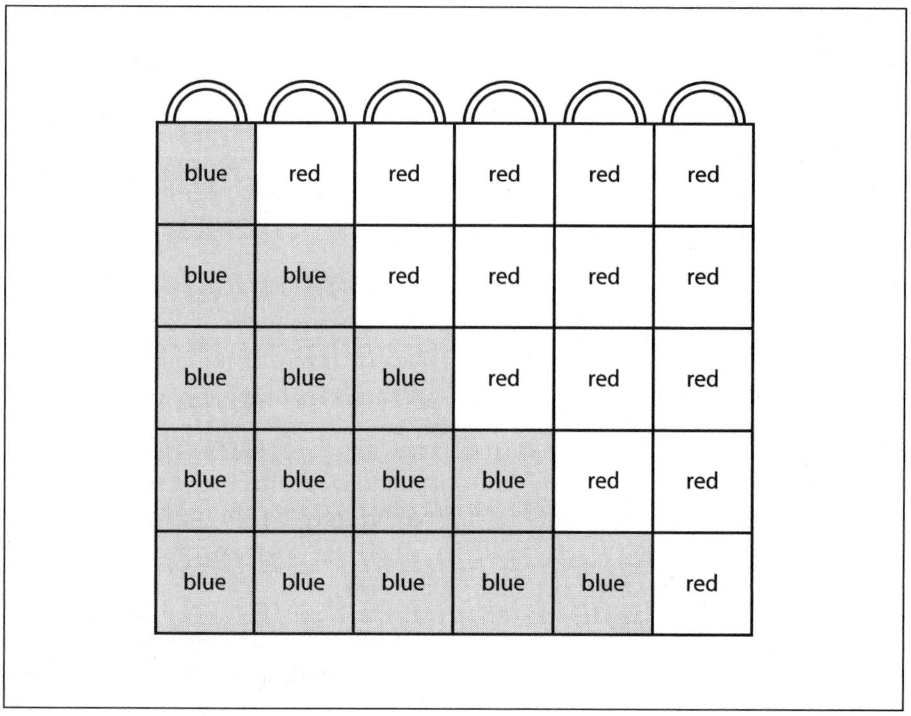

FIGURE 4–9 ◀

Build a number with red and blue cube sticks.

blue	red	red	red	red	red
blue	blue	red	red	red	red
blue	blue	blue	red	red	red
blue	blue	blue	blue	red	red
blue	blue	blue	blue	blue	red

missing. Notice whether the child needs time to determine the answer or can respond immediately.

Counting by 5s

Pattern counting by 5s helps children gain flexibility as they rearrange numbers, take them apart, and combine them in different ways. Proficiency with patterns of five enables them to use groupings of ten more effectively. Young children frequently learn to chant pattern-counting sequences by 5s and 10s. They may recite the words flawlessly, while having little or no idea of the quantities that their words represent. For example, perhaps you've asked a student to count cubes by 5s, and the child has moved each cube one at a time while saying "five, ten, fifteen," and so on.

Parents often introduce an early math idea to babies and very young children by showing them how many fingers to hold up to express their age. However, many teachers try to discourage children from using fingers as they count, to prevent them from becoming overly dependent on finger counting. (Of course, many of us adults may still "count on our fingers" at times! Indeed, our base-ten number system very likely evolved as it did precisely because humans have a total of ten digits on their hands.) Still, you can use the natural context of hands to demonstrate patterns of five.

This simple activity involves using cutout handprints to help children visualize groupings by fives.

Materials

- enough blank newsprint sheets, wrapping paper, wallpaper, and construction paper for each student to trace his or her hand and cut out the tracing to make handprints

Instructions

1. Invite the children to use the variety of types of paper to trace and cut out their handprints. The children can help one another trace around both hands.

2. Ask the children to put the handprints into groups based on an agreed-upon criteria, such as the type of paper, right hands versus left hands, patterned paper versus solid-color paper, and so on. Repeat this process using a different sorting criteria.

3. In each group of handprints, ask how many handprints there are. Then ask how many total fingers (including thumbs) are in the group.

This experience reveals that the total number of fingers will remain the same regardless of how the hand prints are arranged, whether large and small, or left and right. You can also display the handprints in a line, writing the corresponding number of fingers above each hand.

Tally Marks

In this activity, children devise quicker ways to keep track of patterns of five by using tally marks—something that appeals to many children as a means of keeping track of quantities.

Instructions

1. Demonstrate the tally-mark method by drawing four tally marks while counting them out loud and then drawing the fifth tally mark as a diagonal line through the four lines. Or, you can draw the four marks as a square and then draw the fifth mark diagonally inside the square. (See Figure 4–10.) Draw two more sets of five. Then draw a circle around each set of five lines and count out the number of sets by 5s ("Five, ten, fifteen").

2. Have the children practice this technique in their math notebooks. The next time the class is counting a quantity of fifteen or more, encourage them to use tally marks to keep track. Let them know it's

FIGURE 4–10 ◄

Two types of tally marks for counting by 5s.

Keeping track of 5s with tally marks.

||||||| or □/

OK to use the tally-mark style (four lines versus a box with a diagonal line) they prefer. Regardless of which kind of tally style the children choose, many students use this technique in their work once they become comfortable with it.

Extensions

- If you're looking for a more interesting means of generating numbers for tally-mark practice, have the children flip a coin twenty-five times and keep track of whether they get heads or tails.

- Additional practice can be given using tangible objects. Provide the children with Popsicle sticks and have them show quantities by creating tally marks with the sticks. Later in the year, you can use this technique to demonstrate solutions to addition and subtraction problems as well.

Ten Frames

Many students benefit from visualizing geometric images. This activity provides another spatial tool that can help them develop understandings about the key role that the number 10 plays in our number system. Ten frames can also clarify relationships between the numbers 1 through 10.

A "ten frame" is a horizontal rectangle that's been divided into ten squares. (See below.)

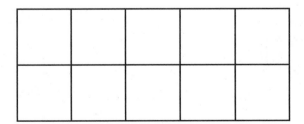

Ten-frame activities provide children with opportunities to build combinations of the number 10 and at the same time see a group of ten represented as a unit. The children can place one object (e.g., a cube) in each square and easily count the total.

The procedure for placing the objects in the squares is quite specific: A student places the first object in the top left square within the rectangle and then proceeds from left to right across the rest of that row. After the top row of five squares has been filled in, the child fills the second row in the same way. You can point out that this idea is the same as writing their names from left to right.

When the children *remove* objects from the ten frame, they must do so in reverse order. Consistent placement procedures will help them visualize quantities. After a good deal of practice, many children will be able to visualize an amount without actually placing the objects.

An overhead projector is a nice way to introduce children to ten frames. If you don't have access to one, you can draw a large ten frame and use easily removable stick-on dots. Whichever approach you use, be sure to spend time demonstrating the placement procedures. During the demonstration, give some class members opportunities to practice and model the procedure for the rest of the students.

Once the children understand how to place objects on a ten frame, they will be ready to practice with partners.

Materials

- pages containing several blank ten frames; 1 page per student (see Blackline Masters)

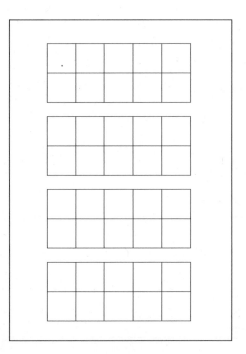

- cards for the numbers 1–20, from a 1–100 pocket chart; or 1 die
- 1 envelope
- 1 set of cubes or other counting objects per child

Instructions

1. Give each child a page that has two, three, or four frames.

2. Put the 1–20 number cards in the envelope.

3. Draw a number out of the envelope (or roll the die to generate numbers), and ask students to place the corresponding number of cubes (or other counting objects) on their ten frames. Remind them to use the correct adding and removing procedures.

4. Have children use the ten frames to demonstrate addition and subtraction problems. For example, one child could roll a die, and the rest of the students could add the corresponding number of cubes to their ten frames. A second child rolls the die again, and the children add the new quantity to their frames. (See Figure 4–11.)

5. Write number sentences (such as $6 + 5 = 11$) on the board as students practice using their ten frames. Once the children feel comfortable with ten-frame procedures, create laminated ten frames for use during partner-oriented menu work. When your students are ready, they can also practice writing number sentences in their math notebooks, or on some other kind of recording sheet.

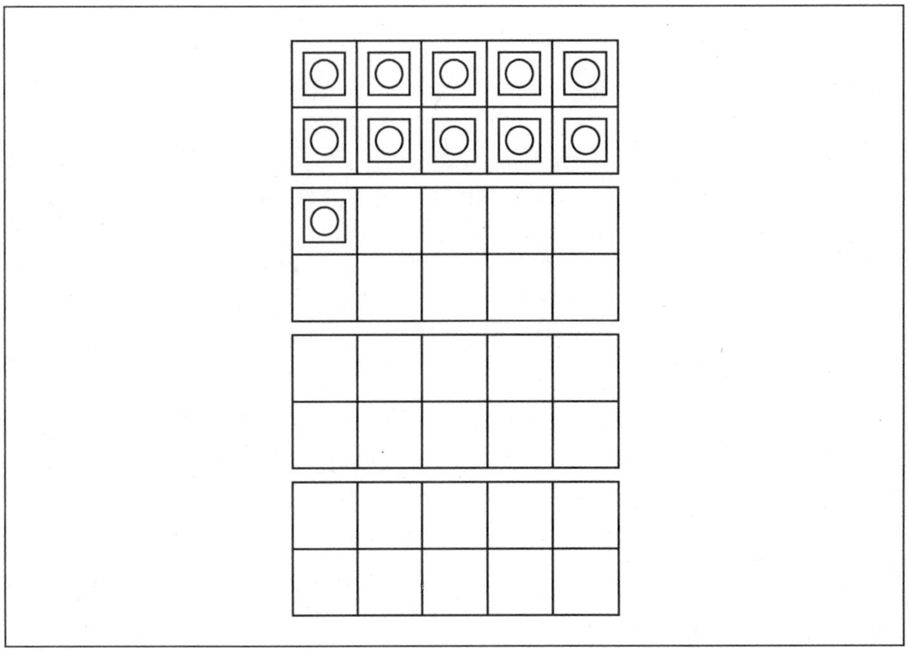

FIGURE 4-11 ◀

Ricardo added six cubes to his ten frame for the first roll of the die, then added five more cubes for the second roll.

Food Math

One of my students' favorite ways to use ten frames is to play *Food Math*—in which they place Cheerios or some other food objects in the ten-frame squares. Consider providing ten frames on recycled paper for this activity, so you can easily wrap up the paper and toss it into a recycling box after removing the food.

Before you even mention the idea of using food in a ten frame, remind children of the required procedures for adding objects to a ten frame and removing objects. Also, review the *Math Words* poster, discussing addition and subtraction symbols in particular. Explain that students will have plenty of opportunities to practice addition, subtraction, and counting during the year, but that you're going to introduce them to a particularly fun math activity—one in which they'll get to eat the "take aways."

Materials

- 1 sheet of four ten frames (total of 40 squares) per child
- 1 small cup per child, filled with dry, easily countable cereal such as Cheerios
- overhead projector

Instructions

1. Give each child a sheet of four ten frames and a cup filled with cereal. Let the children eat a couple pieces of the cereal.

2. Explain that you're going to tell some stories. The children will act them out with you while you model putting Cheerios on your overhead example.

3. Begin telling and acting out addition and subtraction stories. The goofier the stories, the better—for instance: "Once upon a time, there was a little squirrel named Socrates. He was very busy collecting 'acorns.' One day Socrates collected eleven acorns." (Everyone places eleven Cheerios on his or her ten frame.) "Socrates' sister, Susie, came and gobbled up one acorn." (Remove one acorn from your ten frame, and eat it.) "How many acorns did Socrates have left?" Write $11 - 1 = 10$ on the board, saying the number sentence out loud as you write.

4. Continue offering additional stories, until all the Cheerios have been removed. For example, after telling the story about sister Susie, say: "Then Socrates' cousin Sly came and grabbed five more acorns. How many acorns did Socrates have left?" (You'd write $10 - 5 = 5$.) Then

say, "Socrates decided to just start over collecting acorns, so he ate the last five as a snack." (Write $5 - 5 = 0$.)

Be sure to use simple stories throughout the game. Watch as the children add and subtract their Cheerios on their ten frames, and remind them to use the proper procedures. When it's time to state the solution to a problem, ask the children how many Cheerios are on the top row of their ten frames, and how many are on the bottom, then how many are on their ten frame altogether. Also make sure the stories all involve enough subtraction that all the Cheerios end up being removed and eaten.

As the children place their cereal in the squares, you'll find it easy to see who is having trouble keeping track of the amounts. After the first lesson, during which you model the placement of Cheerios on your ten frame, you'll be able to circulate around the room and help out as needed. It's also helpful to verbally describe what the ten frames should look like. For instance, suppose the story is: "Jeffrey had ten basketballs, and his grandmother gave him another one for his birthday." In this case, you would describe the resulting ten frame as: "One ten frame is full, and the next ten frame has the first square filled in."

Food Math helps children overcome the common reluctance to use subtraction and enables them to see quantities clearly displayed. The activity's lighthearted quality also allows you to present and discuss a variety of problems without overwhelming students.

Extensions

Each time you play *Food Math*, introduce a featured math idea, such as "plus 1, minus 1." Here are some additional possibilities:

- different combinations to make a number (i.e., number families)
- plus 2, minus 2
- doubles
- plus 5, minus 5
- plus 10, minus 10
- add and subtract only even numbers
- add and subtract only odd numbers

Ten frames are especially valuable for helping children to visualize 5s and 10s. Give your students copies of ten-frame sheets to tape into their math notebooks. Remind them that they can use ten frames to keep track of amounts while they're adding and subtracting to solve a problem.

Pennies, Nickels, and Dimes

During November, you've focused on building children's awareness of various ways to combine and keep track of numbers. Just as tally marks and ten frames provide tools for managing quantities of 5s, 10s, and 1s, experience with money can help to build these concepts. Money is quite abstract, yet for many children, it is one of the most familiar number-related tools. Some six- and seven-year olds have had enough experience with coins that they can distinguish, name, and identify various coins' worth. Other children have had little exposure to and awareness of money.

For the purposes of learning about coins, it's unfortunate that U.S. coins aren't graduated in size according to their worth (e.g., why is a dime smaller than a nickel?). Even the coins' names seem arbitrary. As we've seen, this month's estimation-jar routine helps children to learn coins' names and monetary value. And if you decide to read the book *A Chair for My Mother*, you'll provide your students with opportunities to discuss the various places families may store coins. One of my students explained that her father empties his pockets each evening. Before he puts the coins in a basket, he helps her count the change.

There are a variety of ways to give children practice with coins. And since the U.S. coinage system is based on multiples of 1, 5, and 10, these activities also enhance their understandings of these numbers. Consider these ideas:

- Provide jars containing real or plastic coins that the children can sort, name, count, and combine in various ways. BandAid boxes and small coin purses also make appealing coin containers.

- For children who have learned the names and value of pennies, nickels, and dimes, give them a copy of a 1–100 chart. Ask them to color in numbers related to a coin's value. For example, they could color the number 5 and all its multiples to show understanding of a nickel's value.

- Have students write the sequence of numbers they would count out to add up the total value of a group of coins; the total value of a particular coin value could be circled. To illustrate, for two dimes, a nickel, and two pennies, a child would write *1, 2, 3, 4, 5, 6, 7, 8, 9,* ⑩(for one dime); *11, 12, 13, 14, 15, 16, 17, 18, 19,* ⑳(for the second dime); *21, 22, 23, 24,* ㉕ (for the nickel); and ㉖, ㉗ (for the two pennies). You can provide children with a piece of adding machine tape to record the numbers as they count. Instruct the children to write the numbers vertically, so that digits don't run together like one long number.

- Play store with plastic pennies, nickels, and dimes to provide practice with 1s, 5s, and 10s. (Quarters provide a valuable relationship to 100, but it may be too complex at this time of the year.) Collect sets of about a dozen little items—such as a spinning top, a ring, a barrette, a little plastic figurine, a small stuffed animal, etc.—and attach a price tag to each item. Prices can reflect the appropriate number range for your students. For example, you could price the most expensive item at around 12 cents. (Include and discuss money symbols such as "$" and "¢" on the price tags, and ask students to record these symbols in their math notebooks along with information about the worth of pennies, nickels, and dimes.)

Have children work in pairs. One partner child "sells" the items; the other "buys" them with plastic coins. Both children count the money for each exchange, naming the coins as they do so. After the transaction, the children switch roles.

As you circulate among the children, notice who needs more support and instruction in learning the names and value of the coins. You can also note who is counting on, combining numbers, using estimation, and trading for new coins (e.g., a child may select a dime and one penny rather than counting out eleven pennies) when appropriate.

Chapter 5

December

GEOMETRY

The Learning Environment

December is always an exciting and busy month. At this time of year, many teachers find it a real challenge to maintain a rigorous academic program while accepting and incorporating children's high spirits. Here's one way to approach this: Shift your students' focus to something new or unexpected. Geometry is rich in mathematical possibilities and can include abundant real-life connections while providing an interesting change of pace. Your planning for the month will involve pushing beyond shape identification to helping students clearly define the attributes of particular shapes. ■

This month, children will again have opportunities to count, compare, sort, create patterns, and look for symmetry. As they make designs with a variety of shapes, they'll be keeping track of the parts within the whole. The activities described in this chapter offer real-life connections and link one strand of mathematics to another. They also encourage numerical reasoning, by prompting children to answer questions such as, "How many sides are on a triangle? How many sides are on two triangles?"

December is also laden with religious holidays. Rather than focus on a particular holiday, continue building on the topic of families and encourage the children to explore their families' traditions. One particularly powerful activity that connects families and geometry is quilt-making.

Many children find geometry very appealing. You'll likely spot someone in your class who particularly shines when engaged in spatial tasks. Some of the children who perform with ease and expertise when working in a geometric or spatial realm may be the same students who struggle when confronted with numerical work, or with reading. Experiencing success in geometry can exert a positive impact on children's view of mathematics and their perceptions of themselves as learners.

Your district or state recommendations may designate specific shapes first graders are expected to study in their introduction to geometry. Regardless of the particular shape names, you'll want to ensure that your students develop the following geometric understandings:

- Shapes have carefully defined names.
- Shapes have variability (e.g., there are different kinds of triangles).
- Shapes can be taken apart and put back together.
- Shapes can be made from other shapes.
- Shapes have sides and corners (or angles).
- Shapes are all around us.

Routines

Calendar

Months of the Year

The last month in the calendar year, December particularly helps children realize that a year is a repeated pattern. Encourage them to visualize the months as a cycle. One way to approach this is to use pictures from old calendars or magazines to depict each month visually, for example, seasonal pictures of animals during various months. Mount the pictures on large index cards and write the appropriate name of the month on each card. Display the cards in chronological order, and include the number of the month within the year's sequence. To reinforce the order, list the names of the months on a large piece of paper, and post the list near the calendar. When you have extra class time, mix the month cards up and have the children help to rearrange them in their correct order. Or, remove a card and see if the children can tell what month is missing.

Large Calendar Display

Have the children help you create the large calendar display for the month. Show the children the blank calendar grid and point out that all the November pieces have been removed. Look at last month's calendar page on a smaller calendar and discuss how to determine where the Day 1 calendar marker should go for December.

To get the children thinking about geometry, ask them to look at the empty grid and tell you what they notice about the shapes they see on it. The words *rectangle* and *square* will likely come up in the conversation. Include shape names on your math vocabulary poster. Then ask what makes a rectangle a rectangle, and a square a square. This is an ideal opportunity to mention that a square is a particular *type* of rectangle. Ask whether the children think other shapes would work well to create a calendar. Entertain the idea of circular or triangular spaces on a calendar. Discuss the number of days in December and talk about special events that are of interest to the children.

Distribute pre-made calendar numbers and have the children take turns tacking them to the grid. Ask each child to check the words at the top of the grid and determine what day of the week his or her particular number will fall in the month.

You might also have the children create their own calendar markers instead of using the pre-made ones. They can do this fairly easily by using shape designs such as triangular pine trees and circular snowmen. (If these seasonal figures don't fit your setting, select other geometric alternatives that the children can manage independently.) Allow each child to determine which *one* of two alternatives he or she would like to create. Provide the students with blank precut squares of two colors, from which they can cut their shapes. This will ensure that the resulting markers fit into the calendar squares on the grid.

After everyone has finished creating markers of their choice, see how many children have made which kind of marker, and how these new markers might be arranged on the calendar grid. The number of days in the month will likely differ from the number of students in your class. The children can discuss how they would like to complete enough markers for the entire month.

Once the children have created their markers, ask those who created trees (for example) to stand and be counted. Record the number of tree markers on the board. Next have those who created snowmen (for example) stand to be counted. Record that number as well. Ask the children if there is the same number of trees as snowmen. Discuss whether it would work to have a "tree, snowman, tree, snowman, tree, snowman" (i.e., an *ab*, *ab*, *ab* pattern) in the calendar grid. If they think such as pattern is feasible, have them line up next to each other, with their calendar markers, to demonstrate the pattern. If you don't have the same number of trees as snowmen, have tree makers and snowmen makers stand in two separate groups. Compare the numbers and discuss a different pattern that might work. The children can arrange themselves to check how the pattern looks.

Once the class has found a solution, write the numerals on the calendar markers and display them on the calendar. (Make sure the numbers are big enough and are all positioned in the same way on the markers.)

Children enjoy the active, investigative nature of this activity. Often, they'll create wonderful, authentic artwork for the calendar. As they're tackling this task, they create shapes and work with numerical relationships, such as even and odd numbers and number sequences. They also gain exposure to the fact that the outcome to a problem is not always clear in advance.

Calendar Countdowns

Since there is a great deal to look forward to this month, consider creating a paper chain so the calendar routine can include some subtraction (as you did in November). This time, count down to winter vacation. Instead of using a paper chain made up of groups of ten links (as described for last month), you might use groups of five links.

Another possibility is to create a large ten-frame display. You can use taped paper markers on an enlarged ten frame (see Chapter 4) to show how many days remain until the vacation. For each day that passes, you can remove a marker, much as you detach the links of a paper chain. The remaining markers in the ten frame show how many days are left in the countdown. Even though this month's math focus is geometry, include a daily conversation about subtraction.

Estimation Jar

During December, feature a particular shape in the estimation jar each week. In most classrooms, math manipulatives provide small geometric objects. These objects come in a wide variety of shapes and sizes, enabling you to use estimation jars of varying sizes from one week to the next if you wish. You can again use a clipboard as a central location for children to record their estimates.

If you used coins in the estimation jar last month, you may have displayed the name and symbol for the featured coin (e.g., the word *penny* and a picture or example of a penny) on the jar to help the children learn the vocabulary. You can continue this practice in December with geometry.

Draw the featured shape and print its name on a label, then attach the label to the lid of the jar.

Extensions

- Use two identical estimation jars and display the same type of similar sized shapes inside both. But double the number of shapes in one of the jars. Have the class help you count the number in the smaller jar. Label that jar with the number and have the children use this information to estimate the second jar's count.

- Fill two same-sized jars with two different shapes, but use the same number of objects in the two jars. Discuss the shapes' attributes and sizes when speculating about the amounts and making comparisons. This activity encourages understandings about conservation of number.

- In addition to asking the children to predict how many shapes are in the estimation jar, ask them whether they think it would be possible to use the pieces in the jar to create another shape that looks just like the shape in the jar—only bigger. Have the children count the shapes, then invite them to make new and larger versions of the shape. Using an overhead projector, show how to create a big square from smaller squares, or a large triangle from smaller triangles.

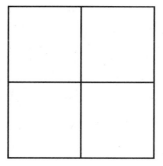 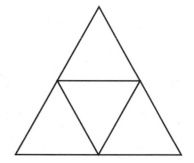

If the children succeed in creating a larger version of a shape, ask if they have any advice for someone who has never done this. Ask, "What worked? What was difficult?" "Do you think that this process is possible for any shape? Why or why not?" This activity could become a menu possibility later in the month.

Math Notebooks

This month's work will expand geometry beyond naming shapes—to defining the attributes of those shapes. Students can use their math notebooks to keep a record of this information. Remind class members about the number recordings they've made based on the day's featured number. Explain that this month they'll do something similar, but now they'll be thinking, writing, and drawing about shapes.

Most first graders can correctly identify circles, squares, triangles, and rectangles (though they may confuse the language of these last two). To start things off, have the class generate a list of all the shapes they can think of. Select a shape from the list and ask someone to tell you about that shape. On large chart paper, record the children's ideas. Draw and record the name of each shape as it's discussed. Include some nonexamples, placing an X through each to show its status. Discussing what a shape is not, as well as what it is, can help clarify attributes. During the discussion, also identify the sides and corners of each shape and begin using the word *angle* in talking about corners. Consider developing and posting a geometry vocabulary list, and adding to it during the month.

As you discuss each shape, ask the children to think about where they might see that shape in day-to-day life. Responses might include "Our door is a rectangle"; "The clock is a circle"; or "We have squares on our calendar." Include those ideas on the chart paper as well.

After each class discussion about a particular shape, give the children time to record ideas in their math notebooks. Then notice who is able to draw the shapes. You may need to help children write words like *rectangle*, *triangle*, *hexagon*, and so forth.

Use this same routine to discuss the shapes that your district or state has identified as mandatory to cover. Once the routine is established, you might introduce a shape by giving clues. For instance, say, "I'm thinking of a shape that has four sides, and four corners, or angles." Draw the shape as you give the clues. Discuss the similarities and differences between shapes. For example, perhaps a featured four-sided shape is actually a trapezoid rather than a rectangle or a square.

Perceptual Number

If the children have not yet had experiences glimpsing small quantities of objects arranged on the overhead projector, see the "Perceptual Number" section in Chapter 4. You can give students regular practice with perceptual-number quantities by using quick-image "dot cards" created specifically for this purpose. (See Figure 5–1.)

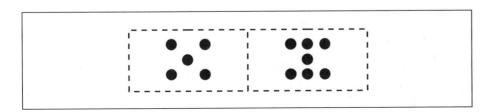

FIGURE 5–1 ◀

Perceptual dot cards.

FIGURE 5–2   ▶

Dominoes.

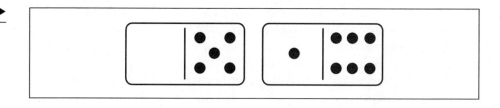

Select a dot card and display it briefly on the overhead projector. Then ask students to draw what they've seen. Discuss the kinds of shapes that would emerge if the children used lines to connect various dots.

You can also use dominoes to similar effect. (See Figure 5–2.) Consider reading the book *Domino Addition* by Lynette Long to provide the class with basic information about how dominoes have been designed. Give the children time to examine a set of dominoes, then have class members discuss shapes they notice within a domino. Next, flash domino images on the overhead projector. Begin by showing just one half of a domino. When the children are proficient with these images, try showing a whole domino. Discuss ways to determine the total number of dots shown on a particular domino.

The Mathematics

The geometry lessons in this chapter focus on two-dimensional shapes. These activities will support children's future understandings about three-dimensional shapes. (Later in the spring, you'll introduce the topic of neighborhoods—and three-dimensional geometry will be an ideal mathematical focus at that time.) The lessons also have been arranged in two categories: activities based on children's literature, and those requiring math manipulatives (such as pattern blocks, tangrams, Multilink cubes, geo boards and blocks, attribute blocks, color tiles, Cuisenaire rods, and dominoes). Base your selections on accessible materials as well as the relevance of the contexts for your class.

Literature-Based Activities

Shapes

The Greedy Triangle by Marilyn Burns provides a particularly appealing introduction to the vocabulary of shapes and their attributes. The rich and playful text relates various geometric shapes to one another. The story features a main character (the Greedy Triangle) who is dissatisfied with being a plain old triangular shape and yearns for other possibilities. The wise and powerful Shape Shifter helps transform the Greedy Triangle by adding sides to the triangle. Each time a side is added, the Greedy Triangle becomes a new shape. In the end, the Greedy Triangle decides that it's best to be who and what he really is, and is content to return to his original form.

As you read the book to your students, name and describe the new shapes that emerge, and connect them to real-world examples. For example, "Quadrilaterals can become baseball diamonds, television screens, windows, and much more." As the story progresses, children begin making predictions about what will happen as more and more sides are added to the shape.

This story offers first graders lots of information to discuss and absorb. After reading the book, revisit the illustrations and begin itemizing the shapes that appear in the text. The children will be familiar with the idea of symmetry from earlier in the year and will likely discuss this attribute as well. If you've begun developing a geometry vocabulary list for display in the room, refer to and extend it each time a new shape is explored.

As you discuss and write about shapes, keep using descriptive words like *side*, *corner*, *angle*, *line*, etc. Repetition with this language helps students to make it their own. They begin to take pride in the sound and complexity of terms like *trapezoid* and *hexagon*.

More Literature Possibilities

There are many excellent children's literature resources that can be used to help the children with shape identification. Perhaps your math notebook shape recording routine will involve reading a shape book before generating ideas about a particular shape. Here are some suggested possibilities for this purpose:

The Shape of Things, Dayle Ann Dodds

My Very First Book of Shapes, Eric Carle

A Secret Birthday Message, Eric Carle

Ten Black Dots, Donald Crews

The Wing on a Flea, Ed Emberley

Color Farm, Lois Ehlert

Color Zoo, Lois Ehlert

A Cloak for a Dreamer, Eileen Friedman

Look Around: A Book about Shapes, Leonard Fisher

A Triangle for Adora, Ifema Onyetulu

The Boy with the Square Eyes, Snape and Snape

Author Studies

If you are interested in combining the study of shapes with literature and/or art, there are several children's author/illustrators who regularly feature geometry in their work. Ed Emberley, Tana Hoban, and Brian Wildsmith offer a variety of interesting possibilities. Each of these authors books have long been featured in collections of children's literature. You will want to request that your media specialist or librarian maintain and assist you with this collection since many of these books may go in and out of print.

Ed Emberley is known for making his artistic methods accessible to his young readers. Perhaps his best known book is the *Thumbprint Book*. Some of Emberley's works, including *Picture Pie,* which includes fractions such as halves and quarters; *Make a World;* and *The Wing of a Flea* specifically feature geometry as a topic and provide step by step instructions for children to create a variety of very satisfying pictures. Emberley has also created a playful shape book called *Go Away Big Green Monster*. This book features cut out shape holes in each page that become parts of interesting pictures.

Some children who have felt reluctant to draw, have remarked that these books helped them feel like real artists because the directions allowed them to make things look the way they do in real life. The step by step development of the pictures often begins with a simple geometric shape. The drawing sequences are actually developed through growth patterns, adding one feature to the shape in each step. Once the children notice how this pattern develops, they are able to use the idea to create their own geometric growth patterns. The class will enjoy everything from drawing and painting, to stamp printing, through Mr. Emberley's examples.

Tana Hoban has created many powerful geometric books through use of photography. Some examples of her picture books include: *Circles, Triangles, and Squares, Shapes, Shapes, Shapes, So Many Circles, So Many Squares,* and *Cubes, Cones, Cylinders, and Spheres*. Digital and disposable cameras, are now available at reasonable costs, so photography has become accessible for classroom exploration. Children can explore the environment in and around the school while creating class books that view the world through Tana Hoban's geometric lens.

Brian Wildsmith creates illustrations by painting collages of shapes within the outline of other forms. The books *Brian Wildsmith's 123s* and *Circus* go in and out of print, but are very frequently included in children's literature collections in libraries. *Puzzles, Jack and the Meanstalk,* and *The North Wind and the Sun* exemplify Brian Wildsmith's unique geometric painting style. Children enjoy the free form designs that are created by making an outline, then filling it in by drawing an array of triangles, diamonds, and other shapes. Once the outline and shapes have been completed, children can paint or use markers to color the interiors of the shapes creating colorful products. This format can easily be used to compile an interesting class shape book.

Object Attributes

Margaret Wise Brown's book *The Important Thing* was featured in Chapter 2. The book looks at specific objects and examines their attributes. It then uses a repeating textual pattern to identify each object's most important attribute. This month, you could revisit the book but use shapes and their attributes as your focus.

For instance, if you're discussing squares, students could cite various places they've noticed squares in the world—such as floor and ceiling tiles. They could then identify the specific attributes of squares. Again, the text's refrain can help them prioritize their ideas by encouraging them to recite, "But the important thing about squares is that. . . ." This activity also provides another opportunity to create a class book of student responses.

I Spy

Play *I Spy* by selecting shapes in the classroom and inviting students to locate the shapes. Give several clues at a time to move the game along quickly. For instance, if your target object is a table near your desk, say, "I spy a large circle in the front of the room." The children then move toward what they think the target object is. You can use "warmer" and "colder" to indicate proximity to the targeted object.

Also consider making an *I Spy* class book using shapes, in which the children draw the shapes of the game's target objects. The book *Eye Spy Shapes* by Debbie MacKinnon provides a nice example. Other books, such as Brian Wildsmith's *Circus*, can help children envision the use of shapes in pictures. However, note that some children feel the need to draw with accuracy in order to be satisfied with their product. Offer straight-edged rulers, shape stencils, or cookie cutters to support such students. Once the children have finished their illustrations, help them create text explaining the shapes that readers should find in each picture. If you wish to increase the level of complexity, the class can work to create rhyming text.

Quilts

For many children, this time of year is laden with celebrations that are as unique as families themselves. Such traditions can help children conceptualize predictable patterns. Yet most young children have a limited awareness of traditions because they haven't lived long enough to observe many repetitions of various celebrations or rituals. Telling family stories through quilts is one way to make the past both personal and tangible. There are a variety of fine children's books that feature such quilts. *Eight Hands Round*, by Ann Whitford Paul, provides historical and geometric information about a range of traditional quilt patterns. *The Quilt Story*, by Tony

Johnson and Tomie De Paola, nicely complements *Eight Hands Round*. *The Quilt Story* traces a family quilt through generations of personal and historical changes.

One of the most effective ways to help children understand the historical significance and geometry of quilts is to invite a guest with quilting experience to come speak with the class. If you have a parent, friend, or colleague with a collection of quilts, see if they'd like to bring them in and show them to your students. This kind of visit can be informative and inspirational for everyone.

Quilting is all about part/whole relationships. Showing the children how quilt squares are created helps them to see these relationships. Inviting people to share baby quilts can encourage children to think about their own histories and family stories. Baby quilts are also a manageable size for classroom display. If actual quilts are not available, you can often find calendars that have large photographs of various quilt patterns. These can be mounted to create a bulletin-board display.

Once your students have some awareness of quilts, encourage them to create their own paper quilt squares. Keep initial attempts simple, so patterns and symmetry can emerge. As the children work, they will be turning shapes to orient them in various ways. They'll also be visualizing the spatial relationships, matching sides and angles, and noticing symmetry as well as patterns.

Materials

- several 6-by-6-inch white construction-paper squares per student
- about 8 2-by-2-inch colored construction-paper squares per student; half of the squares should be one color (e.g., red), the other half a second color (such as blue)
- an array of 2-by-2-inch construction-paper squares of various additional colors
- 1 glue stick per student
- overhead projector
- 1 roll of sturdy bulletin board paper (or whatever large paper is available), or 1 paper punch
- a ball of yarn

Instructions

Part 1

1. Have the children experiment with positioning the smaller colored squares on a 6-by-6-inch white square to create various combinations. Ask them to generate as many variations as possible.

2. Invite each child to select his or her favorite design and glue it to the 6-by-6-inch white square.

3. View and discuss the range of designs. Ask the children to look for the design that used the most colored squares. Ask which design used the fewest. (Often, designs using the fewest squares have one colored square or "diamond" placed in the center of the white square.)

4. On the back of each quilt square, write the number combinations of the two colors; for instance, *4 red + 5 blue = 9 small squares.*

Part 2

1. After a couple of days, explore quilt patterns again. Tell the children that this time they can make one cut in each small, colored square if they wish. Demonstrate cutting a square on the diagonal and discuss the two resulting triangles. Ask the children to predict what shape would emerge if they made a cut down the center of a square. (You don't need to restrict the cuts to halves; the single cut could be made in another way as well. But the one-cut rule does reduce the likelihood that the children will make so many tiny pieces that they'll end up with something that looks like confetti!)

2. If you have an overhead projector, arrange the triangles and rectangles you created in Step 1 in a variety of ways and show them on the projector. (See below.) Discuss the different designs that can be made by placing the triangles and rectangles on a 6-by-6-inch background.

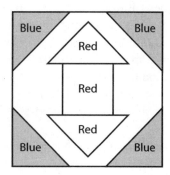

3. Once again, after the children have had an opportunity to try a number of arrangements, have them glue their favorite designs onto a background square. Display these "quilt squares," so each child has a chance to see how others approached the assignment. Children enjoy discussing and admiring their own and others' work.

Part 3

1. Now create a classroom paper quilt. Have a class meeting so the children can discuss specifics for the final product. Frame the discussion with questions like the following:

   "Would you like to have a particular color scheme, or some kind of theme for the quilt?"

   "What colors will you need? Does it matter how many different colors you use on your squares?"

   "Can people use triangular and rectangular halves?"

2. Invite the children to create new quilt squares for the class project.

3. When the squares have been completed, the glue has dried, and everyone is satisfied with his or her work, assemble the quilt. You can use a paper backing of rolled paper to create one big backing piece. A second option is to use a paper punch to make two evenly spaced holes on each side of every quilt square. Attach the squares by tying yarn knots. This is fairly time consuming, but it does produce a realistic effect.

When the quilt goes on display, the children get a great deal of satisfaction from finding their own contribution and admiring the large-scale effect of the group effort.

Paper Folding

Origami, the art of paper folding, is appealing for its beauty, geometric challenge, and cultural connections. After being exposed to some advanced paper-folding examples through children's literature, your students can achieve success with beginning origami work. As the children fold paper to create new shapes, they will encounter part/whole relationships, fractions, spatial visualization, and directionality.

The following two books have been written specifically for young children and feature the art of origami. Either, or both, can help you introduce the topic to students:

■ Rosemary Wells's *Yoko's Paper Cranes* tells of the family traditions and bonds that connect generations. In the book, Yoko is a youngster who has spent her early years growing up in Japan with her parents and grandparents. Yoko and her parents move to the United States. The little girl misses her grandparents and decides to send them some mail. She creates delicate paper cranes just like the ones her grandparents had made for her.

■ Laura Melmed is well known for her 1992 book *The Rainbabies*. In 1997 she wrote *Little Oh*. Like *The Rainbabies*, the new book has been beautifully illustrated by Jim Lemarch and has a similar theme involving a loving adult who longs for a child. In this case, the setting is Japan, and the adult has created an origami child named *Little Oh*. After a series of adventures, Little Oh eventually takes human form and becomes a member of a real family. Children are delighted by the story and amazed by the origami shown in the illustrations.

Of course, paper cranes and origami children are examples of advanced origami. First graders should try making simpler forms such as kites, cups, hats, cats, fish, and dogs. (See Figures 5–3 and 5–4.)

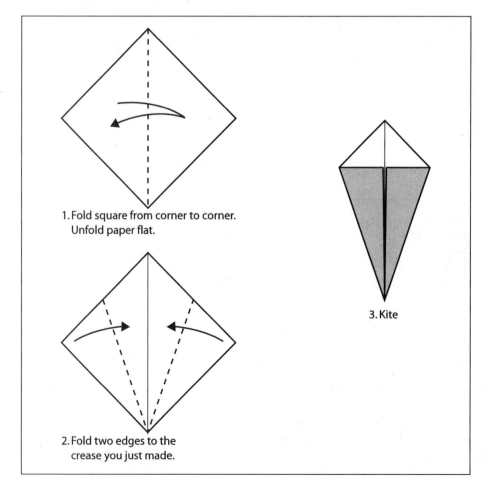

1. Fold square from corner to corner. Unfold paper flat.

2. Fold two edges to the crease you just made.

3. Kite

FIGURE 5–3 ◀

Instructions for an origami kite.

FIGURE 5–4 ▶

Instructions for an origami dog.

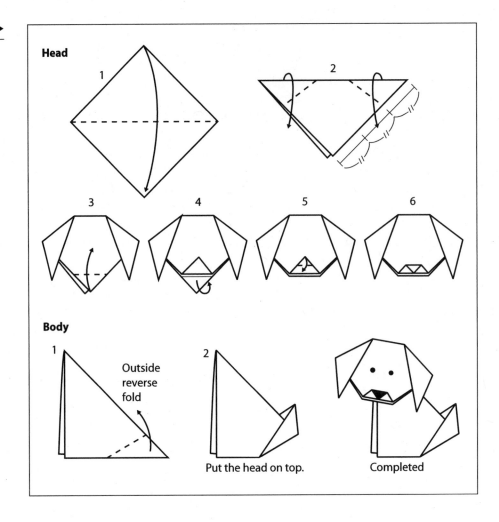

Some children become quite intrigued with these creations and develop a special interest in origami. You may find "class experts" emerging over time if you make materials and examples available. Because of the literature connections, you might also explore origami during language-arts time. Invite the children to build construction-paper settings for their origami creations, mount the origami in the settings, and create stories about the characters.

Tangrams

Tangrams, also of Japanese origin, are puzzles that begin in the form of a square. The original square is divided into seven distinct geometric pieces. *Grandfather Tang's Story* by Ann Tompert has been used for many years to introduce tangram puzzles. Scholastic's tangram book, *Three Pigs, One Wolf, and Seven Magic Shapes* by Grace Neuhaus, provides another possibility for initiating tangram exploration.

Materials

- 2 copies of a tangram puzzle per child (see Blackline Masters)

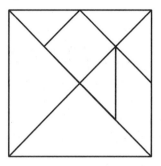

- 1 envelope per child

Instructions

1. Read one or both of the stories recommended above. Discuss the remarkable variety of forms that can be made by combining tangram pieces in different ways.

2. Give each student two copies of the tangram puzzle and one envelope. Invite them to carefully cut one of the copies apart and to store the pieces in the envelope. Suggest that they tape the other copy of the puzzle into their math notebooks to remind themselves what the original puzzle looks like before it's cut up.

3. Suggest a shape (e.g., a house), and ask the children to arrange their tangram pieces to match the shape. You can select varying degrees of complexity for this. For instance:

   - Give each student a "tangram house" (see Blackline Masters), and ask each to put his or her tangram pieces on top of the corresponding pieces shown in the house.

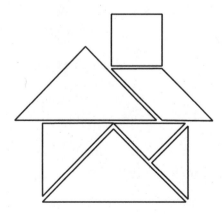

- Show just the outline of the design, but not the lines for individual pieces, and have the students fill the outline with their tangram pieces.

- Ask children to arrange their puzzle pieces without any outline, drawing on their memory or their own imagination.

4. Consider creating a class book or other display using the children's favorite tangram pictures. If there are volunteers available, the text can be dictated by the children and written by adults. Otherwise, create a *word bank*, or listing of unknown and needed words, by having the children generate ideas for their pictures. If this doesn't seem plausible, text can simply be kept to a minimum.

Extensions

Children can make their own puzzles from squares. But agree in advance about how many pieces will be acceptable for these puzzles. Begin with a few cuts and work up to no more than seven pieces. Making puzzles from squares and other shapes can serve as a valuable geometry menu possibility.

Whole-Class/Menu Activities

Pattern-Block Sets

Pattern blocks are remarkably versatile and popular. The colorful, artistic designs that can be created using these math manipulatives delight learners of all ages. Pattern blocks offer opportunities to learn about a wide variety of mathematical concepts and activities, such as shape identification, part/whole relationships, fractions, area/perimeter, and sorting and counting. Small groups of children can comfortably share a set of pattern blocks; thus you can design activities ideal for whole groups, small groups, or menu choices.

If your first graders have not had much experience with pattern blocks, provide several occasions for exploration. Encourage the children to discuss what they notice about each type of pattern block. As students work with the blocks, circulate and observe. Some things to consider:

- Do the children have sufficient materials?
- What types of things are the children doing with the blocks?

- Are the children using mathematical language?
- Are they engaged?

Some children may be creating symmetrical designs, some may be looking at ways to create similar shapes by using combinations of blocks, and others may be creating patterns. Observing the children while they're working can help you generate discussion questions for the processing time that comes at the end of each work session. It's important that the children share ideas and verbally communicate about what they have done. These exchanges help them build a working vocabulary and can benefit the entire class. After a work session-and before the children pack up the blocks— take a few minutes for a class "walkabout." Invite the children to stroll around the room and view each other's efforts, asking questions and discussing what they notice.

If you'd like to create smaller sets of pattern blocks from the complete sets, have the children assist with this task. Here's how:

Materials

- 1 pattern-block set per small group of 3–4 students
- 5–6 small plastic bags per group of students
- 1 piece of poster paper

Instructions

1. Ask students to organize themselves into small groups of three or four.

2. Give each group a pattern-block set.

3. Ask each group to sort the blocks in the set by shape and color. Have students record the quantities of each type of block in their math notebooks.

4. Discuss whether each of the shapes has the same number of blocks and why the sets might have been created as they were (for example, more green triangles and fewer yellow hexagons).

5. Have the children divide each type of block (for example, take the green triangles and parcel them out) into three or four (as you see fit) groups that have the same number of blocks. If there are "leftovers" or remainders that don't fit in a group, discuss the most reasonable spot for these extra pieces. For instance, if one person gets an extra yellow hexagon, the group can decide if that's OK or if the block should be returned to the class collection.

6. Now have the children create smaller sets by placing the divided groups of each color in the bags. This produces small pattern block sets with proportional quantities of each shape.

Pattern-Block Graphs

This activity enables your class to create a graph of pattern blocks.

Materials

- 1 pattern-block set
- 1 cloth bag

Instructions

1. Place an assortment of each type of pattern block into the bag. Include a few more blocks than there are students in the class, so all the children will have an opportunity to pick a block out of the bag.

2. Invite the children to sit in a circle and take turns reaching into the mystery bag for a pattern block. When everyone has taken a block, go around the circle and ask each child to show and identify his or her block. (At this stage, color names are fine.) You can also ask each student to describe one way that his or her block is similar to that of the last person who picked a block. If children who are sitting next to each other have identical blocks, they can describe a shared characteristic or attribute of that block.

3. On the board or a large piece of poster paper, create a graph representing the blocks picked by all the children. (See below.)

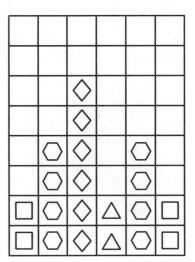

4. Ask the children to make true math statements about the graph. For instance, they may notice how many sides or corners (angles) each

shape in a particular category has. Label the block categories with both the geometric and color names; e.g., *yellow hexagon*, *red trapezoid*, *blue rhombus*, *white rhombus*, *green triangle*, and *orange square*. Say these terms as you write them, to give students access to the vocabulary and encourage usage of the words.

Guess My Block

Guess My Block is a partner game that involves guessing a particular pattern block by using the sense of touch. The previously described pattern-block graph lists vocabulary words for the various shapes and will help to build vocabulary for this activity.

Materials

- 1 small set of pattern blocks per pair of students

Instructions

1. Give each pair of students a small set of pattern blocks.

2. Player 1 selects a block while Player 2 closes his or her eyes.

3. Player 1 then holds the block over Player 2's head.

4. Player 2 reaches up to feel and explore the shape. He or she then describes the shape's attributes and guesses which block it is.

5. The players trade roles and repeat the process to explore each type of pattern block.

As the children play, walk around observing and listening. Encourage students to describe and discuss the sides and angles of the shapes. If a student identifies a shape by the color name, confirm the color name and add the geometric name: "Yes, it *is* the red trapezoid! How did you know?!" The children may struggle with the geometric words at first, but it doesn't take long before one or two of them pick them up. Soon accurate usage will become part of the class culture. After all, if children can master the names of a wide variety of long-extinct dinosaurs, it's not surprising that they can also learn geometric vocabulary.

Make a Twin

This game is especially appealing to children after they've had some experiences with shapes. The children play in pairs—without seeing one another's work. One partner creates a design out of pattern blocks and gives instructions to the other to copy it—but without seeing the first partner's work.

Materials

- 1 overhead projector, for demonstration
- 1 small set of pattern blocks per student; 1 set for you, for demonstration

Instructions

Part 1

1. Ask for a confident, resilient volunteer to come up to the projector to help you demonstrate the game. Create a barrier down the middle of the overhead projector with an inverted "v" made with a folder. Position your partner on one side of the barrier, so that he or she can't see the other side of the barrier. Give your partner a set of pattern blocks. Tell the partner that he or she must not look up at the screen once the demonstration begins—but must look only at his or her work on the projector glass.

2. Tell the rest of the students that this is a tricky game and that they should try to be "silent observers." That means refraining from shouting out any clues as you and your partner play the game.

3. Tell your partner that you are going to give directions for making a pattern-block design. Each time you put a block down, you will tell your partner what you are doing, so he or she can do the same thing. Reiterate that neither of you can peek at the screen to see if you actually are creating twin designs.

4. Explain that the rest of the students will be listening to your instructions and watching the screen as the demonstration proceeds.

5. Begin by placing a hexagon block on the overhead projector, and instruct your partner to do likewise.

6. Then add another block to your design. To show the need for clarity and specificity in your directions, give clues at first in the form of vague directions, such as: "Put a green triangle next to the hexagon." Then provide more specific instructions, such as "Put an orange square on top of the hexagon." Clarity of language and comprehension of conceptual vocabulary such as *over*, *under*, *beside*, *above*, *left*, and *right* are key elements to this game.

7. After you have placed five or six pieces, raise the barrier to see if you and your partner have made twin shapes. (See Figure 5–5 for an example of what constitutes twins and what doesn't.)

8. Play one more round, this time led by your partner. After this second round, you and your partner might discuss whether it would be a good idea to let partners ask questions while they're playing the game. Some groups of children feel that this is the only sensible thing

Twins!

Not Quite Twins

to do, while other groups may decide that it makes the game too easy. The class should agree on this aspect of the game before students begin playing.

Note: The introduction to this game should be playful and brief—just enough to get the idea. You may consider unintentionally misunderstanding a direction that is given to you, and then discussing the challenges of giving helpful, clear instructions.

Part 2

1. Once everyone has the general idea of how the game is played, have students pair up. Give each pair some pattern blocks and have them divide the blocks into two identical sets, one set for each partner.

2. Tell the partners to sit side by side. (This positioning helps them have the same visual perspective while following directions.)

3. Have the partners place a visual barrier, such as a tall book or a folder, between themselves.

4. Invite the partners to begin playing a round.

5. Use some sort of signal, such as ringing a bell, to let the children know when it's time to lift their barriers and switch roles. Each child should have an opportunity to be the direction giver and the direction receiver. It's interesting to ask them which role they think is harder.

6. After everyone has had a chance to serve in both roles at least once, stop the game and have the children discuss the activity's pleasures and challenges. Add any relevant terms to the *Math Words* poster. Consider offering the game as a menu choice.

Pattern-Block Designs

In this activity, students again work in partners and use pattern blocks to create designs. The object of the activity is to recreate the shape of your partner's design, by making some substitutions and using some different types of pattern blocks.

As with *Make a Twin*, demonstrate the game using the overhead projector. Begin with a simple design such as a flower. Discuss possible substitutions for the various pieces. For instance, if the first design used six green triangles, perhaps your partner could use blue rhombuses instead. (See Figure 5–6.)

As the children practice, the designs will grow more complex. Consider supplying a recording sheet so the children can indicate how many pattern blocks of each color they used. You can compare and total numbers to show how many shapes were used in each design and version.

Pattern-Block Mobiles

Creating mobiles has long been an appealing primary-school activity, because balancing a mobile involves scientific principles and the final product can be beautifully artistic. This activity incorporates mathematics by creating a mobile from geometric shapes. The shapes can be pattern-block representations cut from card stock (see Blackline Masters and Figure 5–7)

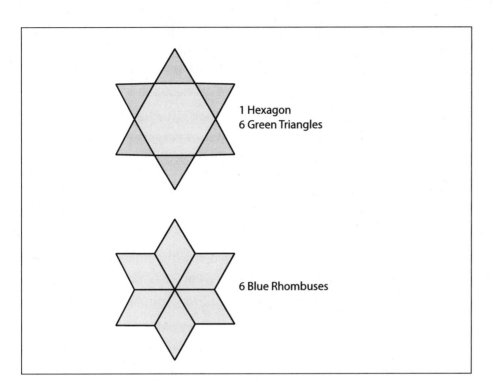

FIGURE 5–6 ◀

Pattern-block designs using triangles, a hexagon, and rhombuses.

1 Hexagon
6 Green Triangles

6 Blue Rhombuses

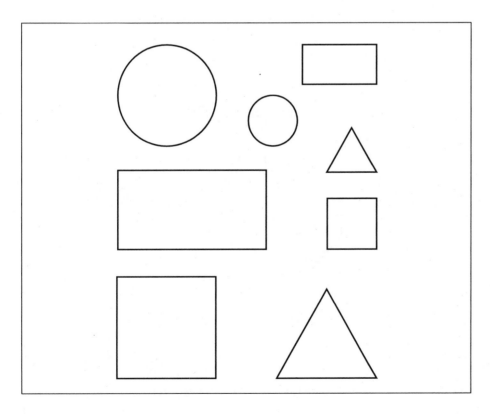

FIGURE 5–7 ◀

Pattern-block shapes can be used to create mobiles.

or drawn using stencils. Children can also look for objects to trace, such as jar lids, pencil boxes, and other objects from around the room.

This activity offers several options. For example, each child could make a mobile, or small groups could work together on a product. Or, you can create a class mobile for display in the room. To make the mobiles, the children could tie the shapes at varying lengths to hangers. Or they could cut spirals from paper plates, attach strings of varying lengths to the spiral, add their shapes to the strings, and then hang the spiral with yarn.

Once the children have cut out their shape pieces, they can decorate them in ways that show examples of those shapes in the real world. For instance, they come up with some very creative ideas including buildings, faces, and furniture. Students can also hang shapes individually or attach several shapes along one piece of string.

When the mobiles have been completed, ask the children to determine how many shapes they used, how many of each type, and (if you are interested in extension questions) how many sides and angles were involved. You can create a class mobile by hanging shapes from wooden rods that you can purchase at a hardware store, or from pieces of wood about the length of walking sticks. (See Figure 5–8.) These larger mobiles can be quite dramatic. The class can use the mobile to determine how many types of particular shapes were used. (See Figure 5–9.)

FIGURE 5–8 ▶

An example of one class's multi-dowel shape mobile.

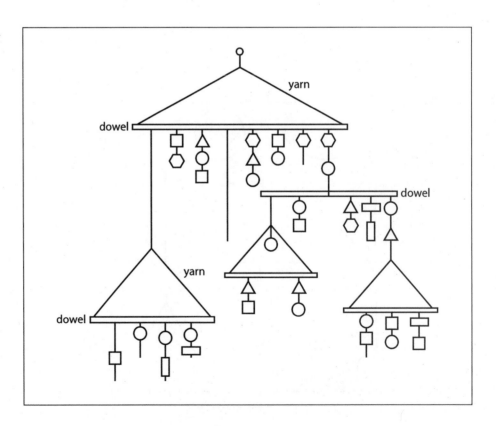

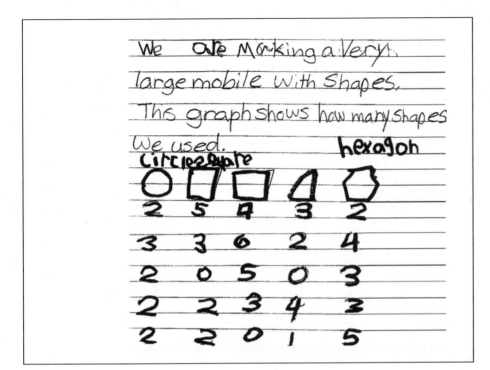

Questioning

Each of the activities described in this chapter offer opportunities for you to observe your students, listen to them, and ask questions while they work. The following general geometry questions may be useful to keep in mind as you circulate among the children:

"Are these alike or different?"

"How are these alike (or different)?"

"Where else have you seen this shape?"

"What does this look like to you?"

"How many sides does this have?"

"How many corners (or angles) does this have?"

"If we had two of these shapes, how many sides and angles would they have altogether?" "What if we had three (and so on) of these shapes?"

"Could you make this same shape, but make it larger?"

"Could you make this same thing using different pieces?"

"What would happen if . . ."

"Can you draw an imaginary line that would divide your shape in half?"

"Is it symmetrical?"

"Is there more than one line of symmetry?"

"Can you predict what should go in this particular place?"

"Could you describe this shape to someone who couldn't see it?"

"What would it look like if you could flip this shape and have it face the other way?"

Chapter 6

January

ADDITION AND SUBTRACTION

The Learning Environment

As you help your students work toward computational proficiency and efficiency, you may feel tempted to try to simplify the process by relying on drills and quizzes. Children build meaning in a variety of ways and at different rates, however, so although shortcuts and strict sequences of strategies may help in the short term, they do not help children construct meaning. Partial understanding is a natural aspect of learning, and premature demands for quick performance can undermine student understanding. While respecting individual thought processes, the activities described in this chapter expand students' ability to add and subtract using a variety of flexible strategies. Flexibility and variety in turn will help children succeed when they encounter increasingly complex ideas. ∎

In January, you'll encourage your class to tackle problems without giving students a singular technique or procedure. Once the children have arrived at solutions, you'll ask them to describe how they thought about a particular problem. The resulting discussions will encourage your first graders to articulate their thinking, and will build their math vocabulary. As the children seek their own solutions, you'll continue to probe and ask questions to help them think logically, look for patterns, and use manipulative materials to explore ideas.

This month's math work will focus students' attention on:

- combining numbers.
- taking amounts away.
- separating quantities (parts and wholes).
- determining "how many more."
- understanding the relationship between addition and subtraction.

Many of the same ideas that were relevant to developing number sense remain central to January's work. These include:

- counting all.
- counting on.
- counting up (for subtraction) from the smaller number to the larger number.
- counting back.
- pattern counting.
- use of doubles.
- use of 10s.

As January proceeds, keep using familiar activities so students move smoothly and naturally from one topic to another. For example, the children could use pattern blocks to continue working with addition and subtraction and to sustain the understandings about geometry they gained during December. Initiate discussion of addition and subtraction by asking the children to make a design using two types of pattern-block shapes. Have students count and combine the two kinds of blocks to find the total. As children describe their work, consistently articulate ideas using mathematical terms and concepts and remind them of the addition and subtraction symbols.

Routines

Calendar

Routines offer whole-group experiences that children can have on a regular basis. This month, as you identify the day of the week, the month, and the year, ask your students to tell you about something that happened yesterday, something that is happening today, and something that probably will happen tomorrow. Expect that some children may still be confused by time-sequence language.

Days of the Month

Number lines can strengthen students' calendar understandings. As part of this month's calendar routine, help the children to create a tally-mark number line of the days in the month. Place a long, horizontal strip of paper in a spot where the children will have easy access to it. Draw a row of thirty-one squares on the paper, and number them 1 to 31. (See Figure 6–1.)

Each day, have the student responsible for keeping the calendar make the appropriate number of tally marks above the corresponding number of the month. Each Monday, the class can discuss the tallies and ways to adjust for the weekend days. This routine exercise enables class members to practice keeping track of the abstract quantity of the days of the month using a simple but effective tool.

Seasons

In many parts of the United States, January marks more than just the beginning of a new year; it also firmly establishes the season of winter. For many students and teachers, January is a perfect time to focus on the topic of seasons. Last month, your calendar routine featured the months of the year. You can use some of December's materials (e.g., the month identification cards with pictures) again to shift attention to seasons. The environmental changes you and your students observe outside your school building will dictate your focus during the exploration of this topic.

Even if your region sees limited seasonal changes, you can still help children learn about how such changes affect other parts of the world. We live in an era of commonplace travel and immediately accessible information. Thanks to frequent communication with friends and family who may live in a variety of locations, many children know a fair amount about what is happening in other parts of the country and even around the globe. You may wish to get a map and mark places on it that are of particular significance to your students. Inquire about what is happening in those settings

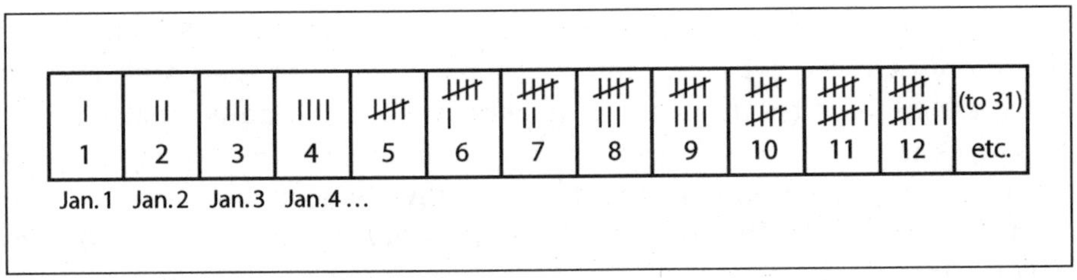

| I | II | III | IIII | ⊔⊔⊔ | ⊔⊔⊔ I | ⊔⊔⊔ II | ⊔⊔⊔ III | ⊔⊔⊔ IIII | ⊔⊔⊔ ⊔⊔⊔ | ⊔⊔⊔ ⊔⊔⊔ I | ⊔⊔⊔ ⊔⊔⊔ II | (to 31) |
| 1 | 2 | 3 | 4 | 5 | 6 | 7 | 8 | 9 | 10 | 11 | 12 | etc. |

Jan. 1   Jan. 2   Jan. 3   Jan. 4 …

FIGURE 6–1 ◀

This number line represents the calendar days in the month of January.

during the month of January. If this kind of exploration sparks an interest, have children watch a weather channel to learn more. Many excellent books, such as Gail Gibbons' *The Reasons for the Seasons*, can also help children develop understandings of seasonal cycles.

Graphing Possibilities

The topic of seasonal changes offers many possibilities for graphing. For example, students could document the following information on graphs:

- favorite seasons
- favorite winter activities
- mittens, hats, or other winter clothing categorized by style, color, or other criteria
- daily outdoor temperatures
- daily weather
- number of indoor-recess days
- indoor or outdoor recess preferences
- favorite indoor-recess activities
- the hour that the sun rises every morning
- the hour that the sun sets every night
- birthdays
- things you see in winter that you don't see during other seasons
- things you don't see in winter that you do see during other seasons

Regardless of the graphing topics you select, take advantage of the part/whole relationships within the graph and explore addition and subtraction problems. Use a variety of graphing formats. (See Figure 6–2.) As always, have students express their understandings in the form of true math statements about each graph.

Estimation Jar

This is a good time of year to emphasize the importance of estimation. Reiterate that sometimes an estimate is sufficient, and that we often estimate before we determine an exact answer. Remind your students that it is not only OK to revise an estimate, but that revising is a good strategy for getting closer to an accurate answer. Talk about additional real-life examples of estimation. For example, you might ask if anyone's parents count out spaghetti noodles to make sure they have enough for the family's dinner. Discuss various contexts in which people make estimates involving money.

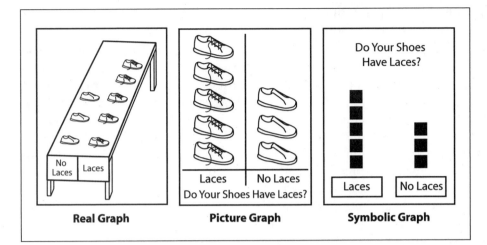

FIGURE 6–2 ◀

A variety of graph formulas.

Here's an easy estimation activity involving something that you and your students use every day. Gather up an armload of books from around your classroom and bring them over to the circle area. Ask the children if they think there are enough books in your pile for everyone in the class. Ask how many books they think might be in the pile. After listening to their guesses, ask them to think up a guess that is *not* reasonable. Often, someone will offer a number like "a million." When this kind of extreme quantity comes up, everyone laughs and easily agrees that there couldn't possibly be that many.

Narrow the gap by asking if there could be one hundred books in the stack. Offer lower and lower numbers, until the children are not so sure of their responses. Next ask for estimates that are obviously too low, and work back up to the point where the numbers again begin sounding like reasonable guesses. Once you've found the range that your students consider possible, begin counting the books by putting them into piles of ten. Each time you make a group of ten, hold up the remaining books and ask the children if they want to revise their guesses. Continue this process until you have an actual count. By emphasizing the importance of estimation and helping the children feel flexible with the process, this exercise further develops number sense.

Previous chapters described how students record estimates next to an estimation jar. If you decide to use the estimation jar this month, the quantities can increase. To reduce the pressure to come up with the exact number of objects in the jar, you could instruct children *not* to put their names next to their guesses on the clipboard. However, some children may get carried away and end up writing the largest numbers they can manage on the clipboard. You can deal with this in a couple of ways:

- Consider offering a second clipboard for the special purpose of writing large numbers.
- Ask children to write any number they please, as long as they can read it.

- Ask them to write their names next to their numbers, so anyone else who has a question about that number can ask the writer about it.

- Choose a beginning number and start generating a number sequence for the children to extend. Write the sequence in a vertical list, so the numbers don't run together. For instance, you might write *92, 93, 94, 95, 96, 97, 98, 99, 100, 101, 102, 103* and ask the children to keep the pattern going.

Encourage the children in their enjoyment of large numbers, even though such figures may have limited meaning to the youngsters at this point. Acknowledge that reading and writing large numbers is both fun *and* good practice. Meanwhile, reserve another clipboard for reasonable guesses about the contents of the estimation jar. If you continue to get random guesses, have children write their estimates during a time when you will be able to hover near them and observe them as they record. This tends to help keep estimates in the reasonable range.

Here are some estimate-jar activities that involve addition and subtraction or number combinations:

- Use one jar filled with two different-colored objects, such as color tiles. Determine appropriate quantities based on your class's previous experiences with estimation-jar activities. Then, on the estimation-jar clipboard, create several sections on the top page asking questions like: "How many red tiles?" "How many blue tiles?" "How many tiles altogether?"

- To maintain interest in the estimation jar, include a few written clues about the contents. Many students may be reading by this time of the year, and all of them have experienced classroom routines involving estimation. So the children should feel fairly comfortable with written clues. Examples of clues might include: "There are twice as many red tiles as blue tiles." "There are ten blue tiles in the jar, and there are two more blue tiles than red tiles. How many tiles are in the jar altogether?" "There are fifteen tiles altogether, and five of them are red. How many are blue?"

- Use two jars. Place fewer than ten objects in each. Put a blank equation on the clipboard and invite the children to insert the appropriate numbers into the equation. For example, you might write __ + __ = __, or __ + __ = *10*, or __ + *5* = __. Vary the equations so the children take time to think about their meaning. Discuss and model the process of using "number sentences" each time you introduce the estimation-jar routine.

As in previous months, each day one or two children will have the responsibility of removing and counting the objects in the estimation jar. Make sure the children have made predictions before the count begins. Consider providing ten frames for the children to use as an organizing device.

At the end of the week, the children who counted the jars can report their findings to the class.

Perceptual Number

Continue to use perceptual-number cards or quick-peek transparencies on your overhead projector. But instead of showing black dots or shapes, use transparent counters of two colors, and show combinations of numbers. You can also show the children a quantity then cover part of it and ask, "How many are missing?"

1–100 Chart

The 1–100 pocket charts make it easy to stimulate class discussions about numbers and their relationships. Children can clearly demonstrate their thinking by going to the pocket chart and identifying numbers that are relevant to their work. If you don't have a chart available, use 1–100 on an overhead projector to demonstrate while the children refer to copies of 1–100 charts that they have taped into their math notebooks.

You can use the number chart to provide a variety of opportunities for students to practice adding and subtracting numbers. For instance, the class can demonstrate ideas like "plus one," "minus one," "plus two," "minus two," "plus ten," "minus ten," and so forth. They can also use the chart to count backward.

As one way to initiate this type of activity, create some problem cards, or "tickets," that can be used in whole- or small-group settings. The tickets can supply written directions, such as, "Add one," "Subtract two," "Add ten," "Subtract ten," or "Count backward to zero." As students sit together in a circle, invite a child to remove a number from the 1–100 pocket chart. (If you are using the chart to count down to the 100th day of school, some numbers may not yet have been added to the chart. But that's OK.) After the child removes the number, he or she or another person picks a ticket from a stack or small container. You can decide whether the student who selected the number and ticket responds to the ticket directions, or another child does so. If the direction on the ticket is complex or demanding enough, it may warrant a whole-class discussion and solution. Provide enough tickets so everyone can have a turn engaging in the activity.

Ten Frames

For many children, a visual geometric model brings clarity to abstract numbers. If possible, give the children weekly opportunities to use ten frames. (See Chapter 4.) The more repetition children have with this tool, the more likely these mental images of 5s and 10s will become automatic. Ten frames also help children solve place-value problems more easily. Once the children have experience with ten frames, ask them to close their eyes and imagine, or visualize, how a specific number would look on a ten frame. For example, if you propose the number 36, ask how many rectangles of ten boxes are filled and how the 6 from the 36 is arranged on the ten frame.

You can also encourage children to use ten frames in estimation-jar or other counting activities involving small objects.

Math Notebooks

You may wish to revisit the numbers 1 through 10 by featuring them as "numbers of the day." Invite your class to generate as many addition and subtraction equations for a given number as possible, and to write them in their notebooks. Encourage the children to physically act out their ideas using tiles on ten frames or small objects like erasers or cubes. The children can also create stories to match an equation. For instance, if someone has identified the equation $7 + 3 = 10$, ask someone else to begin a story to show that action: "Once upon a time, there were seven boys and girls on a school bus. Three more children got on, and then there were ten."

Students can use their math notebooks to practice using addition, subtraction, and equality symbols. As the children engage in problem-solving activities, ask them to continue to show their thinking in their notebooks. As in earlier months, the results will likely be rough. First graders are just beginning to develop written organizational skills and are gaining experience with the use of math symbols. Just as children use approximations while they are learning to write, they will need lots of practice to communicate mathematically. As you record math sentences and ideas on the board or chart paper, have the children write along with you. This active participation may help them clarify ideas and develop a sense of ownership over the writing topics.

The Mathematics

January's lessons are intended to help children construct understandings of the operations of addition and subtraction. Constructing meaning involves more than remembering content information—facts and symbols. First-grade work with addition and subtraction will lay the foundation for making sense of more complex understandings about larger numbers, multiplication, and division later. Addition and subtraction are abstract ideas involving specific types of relationships between numbers. The activities described below can encourage children to begin grasping those relationships.

As in Chapter 5, the activities are organized into two categories: literature based, and games.

Literature-Based Activities

Transitioning from Geometry to Number

In *Neil's Numberless World*, Lucy Coats introduces us to Neil, who finds numbers unfriendly and incomprehensible. Neil decides that he would be better off without the complexity of numbers, so he makes a birthday wish to have all numbers simply disappear. When his wish comes true, the results are dramatic and not nearly as pleasing as he had anticipated.

This book encourages exploration of the wide variety of ways in which numbers affect our lives. By thinking about the many purposes numbers serve, children can begin making the transition from last month's focus on geometry to this month's number work.

Counting

Most children are familiar with a range of counting books, songs, finger plays, and rhymes. Many of the stories described below involve adding one of something on each page. To introduce the topics of addition and subtraction, offer your students a variety of types of number books, and give them time to explore the collection. Then discuss what the children notice about the books. Ask how the books are alike, and how they're different. Discuss what is happening in the stories. Dramatize a favorite selection.

At some point during these discussions, someone will likely mention that some books show things that are being added or taken away. In the event that this observation does not come up, ask the children what is happening with the numbers or amounts in the story, and inquire about noticeable patterns. During these conversations, revisit the symbols for addition, subtraction, and equality. Following are brief descriptions of recommended books.

Eric Carle's Roosters Off to See the World

This book may already be familiar to many students. As you read or reread the story, encourage the children to use cubes or other objects to act out the story's addition and subtraction events. The book uses miniature pictures in the upper corner of each page to identify the story's addition and subtraction events.

Because the numbers in this book are manageable, children will find it comfortable to dramatize the action. They might want to play the parts of the characters and act the story out in the form of a play as you narrate.

And perhaps a student could hold up large addition or subtraction signs at appropriate moments to demonstrate the mathematical operations unfolding in the story.

Donald Crews's Ten Black Dots

This title is an old favorite that can teach everything from counting by 1s and identifying circles in the world, to exploring combinations of numbers that make up a particular total. You can use this book for several whole-class activities. For instance, students can make a class book containing their own ideas for pictures that include a specific number of ten black dots. Or each child can construct a book of pictures made of small black-dot stickers, which you can find in most office-supply stores.

To introduce the concepts of addition and subtraction, you might have the children create pictures consisting of two different dot colors. When the class looks at the pictures and discusses the dots, you can write their ideas on the board to match the illustrations, using words as well as number sentences. For instance, a page might include something like: "One red wheel on a tricycle and two black wheels make three wheels altogether, $1 + 2 = 3$." A subtraction example might read, "There were three wheels on a tricycle, and the red one fell off. The two black wheels were left."

Children generally find it more natural to begin working with addition than with subtraction. They often prefer to consider the parts that, when combined, create a whole, rather than beginning with the whole and then subtracting. Class discussions about part/whole relationships can boost the problem-solving-skills they'll need during their independent work.

Atsuko Morozuma's One Gorilla

This is a beautifully illustrated picture book that explores accumulation of numbers. Discuss similarities and differences between this and *Rooster's Off to See the World* and *Ten Black Dots*. This particular story shows all of the characters together only on the very last page, where they are depicted in a triangular growth pattern. Discuss the characteristics of this illustration with students. Brainstorm a variety of methods, such as drawing quick pictures, counting cubes, or making tally marks, that the children could use to keep track of quantities while listening to number-related stories. Reread *One Gorilla*, this time asking the children to keep track of how many animals are in the story. (See Figures 6–3 and 6–4 for examples.) The class can then check for accuracy by referring to the excellent graphic on the book's last page. Since the gorilla is mentioned on every page, but is only one character, have the children discuss when and how often they counted him.

Jim Aylesworth's One Crow: A Counting Rhyme

This title includes summer and winter scenes of farm animals. You can easily use the book to initiate discussion of annual seasonal patterns. As in

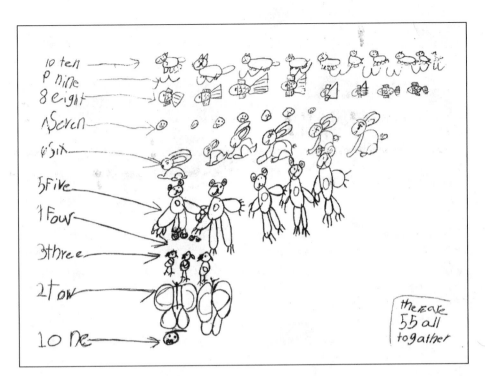

10 ten ⟶
P nine
8 eight ⟶
Seven ⟶
6 six
5 Five
1 Four
3 three
2 tow
10 ne ⟶

there are
55 all
togather

we tried to find out
how meny anamoles
& how meny all together.

g1
bb2
bbb3
SSSS4
DDDDD5
RRRRRR6
FFFFFFF7
FFFFFFFF8
bbbbbbbbb9
cccccccccc 10

55

One Gorilla, each page is devoted to a new type of animal and builds up to the number 10. You can ask students to determine how many characters appear—in this case, by the end of each season. Because the book includes animals, it lends itself to generating problem-solving questions such as: "There are four sheep and three ducks in the barn. How many animals are there altogether?" or "The three ducks went out to the pond. How many animals are still in the barn?"

You can also have the children keep track of groups. For example: "There are four sheep and two ducks in the barnyard. How many feet do the animals have altogether? How many tails? How many beaks?" The book's summer/winter format also provides an opportunity to ask, "Which seasons are missing?"

After reading the book, draw four large, horizontal squares on the board, or divide a large bulletin board into fourths, and have the children create a series of seasonal scenes in them. Children can work in teams to create the four scenes in the style of an *I Spy* book. (*I Spy* books use complex photographs to invite readers to search for specific items. They are extremely popular with children.) Each group of students will create a seasonal scene containing appropriate images, such as snowflakes and snowmen for winter. *One Crow* also makes use of the daily pattern of the sun—another seasonal pattern that could be incorporated into all four scenes.

Lois Ehlert's Fish Eyes

This is a 1 to 10 counting book adorned with colorful illustrations. The text includes the words *plus one*, so you can use the book to bridge the gap between written words and number sentences; e.g., $1 + 1 = 2$, $2 + 1 = 3$, and so forth. Fish are particularly easy for young children to draw, so this book serves as an ideal resource.

The children can make "plus-one" pictures by drawing a designated number of fish using a particular color or design and then adding one more fish in a new color. Or perhaps the fish that is being added could be swimming in a different direction. (See Figures 6–5 and 6–6 for examples.)

As Figure 6–6 shows, you can also use this book to talk about subtraction. Invite the children to make "flap pages," in which they create a scene and disguise part of it by taping a colored flap over a portion of the picture. The book series Where's Spot? by Eric Hill provides examples. The children can draw fish scenes and camouflage some of the fish with a piece of paper colored to match the rest of the scene and then taped over one or more fish. When the children reveal their pages, everyone will be delighted by the surprises, and you'll have an opportunity to demonstrate addition and subtraction equations. You can also encourage students to explore doubles and number patterns by creating a T-chart showing the total number of eyes for certain counts of fish. (See page 132.)

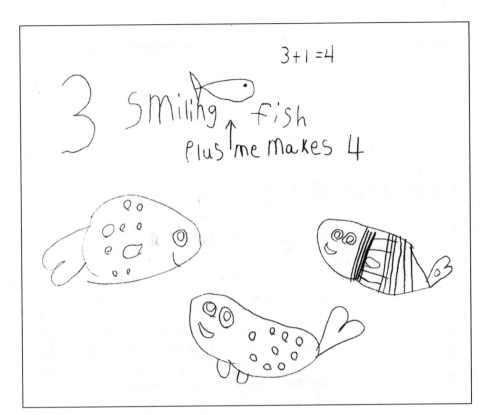

FIGURE 6–5 ◀

Tara added one to her three smiling fish.

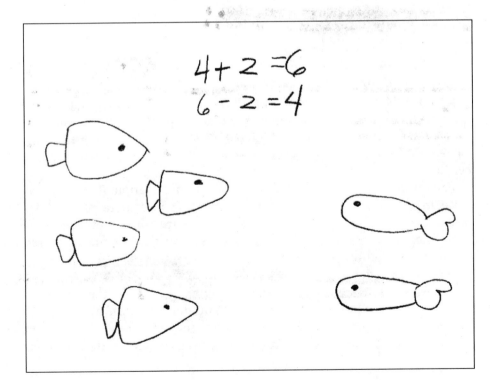

FIGURE 6–6 ◀

Nathan showed how adding two new fish to four fish made six, and how removing them made four again.

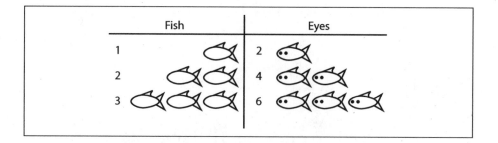

Mitsumasa Anno's Anno's Counting Book

This book provides an illustrated country scene that progresses through the seasons and through the numbers 1 through 12. In addition to clearly depicted, large-print numerals, the book includes a graphic that colors in the quantity for each page on a stick of ten squares. Once the number 12 is reached, the two remaining squares are shown in their own stack.

These graphics enhance children's place-value understandings. Counting the various images within the scene is fun, because sometimes the counting is blatantly obvious. Yet when viewers look carefully, they notice many subtle aspects of the pictures; for example, the time recorded on the church tower. Children enjoy finding similarities and differences from one page to the next. Much like *One Crow*, *Anno's Counting Book* supports understanding of seasonal change and numerical relationships.

Vickie Leigh Krudwig's Cucumber Soup

This story begins with an enormous cucumber falling on an anthill and blocking the only entrance into the ants' home. Ten desperate ants push and pull on the offending fruit, but it's no use—they can't budge the cucumber. They call for help. Gradually, nine noisy mosquitoes, eight orange ladybugs, seven hairy garden spiders, six fuzzy bumblebees, five purple butterflies, four bright fireflies, three yellow grasshoppers, two green praying mantises, and one tiny flea come to the ants' aid. At long last, the cucumber finally moves.

Each page in the book provides nonfiction information about the featured insect. If you're interested in introducing measurement activities through cooking, the final page offers a nice recipe for cucumber soup.

In listening to this story or reading the book for the first time, children can make predictions, look at the illustrations, or simply enjoy the tale. Multiple readings will help students keep track of the cast of characters and become comfortable counting down from 10 to 1. The class can then retell the story by looking at the pictures and describing the action. Once the children are comfortable with the story, you may wish to have them keep track of the quantities of different groups of insects, and depict their findings in an illustration. (See Figure 6–7.) This isn't as easy as it might seem. When the children have finished their illustrations, ask them to share the methods they used to organize their pictures.

Going Beyond Counting

The following books take the challenge up a notch, encouraging students to engage in more sophisticated addition and subtraction.

Ann Jonas's Splash

This book bursts with addition and subtraction action. A variety of characters appear and disappear from a pond setting. The illustrations clearly show which characters are in the pond and which ones are not. After a big splash or two, the story challenges readers to determine how many characters are in the pond. You can record the action on chart paper in the form of number sentences to help children connect action to symbols.

You can also use the "in the pond, out of the pond" idea to have students make a class book about addition and subtraction. Simplify the story

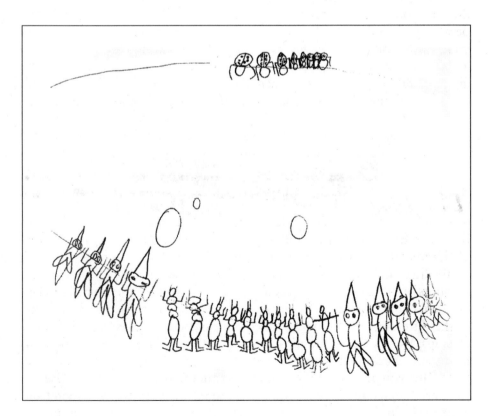

FIGURE 6–7 ◀

Anil drew the various groups of insects in *Cucumber Soup* to keep track of their count.

by using one type of character, such as frogs in the pond. Give the children a page that shows a pond and lily pads. You can put sentence frames on the bottom of the page that say;

"There were __ frogs in the pond. __ jumped out. Now there are __."
"There were __ frogs on the lily pads. __ frogs jumped into the water with __ frogs who were already swimming. Now there are __."

You can also create multiple storyboard cards depicting the pond and lily-pad scene. Have the children use small counters—such as animal-shaped erasers or small plastic animals—to demonstrate addition and subtraction stories. For instance, students could show the various combinations for a particular number by placing the counters in the water or on a lily pad. Fill in the sentences to give the children practice with symbols.

Amy Axelrod's Pigs Will be Pigs

This is one of a series of volumes featuring an amusing family of pigs. This particular story involves collecting and counting money. The story begins with the pigs' realizing that they're extremely hungry but discovering that they have no food in the house. They decide to go out for dinner. To their great disappointment, they discover that they don't have any money. Desperate, the pigs look everywhere for spare change. They find money in a wide variety of places—piggy banks, coat pockets, the washing machine, a toolbox. Each time someone makes a find, he or she announces the amount of money discovered. When the pigs finally decide they have enough money for dinner, Mrs. Pig puts all of the loot in a shoebox, and the family heads for a restaurant. Once they are seated, the pigs peruse the menu and make their selections. Naturally, they overeat, and by the end of the story they're relieved to be going home.

There are several opportunities to explore addition and subtraction through this story. The most obvious activity involves having student keep track of the amount of money the pigs find during their search. You can give each child a small bag filled with plastic or real coins. Students can then act the story out by identifying appropriate coins as the pigs find them. Children could also work in pairs on this task.

To dramatize the story further, selected students can put appropriate amounts of "money" in a shoebox as you slowly reread the story. The class can then help to count the total money in the box while discussing the value of the different types of coins. Once the children have reached their conclusions, use the list of money quantities on the back page of the book to help them check their accuracy.

Finally, you and the children can recreate the restaurant scene. Use toy food or mounted magazine pictures of food to role-play ordering food from a menu. Help the children create a simple menu. The children can participate in pricing the menu items. Along with the toy food or pictures, you can make these restaurant menus available for math menu activities to give students practice with adding and subtracting through a familiar context.

Lily Toy Hong's Two of Everything

This book helps children think about the concept of doubling quantities. This Chinese folktale uses the enticement of magic and surprise to capture readers' attention. In the story, Mr. and Mrs. Haktak live a modest, hard-working existence—until Mr. Haktak discovers a magic pot. When something is put into the pot, it is automatically replicated. This marvelous find is not without its problems, as the couple soon discovers.

Two of Everything sets the stage for several interesting activities. For example, students can use their imaginations to dramatize the story. Have the children find familiar classroom objects to put in the "pot" (which you can improvise from whatever is available) to double the amount.

You can also easily create class books: Take a piece of legal-sized paper, and fold it almost in half. On the resulting front cover, have the children draw and write about what they have put in the pot. On the inside of the folded paper, have them show the doubled amount. You might decide to organize this by having the children use the numbers 1 through 25 and arranging the book so it shows the doubles in order.

You can also use the resulting class book to show doubling information through frame sentences such as: "I put __ in the pot, and __ came out." After class members have explored the concept of doubling, they can create a useful chart showing the patterns that emerge during doubling:

$$1 + 1 = 2$$

$$2 + 2 = 4$$

$$3 + 3 = 6$$

$$4 + 4 = 8$$

$$5 + 5 = 10$$

Ask the children to look for patterns in the above number sentences and to discuss what they notice. Next explore doubles through subtraction:

$$2 - 1 = 1$$

$$4 - 2 = 2$$

$$6 - 3 = 3$$

Create a list of the doubles, and give photocopies of the list to the children to tape into their math notebooks for easy reference.

Whole-Class/Menu Activities

Math games are valuable for several reasons. They provide repeated practice and experience with designated concepts, and they motivate, relax, and engage learners. Many games develop communication skills as well. They also provide teachers with opportunities to listen, ask questions, encourage, make suggestions, and casually conference with students as they work.

The games described below can be used for whole-class explorations, or for menu time. Regardless of the format you select, present the games to students on a regular basis. You can initiate discussions about each game through general questions like: "Who noticed something interesting when we played this game today?" or "Did anyone use subtraction today as you worked on your activity?" Sometimes it's useful to ask about the most enjoyable thing that happened during the work session. At other times, the focus can shift to challenges the students encountered. At still other times, you'll also wish to highlight specific themes, such as using doubles or combinations of ten, during whole-group processing discussions. These conversations can help children make mathematical connections as well as gain insights into their classmates' ideas and experiences.

Five Towers

This game provides opportunities for children to count, consider numbers in groups, and find ways to answer the question, "How many more?"

Materials

- 2 dice per pair of students
- 1 set of interlocking cubes per pair of students

Instructions

1. Player 1 rolls the two dice. He or she adds up the numbers from the dice to see how many cubes to connect to make a tower.

2. Player 2 does the same. Play continues until each player has created five towers.

3. When both players have built five towers, they count the number of cubes in each of their towers. They also determine who has the most cubes altogether, and how many more. They record their findings in their math notebooks.

As the players roll the dice, connect cubes, and write in their notebooks, observe, listen, and watch for ways students are keeping track. Do they count on? Are they able to combine numbers without counting all of the cubes one by one? Do they write numerals independently and accurately? Do they use the numbers to help them determine the total? When the players are determining who has more cubes altogether, and how many more, again see what strategies they're using. For example, some children might line up their combined towers to compare the number of cubes.

When you discuss the game as a class, you may wish to write number sentences as each child tells you how many cubes were in his or her five towers altogether. For example, you might write something like: $5 + 7 + 3 + 10 + 6$. Also discuss ways these numbers might be combined. For instance, someone might mention putting the 7 and 3 together, and the 5 and 6—transforming the problem into $10 + 10 + 11$. Encourage the children to use mathematical tools such as the 1–100 chart, ten frames, tally marks, or a number line to think about these larger quantities. Players can repeat the process and build five towers several times during a math session.

Shake and Spill

One of the most significant addition and subtraction accomplishments for first graders involves learning combinations, or "number families," for each of the numbers 1 through 10. *Shake and Spill* can be played using commercially available two-colored counters (small disks that are usually yellow on one side and red on the other), or using lima beans that have been spray painted one color on one side and a contrasting color on the other side. Children can work independently or with a partner to explore combinations of specific numbers with the two-color counters. They can use a cup or their hands to shake the counters, drop them on a tabletop or the floor, and see how many of each color have been spilled. Players can use math notebooks to keep track of combinations, or you can provide them with a recording sheet to help them organize the information as they play. The resulting data can be displayed and used for discussion as the class investigates the combinations for various numbers.

By this time in the year, first graders have had some experience exploring number combinations for a designated total. In previous months, for example, they participated in activities involving butterflies of two colors landing on a flower, and turkeys with two different colors for tail feathers. These activities helped them begin thinking about combinations for designated totals. Here's a way to build on those earlier activities:

Materials

- 1 cup and 1 set of two-colored counters per student or pair of students
- 2 colored markers; e.g., 1 red and 1 yellow
- 20–30 index cards
- 1 piece of large poster paper

Instructions

Part 1

1. Invite the students to join you in a circle, so everyone can see you.

2. Remind the children of their previous experience with the colored butterflies and turkey tail feathers.

3. Show the children the two-colored counters. Gently toss them so everyone can see how many land with the red side up and how many land with the yellow side up.

4. Shake five counters in your hand and ask the children to predict what's going to happen when you spill them on the floor. Demonstrate dropping the counters in front of you, then invite the children to describe what they see.

5. Use two colored markers to draw on an index card the combination that you have thrown. For example, if three counters fell red side up and two fell yellow side up, draw three red circles and two yellow circles on the index card.

6. Ask the children if they think you will get the exact same results when you toss the five counters again. Discuss other possibilities, and record the children's predictions on index cards.

7. Tape the index cards onto a large piece of poster paper. Ask the students if they think the combinations should be placed in a specific to show a pattern. Arrange the cards to match the students' responses. (See Figure 6–8.) Even if some of the children see a logical pattern for the possible combinations (rrrrrr, rrrrry, rrryy, rryyy, ryyyy, yyyyy),

---

FIGURE 6–8 ▶

Organized pattern for 5—index cards arranged and recorded after class discussion.

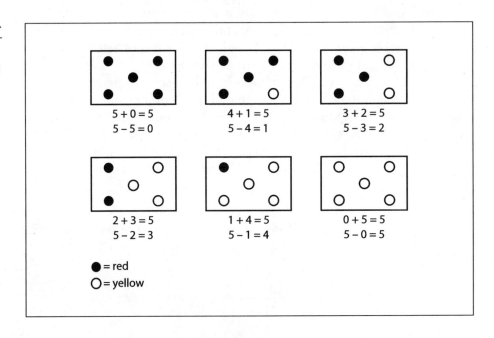

others will not. Gradually, through repeated experiences, they will build on their understandings.

Part 2

1. After recording possible combinations of five, give several children five counters and ask them to gently drop the counters at the same time. Have the class check the results to see if all the combinations that have just been thrown are shown on poster. Add any new ones to the poster.

2. Select one of the combinations—such as three red and two yellow—and ask if anyone can describe how you might write an addition number sentence for that combination. Place three red counters on the floor in front of you and push them together with two yellow counters, so the children see the physical act of combining. Write $3 + 2 = 5$ on the board.

3. Now ask if anyone can say a subtraction sentence for the two colors. Again, show the actual separating action and write $5 - 3 = 2$ (or $5 - 2 = 3$) on the board.

Many children find beginning with the total and removing one of the parts (colors) quite challenging. When they start using the counters independently, check their understanding by walking around and visiting. Ask specific children to demonstrate and talk about this type of subtraction problem.

Part 3

1. During a new lesson with the two-colored counters, have the children divide a page in their math notebooks as if they were making a large tic-tac-toe game, so that one page is divided into nine rectangles or squares.

2. Explain that the students will use red and yellow crayons or markers to show the combinations that they throw with the *Shake and Spill* counters. Remind them to write addition and subtraction ideas beneath each of their drawings. Practice this as a class until you feel confident that the students understand the procedure. (This informal type of recording sheds light on the ease with which individual children are managing addition and subtraction symbols—helping you determine who needs support.)

3. Ask the children to pair up with partners. Assign different combination target numbers to each pair, depending on your sense of what they can handle. For example, you might want some children to work on combinations of five counters while others are working on combinations of ten. You can assign these target numbers by giving the desired number combination to students are they pick up their materials.

4. Encourage students to predict what they think they'll see when they shake and spill the counters.

5. Have the children begin their shaking and spilling, and suggest that they record their results in the tic-tac-toe grid they created in their math notebooks. Remind them to write equations for each illustration. (See Figure 6–9.)

Some children may notice that certain combinations seem to come up more frequently than others. As the students work to make sense of their results and identify patterns in the data, the number fami-

FIGURE 6–9 ▶

The teacher might ask, "Can you show me what 6 – 3 = 3 means?" or, "Do you think you have all of the combinations or not? Why do you think so?"

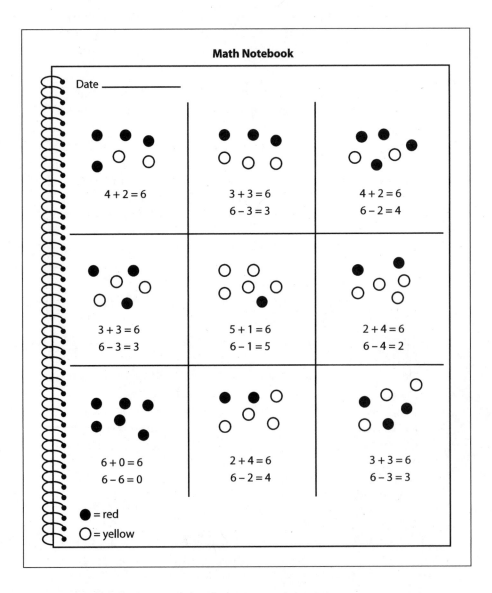

lies (i.e., all of the ways that two numbers can be combined to generate a specified number) will begin to emerge.

6. Conduct a class discussion about the activity when the children have finished playing. Encourage students to discuss their observations and show their recorded information as evidence of their thinking. Ask questions about their reasoning; for example, "Can you show me what 'six minus three equals three' means? Do you think you have all of the combinations? If so, why?" You may wish to post some of the data in the math area of the room, so the students can look at them over time.

Cube Stories

In this activity, the children use interlocking cubes to represent people, objects, or animals, and to act out addition and subtraction stories.

Materials

- 1 set of interlocking cubes per group of students

Instructions

1. Write simple addition and subtraction stories on the board, and say them out loud. Here are some examples from *About Teaching Mathematics* (Burns 2000):

   "There were four ladybugs and three ants in the grass. How many insects were there altogether?"

   "We gave our rat six kibbles. He ate four of them. How many kibbles were left?"

   "There were four horses in the pasture. Two more horses wandered into the pasture. How many horses were there in all?"

   "Seven cars were in the supermarket parking lot. Two people came out of the store and drove away. How many cars are left?"

2. Working in large or small groups, the children act out the stories by snapping cubes together and taking them apart.

If you decide to include this activity as a menu option, you can write the problems on strips of paper and give them to the students who have selected the activity. You can also introduce a storyboard element to this game, by drawing scenes on construction paper or poster board and then using small objects to demonstrate addition and subtraction stories.

Make Ten

Most first graders are somewhat familiar with playing cards. The number relationships inherent in card games offer repeated practice for skills ranging from matching to adding and subtracting. You may wish to begin card experiences with games like *Concentration*, in which you put a bunch of cards face down on the floor or table and children turn them over and match colors, numbers, or suits. You can also play *War*, which requires partners to compare the number values of two cards.

Once the children are fairly comfortable with cards, introduce games that give repeated practice with addition and subtraction math facts. *Make Ten* is a partner game that requires children to look at combinations of cards and determine when the sum of the cards is 10. As with any game that has a specific objective, there's a "winner" and "loser" at the game's end. Explain that whether they feel a sense of triumph or frustration, the children will need self-discipline to enjoy the game. Role-play extreme reactions to winning and losing to provide a light touch with humor and reinforce your point.

Make Ten also involves shuffling the cards, removing face cards and jokers, and putting the cards to be played in one pile. You'll need to show the children how to put the cards on the floor and "stir them up" to shuffle before recreating a pile.

Materials

- 1 deck of cards per pair of students, with face cards and jokers removed

Instructions

1. The game begins with the stack of cards turned face down in front of each pair of students.

2. Each partner takes a turn flipping over one card at a time, placing the overturned cards in a row, and looking for a combination of 10. For example, perhaps the 10 card is flipped over, or a 6 and a 4 are overturned.

To reduce feelings of winning and losing, you may wish to instruct the children to place the combinations of 10 into one shared pile. This removes the natural inclination to keep track of who has spotted the most combinations. Children can also write combinations of 10 in their math notebooks before the game starts and refer to their lists as they play.

How Many Reds?

This is another two-person card game.

Materials

- 20 playing cards per pair of students—2 sets of ace through 10, or 10 cards with a red suit and 10 with a black suit
- 1 recording sheet per pair, divided into 10 rectangles (see Blackline Masters)

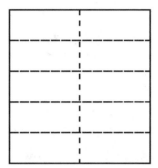

Instructions

1. One player in each pair of students stirs the cards to shuffle them and passes out ten cards to himself or herself and to his or her partner.

2. Each player counts the number of red cards in his or her hand.

3. Player 1 records the total number of red cards from both players' hands on the recording-sheet rectangle; e.g., 4 + 6.

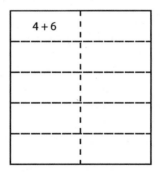

4. The partners shuffle and deal the cards again. This time, Player 2 records the total of red cards in the partners' hands.

5. Play continues until all ten boxes on the recording sheet have been filled in. This game gives children practice with exploring combinations

of 10 and offers an opportunity for them to use standard notation as they record the combinations.

Empty the Bowl

This partner activity strengthens subtraction skills.

Materials

- 20 cubes or tiles per pair of students
- 1 die per pair
- 1 bowl per pair

Instructions

1. Put the twenty cubes or tiles in the bowl.

2. Demonstrate the game by asking for a volunteer to come up, and roll the die.

3. On the board, write *Roll 1*, and record the number shown on the die.

4. Have your volunteer remove the same number of objects from the bowl that's shown on the die.

5. Repeat the process until the bowl is empty, continuing to record each roll and subtracted number. (See Figure 6–10.) You don't need the exact number to remove the last objects from the bowl.

6. Now have children pair up. Have them put twenty cubes or tiles in a bowl and play the game as partners. Suggest that they record their rolls in their math notebooks using the same process you demonstrated on the board.

   This game gives students practice with subtraction and provides an opportunity for them to write the subtraction symbol as quantities are removed from the bowl. After the children have played one round of the game, have a whole-class conversation in which the students discuss the numbers that came up on their dice. Ask these sorts of questions:

   "Which number was the largest, and which was the smallest?"

   "Would it be possible to empty the bowl in one roll? If not, how many rolls would it take?"

   "What would be the *most* rolls that someone might need to empty the bowl?"

FIGURE 6–10 ◄

Roll numbers and sub-tracted numbers.

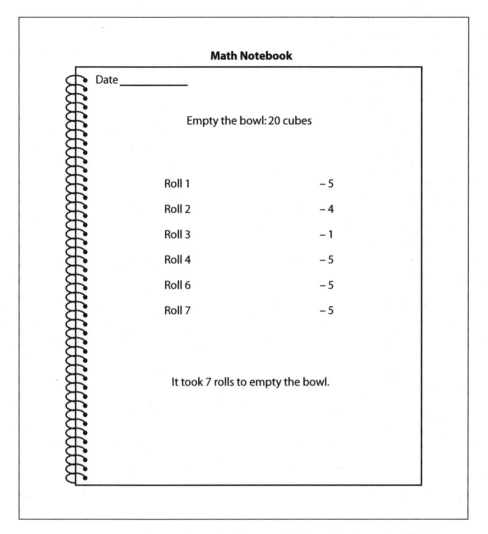

Math Notebook

Date _____

Empty the bowl: 20 cubes

Roll 1   – 5

Roll 2   – 4

Roll 3   – 1

Roll 4   – 5

Roll 6   – 5

Roll 7   – 5

It took 7 rolls to empty the bowl.

Grab-Bag Subtraction

Here's another partner activity focusing on subtraction skills.

Materials

- a collection of cubes or tiles and 1 paper bag per pair of students

Instructions

1. Select a number of objects for the children to work with. Player 1 fills the bag with that number of cubes or tiles.

2. Player 2 reaches in and removes some tiles, showing how many he or she has taken.

3. Both players predict how many tiles are still in the bag and check their predictions.

4. Each player records the equation in his or her math notebook (for example, $15 - 7 = 8$).

Grab a Handful

This partner activity emphasizes comparison and subtraction skills.

Materials

- 1 small bag with about 30 cubes or other small objects per pair of students

Instructions

1. Each set of players gets a bag containing cubes or other small objects.

2. One at a time, both players remove and count a handful of objects.

3. The players count and record the number of objects from each handful and determine which amount is larger.

4. Players then answer the question: "How many *more* objects are there in the larger handful than the smaller one?" They write the information in their math notebooks or on recording sheets.

You can provide ten frames and 1–100 charts for problem-solving support during this activity.

How Much Is Your Word Worth?

This fun activity encourages students to use their addition skills.

Materials

- 1 piece of poster board

Instructions

1. Write the letters of the alphabet in rows on the piece of poster board.

2. Beneath each letter, write a number according to the following pattern: Write 1 under the A, 2 under the B, and so on—until you've gone up to 9, under the letter I. Then start with 1 again under the letter J until you've reached 9, under the R. Finish up with an 8 under the Z. (See Figure 6–11.)

How Much Is Your Word Worth?

A	B	C	D	E	F	G	H
①	②	③	④	⑤	⑥	⑦	⑧

I	J	K	L	M	N	O	P
⑨	①	②	③	④	⑤	⑥	⑦

Q	R	S	T	U	V	W	X
⑧	⑨	①	②	③	④	⑤	⑥

Y	Z
⑦	⑧

C A T
3 + 1 + 2 = 6

FIGURE 6–11 ◄

"How Much Is Your Word Worth?" letter and number board.

3. Post the numbered alphabet so the class can clearly see it.

4. Ask the children to think of two words that have only one letter; for instance, the word *a* and the word *I*. Looking at the poster, discuss how much the word *a* is worth, and compare that number with the word *I*'s worth. Discuss which word is worth more, and determine how much more.

5. Next ask the children to write two words that have *two* letters in their math notebooks. Invite them to decide how much the words are worth. Explore several examples together.

6. When the class is ready, have the children try this same process with slightly longer words or with their first names. After students have explored several words, ask questions like:

   "What small word is worth the most so far?"

   "Do you have any words that are worth the same amount?"

   "Can you think of a way to make sure that words are worth more than ten or less than ten?"

Encourage students to use cubes, number lines, ten frames, 1–100 charts, or other tools to keep track of the numbers as they work.

Chapter 7

February

PROBABILITY

The Learning Environment

Memories of college statistics classes might cause any adult to wonder how the topic of probability could possibly be relevant to first graders. We know that issues relating to probability and the study of data (or statistics) influence each of us on a daily basis. We consider probability every time we make decisions about whether to pack an umbrella, which health-insurance plan to select, and scores of other choices. Our students, too, must learn how to collect and interpret information in order to become confident and productive citizens. ■

We adults analyze data or statistics to cope with uncertainty. In fact, we can think of probability as a way to determine as closely as possible how likely it is that something will or won't happen. In real life, making a decision often involves weighing the available facts. We can't know precisely what events *will* occur, but we *can* make decisions based on what we know about their *likelihood*. Gathering quantitative data about a question is a statistical pursuit. Using those statistics to make predictions, draw inferences, and ultimately make decisions shows the close relationship between statistics and probability.

Young children sometimes make some surprising predictions and may have misconceptions about issues involving probability. As with adults, their thinking can be easily influenced by what they would *like* to have happen, or by personal preferences. This month, your students will have opportunities to make predictions, gather data, and discover that some outcomes can be more likely than others. They'll also continue to encounter numerical relationships and hone their proficiency with numbers.

Creating and interpreting graphs is a powerful way to make sense of data. This month's activities give children opportunities to deal with real numbers and real problems. As in previous months, students will develop problem-solving strategies that help them make informed decisions. Class discussions, games, and children's literature offer practice in creating and interpreting graphs and surveys, analyzing numerical relationships, and considering questions about what is likely or not likely.

Children grasp the basic concepts underlying probability and statistics gradually as they accumulate experiences. As you plan this month's activities, think about ways to help your students understand the following notions:

- Some events are more likely than others, and some events are equally likely.
- We need information (data) to make sound decisions about what is likely or unlikely.
- Probability involves special terms, such as *more, less, how many more, total, some, altogether, likely, not likely, prediction, data*, and *survey*.
- There are symbols, pictures, and tallies that represent particular kinds of data.
- We can look at data and make sense of its meaning.
- There are relationships between data categories and quantities—the amounts within those categories.

Routines

Calendar

For many classrooms, the 100th day of school typically comes sometime in February.

Celebrating the event has become something of a tradition in many primary classrooms. You can plan your 100th Day celebration as an elaborate party, or keep it simple. Regardless of how much emphasis you place on the event, Day 100 provides a variety of opportunities for children to explore patterns within our number system and develop awareness of the numbers 1 through 100. Here are examples of activities you could use to count down to Day 100 or present to your students on the big day itself:

- On a large map of your region, identify and list places that lie within 100 miles of your location.
- Draw or write about something that you could carry 100 of (for example, beans), and something that you couldn't (such as basketballs).
- Complete a jigsaw puzzle that consists of 100 pieces.
- Make paper chains with 100 links and keep track of the ten-link segments in some way.
- Create puzzles by cutting up to five pieces from a 1–100 chart.
- Make a mosaic using 100 paper shapes.
- Make 100 valentines for a nursing home or hospital.
- Collect 100 canned goods to donate to a food pantry.
- Find out how many times you can write your name, count, clap, or jump in 100 seconds.
- Investigate how far you can get when you take 100 steps.
- Look at a set of math materials (cubes, tiles, etc.), and guess how likely it is that the set has 100 pieces. Count to check your guess.
- Ask each student to drop a cube in a container every time he or she leaves the room. At the end of the day, count the cubes and discuss how many groups of 100s there are, how many 10s, and how many 1s.

In addition to the 100th day, February also features recognition of Dental Health as well as Valentine's Day and Presidents' Day. You can easily incorporate all these special events into your class's calendar routines. Create markers for special dates by placing a picture or other kind of symbol on the appropriate calendar square. Children will naturally ask questions like, "How many days until Valentine's Day? How many to Day 100?" As students pose these kinds of questions, they will think about where on the calendar they need to start and stop counting. "Should we count today?" "Should we count the day of the special event?"

By this time of the year, your first graders have experienced keeping track of time by counting down to specific dates using paper chains, and subtracting a link each day. When children consider questions involving the number of days to a special event, remind them of the various tools they have used in the past (such as ten frames, tally marks, cubes, and paper chains). This month, ask the children to decide how they would like to keep track of special events. Perhaps your class will decide on one option, or individual children may elect to keep track of a particular countdown in their own way. By shifting some responsibility for decision making to your students, you increase the mathematical challenge and encourage ownership of the problem.

Weather

In some parts of the United States, February can be an interesting month to focus on weather. Create a weather graph to compare actual weather with class predictions about the weather. List typical February weather events in your area, then use the list to create categories for your weather graph—such as *sunny*, *cloudy*, *snowy*, and *rainy*. You can create a new graph each week. Compare the graphs from one week to the next, discussing similarities and differences as you make predictions.

Weather predictions provide natural opportunities to use terms such as *likely* and *unlikely*. As the children begin encountering this vocabulary, help them grasp the concepts by giving them extreme or even ridiculous scenarios for prediction. For instance, if you live in the north, ask, "Is it likely that we'll have nice, warm picnic weather tomorrow?" If you live in a warmer climate, ask, "Is it likely that there'll be enough snow tomorrow to go sledding?"

As an alternative to creating weather graphs, you can use a regular monthly calendar, as opposed to the bulletin-board display, and organize weather information. Be sure that this calendar is easily accessible to the children. Each day, a child draws a weather picture in the appropriate square on the calendar. At the end of the week, discuss the meaning of the daily pictures and make predictions about the upcoming week. Make comparisons from one week to another. At the end of the month, use tallies to compile data about various categories of weather. Count and compare the types of days that were shown (e.g., number of snowy days versus number of sunny days). Class members can also use a television weather channel, newspaper weather map, or Internet source to compare their weather against that of other parts of the country. This routine offers natural and interesting connections among math, science, and social studies.

Attendance

Attendance and lunch-count data is statistical information required by the school every day, and is a typical routine in classrooms. This month, as you collect this data, discuss reasons that the office needs to keep track of attendance and lunch count. Ask the children if they have noticed anything during the school year that would help them make predictions about attendance—such as classmates with chicken pox—or lunch-count trends—such as a popular meal. Use this familiar topic to discuss unlikely scenarios. For instance, it's unlikely that only two class members will attend school tomorrow.

Many schools offer various food options for lunch, and some children probably bring their lunches from home. Have your students look over the cafeteria's lunch menu for the week. Then ask them to predict which lunch orders are likely to be the most popular—meaning which orders will appeal to the most class members (not which foods a particular individual might prefer). Ask the children if they think other classes are likely to make similar choices. Why or why not? Guide the class to design a weekly recording sheet for keeping track of attendance (the number of children who are present and absent each day) and lunch count (how many people buy lunch, and how many bring lunch from home). Compare the data from one week to the next. As the children become comfortable with this process, discuss what they notice and expect based on the data they've collected so far. Link this process with determining what is likely or unlikely.

Estimation Jar

This month, incorporate probability language and ideas into your estimate-jar routine. Each time we estimate—narrowing the possibilities to a reasonable guess—we go through a process of thinking about what is likely and unlikely. During February, present your students with a variety of estimation questions that get them thinking about what is likely and unlikely. Here are some examples:

> "Is it likely that forty people could fit in this room?"
>
> "What about twenty grown elephants fitting in this room?"
>
> "Is it likely that you could jump five thousand times in one minute?"
>
> "What about jumping two hundred times in one minute?"
>
> "Is it likely that you could stay balanced on a bike for a minute if you weren't moving?"
>
> "What about staying balanced on top of a pole?"

Then ask questions about likelihood and unlikelihood in relation to the estimation jar; for example:

> "Is it likely that we could fit twenty cubes [or beads or tiles] in the jar?"
>
> "What about eighty cubes [or beads or tiles]?"
>
> "What about twenty baseballs [or potatoes or hockey pucks]?"

Begin each week by writing a likely/unlikely statement at the top of a horizontal piece of construction paper. Divide the paper down the center and label one side of the paper *likely* (or *probably*) and the other side *unlikely* (or *probably not*). Have the children use small sticky notes to record their responses and place them in the appropriate categories.

Questions and Surveys

Toward the end of the month, students can use what they've learned through the other routines to think up an interesting question and then develop a plan—a survey—for collecting and tabulating responses to their question. This activity can present quite a challenge, because many children have difficulty distinguishing between questions and statements. You may have seen this during field trips or after the class has listened to a guest speaker. When asked, "Does anyone have questions?" someone in the class will almost invariably launch into a statement that may or may not be related to the topic at hand. Questioning skills can benefit children in many areas besides math, such as language arts. Knowing how to ask and answer questions can also help children become better listeners.

Begin a discussion about surveys by helping children understand what makes a good survey question. Interesting questions have to do with something that you are really curious about, or something that you can't be sure of, like:

"Have you lost more than three teeth?"

"Do you like to ride in the car?"

"Do you have chores/jobs to do at your house?"

Perhaps your class is planning a celebration for Valentine's Day. If so, you might tell the children that you have a question about how you might plan the party. Explain that your question is not something they could answer with one simple piece of information (e.g., "Is Valentine's Day on February 14?"). Mention that it's also not a question for which you could make easy predictions ("Do most of you like treats?").

Point out that this is a different kind of question than what they may be used to. It's a question that requires you to find out what each person thinks—so you can plan the party in a way that will be fun for as many people as possible. Then pose your question. Suppose your question is: "Would you rather frost cookies or play games during the party?" Create two labels—*frost cookies*, and *play games*—and place them in front of two bowls. Read the labels out loud and explain which one goes with which bowl. Then ask the class members to place a cube or some other counter in the bowl that represents their preference.

You may introduce the idea that when people are required to "vote" in front of others, or to sign their names to their vote, they might make different choices than they would if no one knew how they were voting. Ask the children if they can imagine why this might be true. Generate ideas about how you might ask the frost cookies/play games question so that no one would feel influenced by others. Sometimes children suggest putting their heads down and raising their hands (no peekies!) during the vote.

During each day's opening routines, take time to generate additional question examples. Provide some "nonexamples" as well (e.g., statements) and see if the children can distinguish them from questions. Here's one way to do this: When the children are sitting at circle during an opening routine, or as they prepare to listen to a story, make some statements and ask some questions. Have the children give a thumbs-up signal when they hear a question, and to not respond at all when they hear a statement. Talk about questions for which you already know the probable answer (e.g., "Do most of you like recess?") and compare this kind of question with others for which more information is needed ("Did you bring your P.E. shoes today?"). Ask the children to help you think of questions whose answers aren't easily predictable. Write these questions on strips of paper and collect them in a box or basket for later use in case children need extra survey ideas. (The class might decide to collect 100 questions in honor of Day 100.)

Soon the children will feel comfortable generating questions that would be suitable for surveys. Now discuss the idea of creating surveys. Explain that surveys involve organizing a piece of paper to show how people answered your question. Surveys are like graphs and charts, because they show information in a way that's easy to see and understand. Give examples of graphs and charts that the class has worked with before. Remind the students about how they've made "true math statements" about class graphs.

FIGURE 7-1 ▶

My class suggested using tally marks to record responses to their survey question.

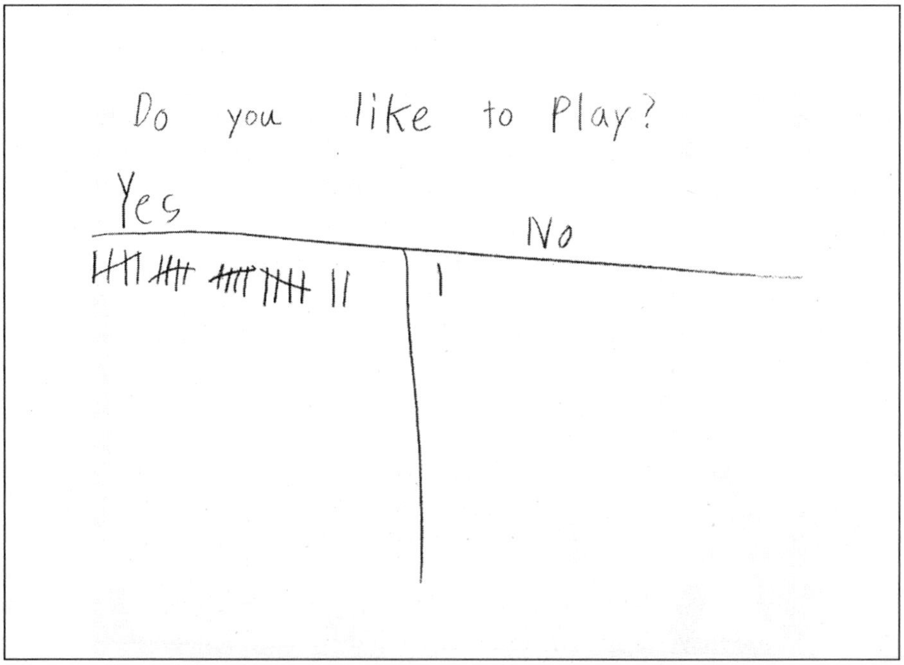

At least once a week, select a question from the collection box and discuss ways that students might organize responses to that question. During these discussions, remind the class about the options of using names, tally marks, *X*s, checks, etc. As you discuss various ways to represent data, have children draw examples of possible surveys in their math notebooks. (See Figure 7–1.) By giving students practice during whole-group discussions, you'll help them develop individual surveys later in the month.

Math Notebooks

This month, the children can use their math notebooks to create surveys and record their thinking from whole-class and menu activities involving probability.

The Mathematics

February's lessons have been designed to give children multiple experiences with:

- comparing quantities.
- communicating and making representations about what they notice.
- predicting likely occurrences.
- drawing conclusions.

Whole-class lessons introduce games and graphing activities to develop probability concepts and vocabulary. Some games provide continued practice with addition and subtraction. As with preceding chapters, the activities are organized into literature-based lessons and whole-class/menu options. Feel free to choose from among the activities described below, or to present them in a different sequence than they're shown here.

Literature-Based Activities

Choosing children's literature to teach probability differs significantly from selecting titles that teach geometry and number. The recommendations in this chapter fall into three categories:

- books that enable you to initiate graphing activities
- books that suggest Day 100 activities

■ books that help students master pairs of contrasting concepts, such as *likely* or *unlikely*, *real* or *pretend*, *possible* or *impossible*, and so forth

Graphing

Losing Teeth

Henry Pluckrose's *Look at Teeth* provides nonfiction information about dental health. Focusing on dental health is particularly relevant for first graders, many of whom are losing baby teeth and learning to take more responsibility for dental hygiene. Discuss the emotions children experience as they lose their teeth, or the fear of never losing their teeth that some youngsters feel. Here are some ideas for processing these emotions:

■ Tell the children that regardless of whether they've lost any teeth or not, they should take pictures of those great smiles—because they're all going to get new and even better smiles soon.

■ Ask the children to count their teeth when they brush them tonight. The next day, discuss the results.

Reading the book and having such conversations will prepare students for making a graph about the number of teeth that class members have lost. Ask for several volunteers to say how many teeth they've lost. List the range of responses vertically (e.g., 1 tooth lost, 2 teeth lost, 3 lost, etc.). Ask the children to predict which number of missing teeth will be the most common. Have them tell you a number that they think is very *unlikely* for first graders. This activity sets the stage for future understandings about *mode* (the most common number), *median* (the middle number in a range), and *mean* (the average). Now make your graph.

Materials

■ paper tooth cut-outs, available from most educational-supply stores
■ 1 piece of dark-colored poster board

Instructions

1. Position the poster board horizontally. Down the left side of the board, list the range of numbers of teeth lost that you discussed with the class earlier.

2. Ask students to find the number on the graph that represents the number of teeth they have lost, and to attach that same number of paper teeth cut-outs to the graph. For instance, if Kamika has lost two teeth, she will attach two cut-outs next to the 2 on the graph. (See Figure 7–2.)

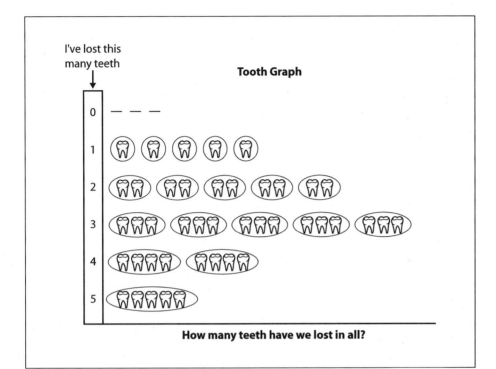

FIGURE 7–2 ◄

Lost-tooth graph.

3. Once everyone has placed paper teeth on the graph, discuss various ways to count the data. For instance, will you add totals from the rows? Count by 2s? By 1s?

4. Invite the class to make true math statements about what they're seeing in the graph. For example:

> "Five people have lost one tooth and five people have lost three teeth."
>
> "Everyone has lost at least one tooth."
>
> "One person has lost five teeth!"

Extensions

Read the book *A Quarter from the Tooth Fairy* by Caren Holtzman. Have the children determine how much money the tooth fairy would leave for the various numbers of lost teeth.

Valentines

Frank Modell's *One Zillion Valentines* tells of a boy who has decided to make his valentines rather than buy them. After you read the story, students will create a Venn diagram of valentines.

Materials

- 1 piece of poster board
- 1 red marker
- 1 pink marker
- 2 or 3 pieces of red construction paper
- 2 or 3 pieces of pink construction paper
- 2 or 3 pieces of red-and-pink gift-wrapping paper or wallpaper samples

Instructions

1. To prepare for the lesson, make a large Venn diagram on the piece of poster board by drawing two big, overlapping circles. Draw one circle with red marker and the other with pink. Label the red circle *red hearts*, and the pink circle *pink hearts*. Label the overlapping area *pink and red hearts*.

2. Fold each piece of the different colored paper and draw fairly small dotted half-heart outlines. (See Figure 7–3.) Make the hearts a size that will fit easily within the Venn diagram circles you've drawn.

3. Ask each child to choose a color paper—red, pink, or red-and-pink—and to cut along the dotted lines to create hearts.

FIGURE 7–3 ▶

Valentine diagrams.

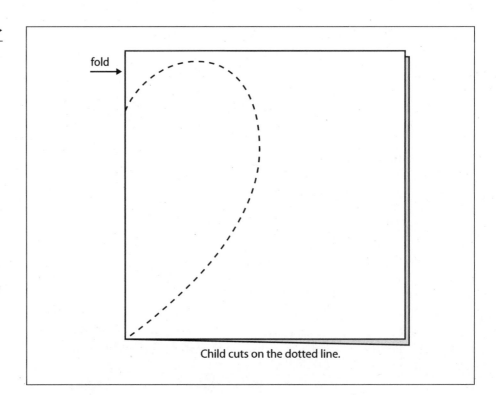

fold →

Child cuts on the dotted line.

4. Invite the children who have created red hearts to hold them up. Do the same for those who created pink hearts and red-and-pink hearts.

5. Place the Venn-diagram poster in a spot that is easily accessible to the children. Invite several children to speculate about where they think their hearts should go on the diagram. Have the children discuss their reasoning.

6. Invite confident volunteers to come up and tape their hearts in the appropriate areas of the diagram. (See Figure 7–4.)

    If a student is unsure or makes an error—e.g., he or she places a pink-and-red heart in the red circle instead of the overlapping area—ask the child to think out loud about the problem. In this example, you could confirm that the heart indeed has some red and does belong in the red circle. But then ask the child if the heart can also go in another spot because it has both red and pink. Venn diagrams help children to think in terms of more than one similarity at a time.

7. Once all the class members have placed their hearts in the diagram, ask them to think of and list true math statements about the graph. Display the list with the graph.

President Lincoln's Beard

Louise Borden's *A. Lincoln and Me* provides biographical information about Abraham Lincoln. The story is told from the perspective of a young

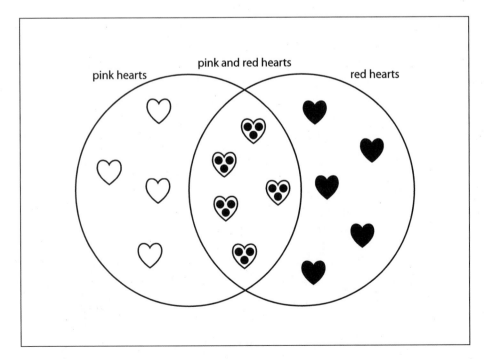

FIGURE 7–4 ◀

Venn diagram of cut-out hearts.

boy who feels a particular sense of identity with this historical figure. After reading and discussing the book, explain to your students that Lincoln was very fond of children and received many letters from them both before and after he became president of the United States. In fact, when Lincoln first ran for a lesser office, a young girl wrote to him and told him that she thought he would look more handsome with a beard. He took her advice and grew one.

This activity provides opportunities for your students to make predictions and practice addition and subtraction (Parts 1 and 2) and then to create a graph (Part 3).

Materials

- photocopies of Lincoln with a beard; enough for everyone in the class
- photocopies of Lincoln without a beard, enough for everyone in the class

Instructions

Part 1

1. Show the children pictures of Lincoln with and without a beard.

2. Ask the students to predict how many children in the class they think prefer Lincoln *with* a beard, and how many prefer him *without* a beard. If your class is large (twenty to thirty or more students), simplify the problem by asking the children to imagine a small classroom with only ten students. Among these imaginary ten students, how many would be likely to prefer Lincoln with a beard? How many would prefer him without a beard?

3. Write number sentences based on the idea of 10 as a total; for example, if the children think that five of the imaginary students would like him with the beard, and five would like him without it, write *5 + 5 = 10.*

Part 2

1. Ask the children how many people are in the class.

2. Write __ + __ = *25* (or whatever your class total is) on the board. (Note: The remaining steps in this extension use 25 as the class total; you'll need to customize the steps based on your own total.)

3. Help the children explain what the blank spaces in this number sentence represent. For example, the first blank could be for the number of people who like Lincoln *with* a beard. (Tape a bearded picture of Lincoln above the first blank.) The second blank could represent the number of people who like Lincoln *without* a beard. (Position the clean-shaven picture above this blank.)

4. Tell the children that you are imagining a situation where one person in the class likes Lincoln *with* a beard. Ask the children to help you fill in the number sentence: 1 + __ = 25.

5. Then ask what number should go in the second blank. Guide the discussion so the children arrive at 24. Discuss how they decided that 24 belongs in the second blank.

6. Now write some new number sentence: *2 + __ = 25*, then *__ + 23 = 25*, and *15 + __ = 25*. Have the children volunteer some of their own number sentences that would also work, discussing their reasoning as you go along. Invite children to use ten frames and cubes or other manipulatives to count and to prove the numerical relationships.

7. Introduce a number sentence involving subtraction; e.g., 25 − __ = 24. Ask what this number sentence means. Help the children figure out that the 25 in *this* number sentence represents the total number of students in their class. Explain that the blank represents the number of people who like Lincoln *with* a beard, while the 24 is the number of people who prefer him *without* the beard. Experiment with more subtraction equations, such as 25 − 24 = 1, 25 − 5 = 20, or 25 − 10 = 15.

Part 3

1. On the chalkboard, write *Do you think President Lincoln looks better with or without a beard?* across the top. At the bottom, write two labels next to each other: *with a beard* and *without a beard*.

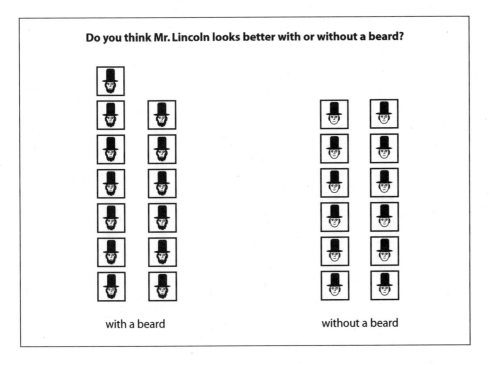

Do you think Mr. Lincoln looks better with or without a beard?

with a beard   without a beard

FIGURE 7–5 ◀

Do you think Mr. Lincoln looks better with or without a beard?

2. Invite the children to select a picture of Lincoln that represents their preference about his beard, and to tape the picture in the appropriate column on the board. (See Figure 7–5.)

3. Ask the children to look at the resulting graph and make true math statements about what they notice. Responses might include: "More of us like him *with* a beard," "The 'without' has the lowest number," and "The 'with' group has one more in it than the 'without' group." Such comments represent understandings about the concepts *more*, *fewer*, and *how many more*.

4. Consider having the children provide addition and subtraction number sentences representing what they see in the graph.

Day 100

Making Plans

The books *Miss Bindergarten Celebrates the 100th Day of Kindergarten*, by Joseph Slate, and *The 100th Day of School*, by Angela Medearis, can generate ideas for celebrating the 100th day of school. During a class meeting, the children can help plan the activities for the big day. Consider using these two books together to open a discussion about the kinds of math activities that the children remember learning and doing in kindergarten, and new things that they're learning this year. Keep your *Math Words* poster handy so you can add new terms that come up during the conversation. This is also a good time to discuss things the children want to learn and math skills they want to acquire. Finally, perhaps your class would like to celebrate Day 100 with a kindergarten class. For instance, they could count 100 things from sorting sets with kindergarten-age partners.

Drawing 100 Faces

Terri Sloat's *From One to One Hundred* (referenced earlier in this book) features sorting and counting. Each page shows pictures focusing on a unique theme. The book's cover depicts the cheerful faces of many children. After rereading the book with your class, ask the children to estimate how many faces they think are on the cover. Are there 100? Fifty? Twenty-five? Invite the children to create a display of 100 faces to celebrate Day 100. Faces are easy to draw, and children come up with an astonishing variety. Here's what you'll need:

Materials

- several 4-by-4-inch or 5-by-5-inch squares of construction paper, in different skin tones, per child

- several drawing and coloring materials (markers, paints, or some other tool) per child

Instructions

1. Decide how many faces each child will create. Use the 1–100 pocket chart as a tool to discuss ways to end up with 100 faces. You might place a popsicle stick in each number pocket and begin passing out the sticks to show how many faces each child needs to draw.

2. Invite the children to start drawing their faces on the construction-paper squares you've provided.

3. After each child has created several faces, designate a large space, such as a bulletin board, for displaying the faces. Have the class suggest ways to arrange the faces so as to make counting them more efficient. Someone will likely recommend arranging them in 2s, 5s, or 10s.

4. Verify the final face count on the board.

Invite children who particularly enjoy this type of art project to make additional pictures of faces if they wish in the weeks that follow. You might also conduct two or three more whole-class "face-making" sessions. This simple, student-created display will provide plenty of entertainment and humor in addition to offering counting opportunities.

Contrasting Concepts

This section features pairs of contrasting stories that enable children to explore the comparative nature of word pairs such as *possible/impossible*, *probably/possibly*, *likely/unlikely*, *likely/not likely*, *true/pretend*, and *fiction/nonfiction*.

Hats and Caps

Ann Morris's *Hats, Hats, Hats* is a beautifully photographed book depicting a wide variety of hats. Each page offers pictures of people who are the same because they wear hats, but who are different because they're wearing different *kinds* of hats that come from different cultures and feature a variety of styles. After reading the book, ask the children if they think the hats shown in the book could be found in real life, or if they're pretend hats. Then invite them to use a map or globe to find the various geographic locations identified in the book.

Esphyr Slobodkina's *Caps for Sale* provides the "pretend" counterpoint to the "real" *Hats, Hats, Hats*. In this popular story, which has delighted children for generations, a peddler who is unable to sell his caps decides to take a little nap. While he's sleeping, monkeys take the cap and then have some fun with the peddler. Children love to dramatize the story and pretend to be the mischievous monkeys. You can expand on the math connections by having the children keep track of the caps that crop up during the story, or by creating a class bulletin board with monkeys wearing stacks of ten caps of varying colors.

Marketing, Marketing

Ted Lewin's *Market* is a visually appealing, factual book that offers marketplace images from places ranging from New York City to Ugandan villages. Like *Hats, Hats, Hats*, this book evokes social studies by showing similarities and differences from regions around the world. Again, you can ask children how realistic they think the pictures are, and encourage them to explore maps and other resources that shed more light on the book's vivid settings.

As the counterpart to *Market*, read Anne Miranda's *To Market, To Market*. This raucous book uses the rhythm of the familiar nursery rhyme *To Market to Market to Buy a Fat Pig*. Children enjoy the humor of the illustrations and can clearly see the contrast between these hilarious pictures and the beautifully realistic paintings in *Market*.

Polar Bears

Polar bears tend to be quite popular among children in the winter, especially students who live in colder climates. Gail Gibbons's *Polar Bears* is packed with interesting information about this remarkable arctic animal. The clear illustrations and informative nature of the text will help children identify this as an accurate source. The class will then enjoy contrasting the book with a fictional account of a polar bear.

Hans de Beer's *Little Polar Bear* introduces an endearing character and provides a distinct counterpart to the previous book. The little bear behaves as though he were a human being. The students can discuss other stories in which animals behave like people (e.g., Winnie the Pooh, Goldilocks and the Three Bears, and the Berenstain Bears). Most children will draw the obvious conclusion that this story is pretend.

Delightful Dogs

Stickeen, by Rubay Donnell, tells the awe-inspiring true story of explorer and environmentalist John Muir and his little dog Stickeen. Muir and Stickeen exhibit extraordinary bravery during this intense Alaskan adventure. From the first page, the author makes it clear that this is a true story. Children become absorbed in the unusual illustrations and amazed by this historical account.

For a fanciful counterpoint, read *Officer Buckle and Gloria* by Peggy Rathman. This charming and humorous story tells of the friendship between a police officer and his dog. In the story, Officer Buckle visits schools to deliver earnest and dull messages relating to safety. Much to the delight of the children, his dog Gloria puts on wildly entertaining shows behind Officer Buckle's back. The illustrations depicting the steadfast Officer Buckle and his dog give ample evidence that the story is fiction.

After experiencing several of these contrasting stories, your students could create a class compilation of likely/unlikely pages using their own ideas, or record the titles of the books. They could also write their own likely/unlikely stories.

Whole-Class/Menu Activities

The activities described below encourage children to obtain numerical information through games and surveys, and challenge them to predict what is likely or not likely based on the data they obtain.

Roll Two Dice

This partner game gives students practice with the concept of likelihood, while also providing practice with addition facts. As two dice are rolled repeatedly, certain sums will be generated more often than other sums. Children can record the sums and then graph them to depict their findings in visual rather than list form.

Materials

- 1 pair of dice per pair of students
- 1 pair of oversize dice
- overhead projector
- 1 copy of *Roll Two Dice* recording sheet per pair of students (see Figure 7–6 and Blackline Masters)

Instructions
Part 1

1. Demonstrate the game to the class. If you have a pair of oversize dice, ask student helpers to roll them ten times and show the results (the total value rolled) to the class after each roll. While your volunteers

FIGURE 7–6   ▶

**Roll Two Dice blank
form.**

2	3	4	5	6	7	8	9	10	11	12

Finish Line

are doing this, record the results on a large piece of chart paper or on the chalkboard. Document results in the form of equations that show how the values on the two dice add up; e.g., 2 + 1 = 3, 5 + 2 = 7, 6 + 6 = 12. If large dice aren't available, have several children roll two dice and report their results as you record them.

2. Once you have the data from ten rolls, stand back and look at it. Ask the children to pair up and discuss among themselves what they notice about the number combinations they see on display.

3. Invite the children to offer comments about what they see. Most likely, they will identify number combinations and totals that occur more than once.

4. Discuss any repeats. Ask the children if they think all of the combinations you can get by rolling two dice have been listed. Ask what the students think could happen if Player A rolled one die and Player B rolled the other die. Some children may begin to realize that it is harder to roll 1 + 1 "snake eyes" than to roll say – a total of 6 or 7.

5. Use the overhead projector to introduce the recording sheet.

6. Once again have some students roll two dice. Record the results in the appropriate space in the recording sheet. For instance, if a student rolls a 3 and a 2, write *3 + 2 = 5* in the first blank space under the "5" column. Invite several students to come up one at a time and take turns trying this recording technique. Keep rolling and recording results until you see some columns start accumulating more entries than other columns.

7. Look at the recording sheet with the class, and ask the children to tell you what they notice. Point out that some columns have more entries than others. Ask the children if this was just luck, or if there is some reason that this happened. Tell them that when they play the game with a partner and record their results, they should pay special attention to how the graph looks. Do they think their graph will look like the one the class just created together, or do they think it will look different? Does anyone want to make a prediction?

Part 2

1. Ask the children to pair up. Give each pair a copy of a blank recording sheet. To play, partners can take turns rolling the dice and recording, or each player can perform the same job throughout the game. Explain that the game ends as soon as one column has been filled with entries.

2. After each pair has played, ask the children to turn in their recording sheets. If possible, post a variety of their results. The graphs will show a rough V-shaped result, and will affirm that there is something predictable going on in this game. (See Figure 7–7.)

3. Invite the children to discuss possible explanations for why there are more ways to roll some numbers—like 7 or 8—more often than 2 or 12. For instance, 7 could come from 1 + 6 or 2 + 5, or 3 + 4 or 4 + 3. Respect that many first graders will not generalize about these relationships.

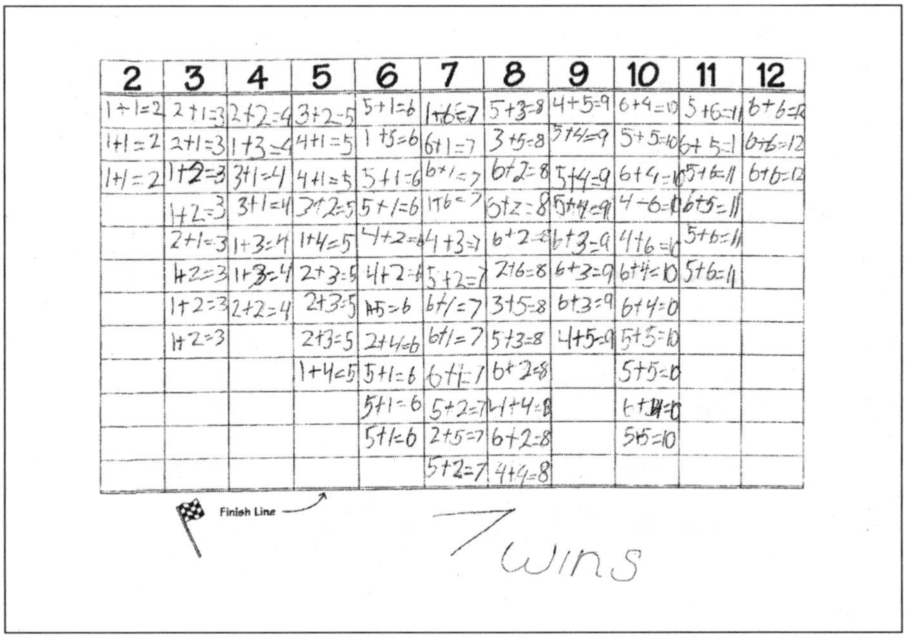

FIGURE 7–7 ◄

Margaret and Pita's recording sheet helped them to predict unlikely combinations.

Egg Carton Shake

This game has some similarities to *Roll Two Dice*.

Materials

- 1 egg carton per pair of students
- 2 small disks, coins, or tiles per pair, to serve as game pieces
- 1 permanent marker
- masking or other opaque tape

Instructions

1. On the *inside* of each egg carton, use the permanent marker to number the bottom of each egg compartment along the inner row 1 through 6. Repeat on the outer row on the inside of the carton.

2. Tape over any holes in the egg cartons' tops.

3. Place two small game pieces in each egg carton.

4. Ask children to pair up. Then explain the rules: Players will take turns shaking the closed carton and opening it to see where the game pieces have landed. They'll then add the two numbers together and record the results in their math notebooks in the same form they used for *Roll Two Dice* (for example, 4 + 2 = 6, 1 + 6 = 7, and so on).

5. Play a few demonstration rounds with the whole class and model writing the number sentences.

6. Instruct players to begin the game. Explain that the game ends after twenty "shakes."

7. Once all the pairs of players have finished the game, ask students to circle the sums they recorded. Then discuss patterns as a class; e.g., whether certain numbers came up more frequently than others.

Two-Card Turnover

Children can play this game in pairs or individually. Players will turn over two cards at a time from a deck, then observe whether the upturned cards show combinations of red/red, black/black, or red/black.

Materials

- 1 deck of cards per pair of students or per student, with jokers removed

Instructions

1. Model the game for the class: On the board, make three columns labeled *red/red*, *red/black*, and *black/black*. Ask students to copy the same labels into their math notebooks.

2. Shuffle the cards, then place them face down in a pile.

3. Invite a student to turn over two cards. Put a tally mark or an X as a recording mark in the appropriate column on the board. Ask students to record the same data in their notebooks. Remind students how tally marks work, and agree on a method for keeping track. (For example, will you make four tally marks and then draw a diagonal line through them to group your marks in 5s?)

4. Have your volunteer do several more turnovers, and keep recording the results. Make sure students are all continuing to record in their notebooks, too.

5. After several demonstrations of turning over and recording, ask the class what they expect to see happen as more cards are revealed.

6. Continue the demonstration until all of the cards have been turned over, and then compare the results in the three columns. Ask the students which column has the highest count, and the lowest. Ask the children if they think the results were just luck or if they expect to see the same results when they play the game in pairs. Discuss their reasoning. Some children may find it easier to talk about their predictions by pretending that they're explaining the game to a family member or friend and trying to help that person understand what will probably happen by the end of the game.

7. Invite the children to pair up and play the game themselves.

8. Regroup, and discuss the results as a class.

Paperclip Toss

This partner game entails active participation and further develops children's prediction and data-gathering skills.

Materials

- 1 large circular target, made of 3 different-colored pieces of construction paper, per pair of students
- 1 paperclip per pair of students
- 10, 15, or 20 counting cubes, in the same 3 colors as the construction paper, per pair of students

Instructions

1. Create one construction-paper target per pair of students. Each target is made of three concentric circles glued to each other, each circle a different color of paper. Be sure the outer circle is significantly greater in area than the middle and innermost circles. The smallest circle should look something like a "bull's eye" target. (See below.)

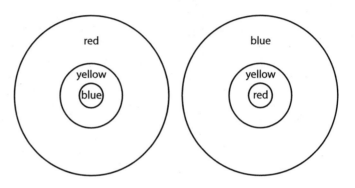

2. Demonstrate the game: Place one target on the floor, and have a paperclip handy for the demonstration.

3. Then invite several students to come up one at a time and drop or toss the paperclip onto the target. Ask for a volunteer to use a colored counting cube to record the area on the target where the clip lands. For example, suppose your target's large circle is red, the middle circle is blue, and the innermost circle is yellow. If the clip lands on red, the record keeper will gather a red cube to keep track of the toss. After each toss of the paperclip, pick up the clip and give it to the next player who wants to try. Have the record keeper continue gathering cubes that match the color of the areas the clip falls into. Ask students what they predict will happen as the game continues.

4. Have students continue tossing the paperclip and gathering the corresponding color cubes until a designated number of cubes (e.g., ten, fifteen, or twenty) has been accumulated. Ask, "How many did we get of each color?" "What color did we have the most often? The least often?"

5. Invite students to pair up and play the game in partners. Suggest that partners take turns tossing the paperclip and gathering cubes to record the results. When they're finished, ask them, "How did your results compare with your partner's?" "Did you get the results you expected?" "How can you tell that you actually had ten [or whatever the target number was] tosses in all?"

During this game, some students will try to hit the innermost circle with the paperclip. That's OK, though it's not the object of the game. The real goal is to try to accurately predict where most of the paperclip tosses will land. If players want to make predictions about how many times they think they will be able to hit the center, that's fine—they'll still be working with ideas of likelihood.

Coin Flip

This game also provides opportunities to practice making predictions and keeping track of results.

Materials

- 1 coin per child

Instructions

1. Show the children the coin and describe its two sides. Use the words *heads* and *tails*.

2. Ask the class to predict what would happen if you flipped the coin twenty times. Discuss the reasoning behind the predictions.

3. On the board, create two columns, one labeled *heads* and the other *tails*. Flip the coin twenty times, and record each result by making a tally mark in the appropriate column. Have the children record the same information in their math notebooks.

4. Give each child a coin and ask the class members to repeat this experiment on their own, flipping or cropping their coin twenty times and making tally marks to show their results. Discuss the results of this larger sample as a class.

5. Ask the children if they think the results would be the same or different if *two* coins were used. Discuss possible results two coins were dropped.

6. On the board, make three columns labeled *heads/heads*, *tails/tails*, and *heads/tails*. Invite the children to gather in groups of three. Give each group two coins. Two players toss the coins, and the third records the results. The children can take turns being the coin tossers and recorders.

All About 10

Here's another partner activity that encourages estimation skills.

Materials

- 1 small bag filled with 15–20 small objects (e.g., Unifix cubes) per pair of students
- 2 recording sheets per pair of student, with the labels *less than 10, exactly 10,* and *more than 10* written across the top of the page

Instructions

1. Ask children to pair up. Give each pair a small bag filled with the objects. Also give each pair two copies of the recording sheet. Invite the children to play according to the rules below:

2. Player 1 makes a prediction about whether he or she expects to grab *less than ten, exactly ten,* or *more than ten* objects from the bag.

3. Player 1 reaches into the bag and grabs a handful of the objects.

4. The players count the actual number of objects from the handful and write the count under the appropriate heading on Player 1's recording sheet.

5. Player 1 puts the objects back in the bag.

6. Players repeat these steps until each player has made and recorded ten grabs. The two players then compare their results.

7. Have a class discussion about the game after everyone has played. Ask students to consider possible ways to alter the outcome they obtained. For instance, what might happen if a smaller or larger child took the handfuls from the bag? What would the results look like if the bags had been filled with objects of varying sizes?

Scoops in a Jar

This activity encourages children to think about the concepts *likely* and *unlikely*.

Materials

- 3 or 4 plastic jars of varying sizes
- 1 small scoop (e.g., from a coffee can)
- a 3-lb. bag of lentils

Instructions

1. Select one of the jars and ask the students how many scoops of lentils they think it would take to fill it. Encourage them to generate several guesses that they know are obviously too large and others that are obviously too small.

2. Then have the students narrow the range between these two extremes until they arrive at a selection of guesses that, to them, seem more likely to be true. Write these guesses on the board. (Your list might include numbers such as 3, 4, 5, 6, 7, 8, and more than 8.)

3. Point to each guess that you've written on the board, and ask children to raise their hands to indicate support for that guess.

4. Start filling the jar with lentils, one scoop at a time. Have the children count out loud as you empty each scoop into the jar. When you've filled the jar about halfway, stop—and ask the children if they want to reconsider their guesses. Point out that estimates are our best guesses *at a given time*, and that it's OK to change your guesses once you have new information.

5. Finish filling the jar, noting how many scoops it actually took. Reassure the children that they all made reasonable guesses. Remind them that most guesses *don't* exactly match the actual outcome in real life.

6. Hold up a jar that's larger or smaller than the one you just used. Ask students if they think the jar is likely to hold more or less than the one that you just filled. Discuss the responses.

If you want to provide this activity as a menu option, offer children a variety of containers labeled *A*, *B*, *C* (or some other system), to help the children identify which jar is being used at any given time. Encourage students to keep track of their predictions and actual counts in their math notebooks.

Surveys

During this month's routines and activities, students have learned how to ask questions. They've also created questions for the class collection box, and have discussed which kinds of questions have answers that can be predicted with some degree of certainty. For instance, suppose a child were asked, "Do you eat food sometime during the day?" In this case, there is a fair degree of certainty about the response to this question. So, someone seeking to conduct a survey of responses could make fairly accurate predictions about what he or she would find out.

On the other hand, if someone poses a question for which he or she has little idea of the likely response, the question can be considered "interesting." This type of question is particularly fun to use in a survey.

Here are some ideas for conducting surveys:

Materials

- 1 survey sign per child, made of a 4-by-3-inch piece of poster paper attached to the top of a Popsicle stick—with *yes* written on one side of the paper, and *no* written on the other

Instructions

1. Pull a question from the collection box—e.g., "Are you afraid of heights?"—and read it out loud. Ask class members to respond silently to the question by holding up their yes/no signs with the appropriate side facing you.

2. Ask for a volunteer to report whether they think more people answered *yes*, more people answered *no*, or the responses were about equally divided.

3. Discuss how the question and its responses could be represented on paper using some sort of graph or chart. Talk about the pros and cons of using tally marks, names, or Xs to record responses. Point out that every graph or chart should have the survey question written across the top, but that the graph or chart itself can have a variety of forms. Discuss different ways of organizing the information. Invite a volunteer to document the responses. (See Figure 7–8.)

FIGURE 7–8 ▶

This class decided to use names to record the responses to the survey question, "Are you afraid of heights?" Responses ranged from "Yes," to "Sometimes," to "No."

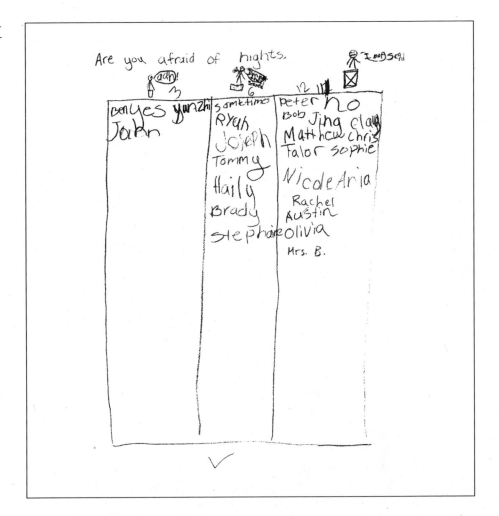

Once they've tried their hand at creating surveys, students often want to create more. Their selected formats can show delightful variety. (See Figures 7–9 through 7–12.)

As children grow excited about doing surveys, you may end up with a bit of chaos on your hands. To keep things manageable, develop a plan for conducting surveys. Here are some possibilities:

- Place two or three surveys at a time near the estimation jar. Review them at the end of the week.

- As a menu option, allow students to think up and gather responses for additional surveys.

- Have a couple of "survey parties." Designate a half-hour every few days for the children to develop, exchange, and respond to surveys. Incorporate class discussions about survey results into morning routines, or math-menu processing times.

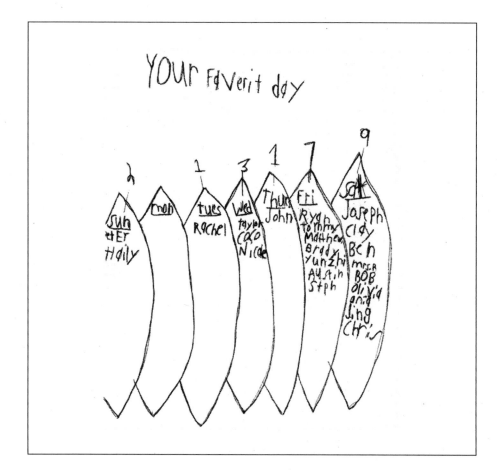

FIGURE 7–9 ◀

Matthew used leaf-like shapes and names to record responses to the survey question, "What is your favorite day?"

FIGURE 7–10 ▶

Sophie listed the names of people who responded "Yes," "Younger," or "Older" to the survey question "Do you like the age you are?"

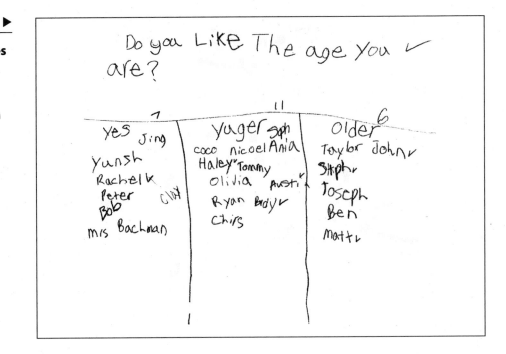

FIGURE 7–11 ▶

Ania used tally marks to record responses to "Do you like your brother or sister better?" Responses included "Sister," "Both," "Brother," and "You don't know."

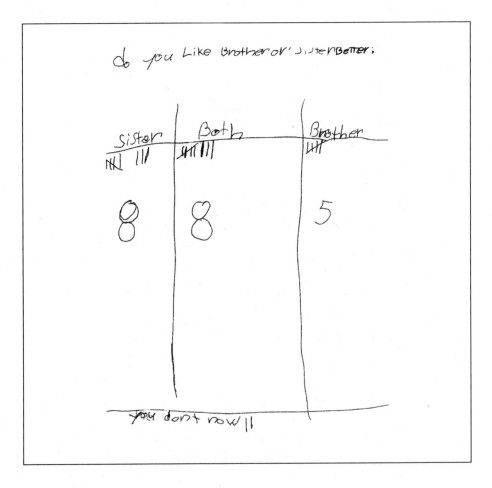

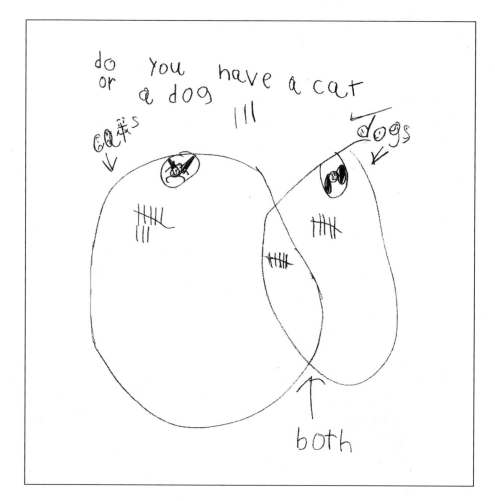

FIGURE 7–12 ◀

Ben created a Venn diagram—complete with tally marks, pictures, and word labels—to show responses to the survey question "Do you have a cat or a dog?"

Shake and Spill Revisited

One of the most significant addition and subtraction accomplishments for first graders involves learning combinations or "number families" for each of the numbers 1 through 10. *Shake and Spill* (see Chapter 6) offers opportunities to master these skills. This version of the game is played the same way as the version described in Chapter 6 and features the same materials. (Children shake and spill two-colored counters such as small discs or lima beans and see how many of each color is showing.) But this month, the game has a different focus: predicting whether you're more likely to shake and spill *certain combinations* of a given number than of other numbers.

Here's how it works:

Materials

- counters colored differently on each side, or lima beans painted a different color on each side, up to 10 per student

- 15 index cards per student (or pieces of paper with the same dimensions as an index card; i.e., 3-by-5 inches)

Instructions

1. Select a special number; such as 6.

2. Have the children gather up that same number of the two-colored objects in their hand, shake them up, then spill them on a tabletop or the floor. Ask them to write their results (e.g., *3 yellow, 3 red*; *2 yellow, 4 red*; etc.) on an index card.

3. Students repeat these steps until they've shaken and spilled fifteen times for the assigned number.

4. Ask students to arrange their cards so similar combinations are placed together. Ask, "Which combinations came up most frequently?" "Why do you think that happened?" "Do they think it's likely to happen again?"

5. Have each child organize his or her cards in some way that makes sense to that individual, and to stack or staple the cards into a little book. This makes the results more tangible and useful for processing discussions if you offer this activity as a menu choice.

Chapter 8

March

MEASUREMENT: LENGTH, HEIGHT, DISTANCE, AND TIME

The Learning Environment

From a young age, children use measurement in very natural ways. For example, during play they might make direct comparisons by placing objects side by side. Or they might make indirect comparison; for instance, by spreading their arms across one space and then doing the same with another space to compare lengths. Nonstandard measurements, such as walking off the length of one room and then comparing the result by walking off the length of another room, might be used as well.

As we know, obtaining a *precise* measurement or communicating easily with someone else about that measurement requires using standard units of measurement. To that end, this month's lessons encourage students to extend their use of nonstandard measures and begin to develop understandings about standard measures. ■

Because measurement has such wide application in everyday life, you might consider inviting some guest speakers to come and talk with your class about how measurement affects their work. For example, the children would probably love to hear an athlete discuss his or her games, accomplishments, and challenges. The school custodian, a surveyor, an architect, or a nurse could also show and discuss some tools of his or her profession. Or you could invite a picture framer, gardener, or quilt maker and ask how that person keeps track of measurements. Inviting retired people to come and visit with the class can be satisfying for all involved.

You'll also want to set the stage for learning about measurement tools. Suggest that the children talk with their parents about the kinds of tools in their homes and jobs. It is helpful to start a class collection of tools from home, such as rulers, tape measures, thermometers, timers, clocks, and scales. You can label each tool with its owner's name and then return the implements to their owners after the class has had a chance to examine them. Begin adding tool names to your *Math Words* poster.

During March, you'll strive to develop the following measurement understandings in the classroom:

- Objects' sizes can be compared directly and indirectly.
- Objects and quantities can be measured using nonstandard and standard units of measurement.
- Different units are used to measure different things.
- We measure things for a variety of reasons.
- We use different kinds of tools to keep track of measurements.
- Measurement involves terms such as *long, tall, short, shorter, shortest, length, height, width, distance,* and *across.*
- Measurement involves patterns and numbers.

During last month's work with probability, your students gained experience and confidence at making predictions. Initiate the transition from probability to measurement by asking the children to make some predictions about distance or length. Many children enjoy counting their steps as they walk from one place to another—pose a question about relative distances in your school building, such as, "Would I need to walk farther to get to the office or to the gym?" Have the class discuss a variety of ways to answer that question.

Routines

Calendar

Understanding Days and Hours

This month, you'll emphasize the concept of measuring time during calendar routines. As the year has progressed, your first graders have developed awareness of time cycles, such as seasons, months, and weeks. Now they'll begin measuring smaller units of time, such as days and hours. First graders have long been aware of the pattern of night and day, and some children may realize that there are twenty-four hours in a day. Others may understand that midnight and noon are significant in some way. Most accept the basic pattern that they go to bed at night and then awake the next morning to a new day.

Calendar routines this month will include making note of specific, significant times in a typical day at school. For example, when it is time to shift from one activity to another, have the class pause to look at both a digital clock and an analog (face) clock. Discuss the five-minute intervals represented by the numbers. Show on a clock that one minute is made of sixty seconds, and one hour is made of sixty minutes. These facts may seem arbitrary and abstract to first graders. Until very recently, most of your students were probably not even comfortable counting to sixty. Mainly, you will want to emphasize hours and half-hours on the face clock as children begin to make sense of the many patterns and relationships involved in telling time.

Using Time

This month, you may wish to begin the morning routines with an activity that relates to using time. For instance, as the children get settled, give the class three extra minutes to visit with one another before the school day starts. Use a clock's second hand to time a minute, asking the children to watch as the second hand makes it circuit around the clock. Then set a timer for three minutes, or use a sand timer, to see whether the children can get ready for the school day within the three minutes.

You might also play a game of timing the children each morning to see how many times they can accomplish some task, such as writing their names, hopping in place, or counting up to twenty by 2s. If you don't already have a large, yellow, wooden, commercially made "Judy clock," consider getting one: Children can easily see and manipulate the clock's hands. You could also invite the line leader for the day to direct you to show a particular time on the clock. As you arrange the hands on the clock, you can discuss the two hands' different functions.

Reinforcing Number Understandings

In addition to routines involving time, you can continue using calendar-related activities to reinforce understandings about number. For example, it's likely that your class has counted down to that all-important Day 100. Now you can help your students move beyond the number 100 and develop awareness of other three-digit numbers. For example, discuss how many days there are in your school year, and show the children what that number looks like (e.g., 180). If you have a 1–100 pocket chart, make sure all of the numbers are in place and remain visible to the children. Rather than covering the numbers 1 through 100 with cards that show 101 through

180, use a separate number chart and place an *X* through the number that represents each school day. (See Figure 8–1 and Blackline Masters.)

The children will need more guidance from you during calendar activities now that the numbers are larger. Be ready to lend support as students engage in whatever counting routines you've established, such as discussing the total number of school days, writing equations for the day's number, trading coins after adding a daily penny to earlier coins, or bundling straws into groups of ten while adding them to the one hundred straws they've already collected.

Estimation Jar

During March, you'll ask the children to make predictions and do some measuring rather than guess the number of objects in a container. Every Monday, invite the children to come up with a "measurement question of the week"—e.g., "How many paperclips will it take to measure this piece of yarn?" Write the question at the top of a piece of paper that has a line

FIGURE 8–1 ▶

Calendar countdown.

101	102	103	104	105	106	107	108	109	110
111	112	113	114	115	116	117	118	119	120
121	122	123	124	125	126	127	128	129	130
131	132	133	134	135	136	137	138	139	140
141	142	143	144	145	146	147	148	149	150
151	152	153	154	155	156	157	158	159	160
161	162	163	164	165	166	167	168	169	170
171	172	173	174	175	176	177	178	179	180
181	182	183	184	185	186	187	188	189	190
191	192	193	194	195	196	197	198	199	200

drawn down the center and includes spaces for predictions and actual measurements. (See Figure 8–2.)

Place the paper and the needed materials for the question in the same place where you had displayed the estimation jar. Children can write their predictions on one side of the paper and the actual counts on the other. **Note:** Students can simply attach sticky notes to the question paper, and they don't need to include their names. Here are some additional "measurement question of the week" possibilities:

"How many times will your hand fit across this desk?"

"How many orange rods will it take to measure this book's width? Its length?"

"How many smaller wooden cubes do you have to add to make this block as tall as that other tall block?"

Math Notebooks

This month, students can write measurement vocabulary in their math notebooks as you introduce new terms and add them to the *Math Words* poster. Even this late in the year, many children continue to need reminders to turn to the next blank page and write the date each time they use their notebooks.

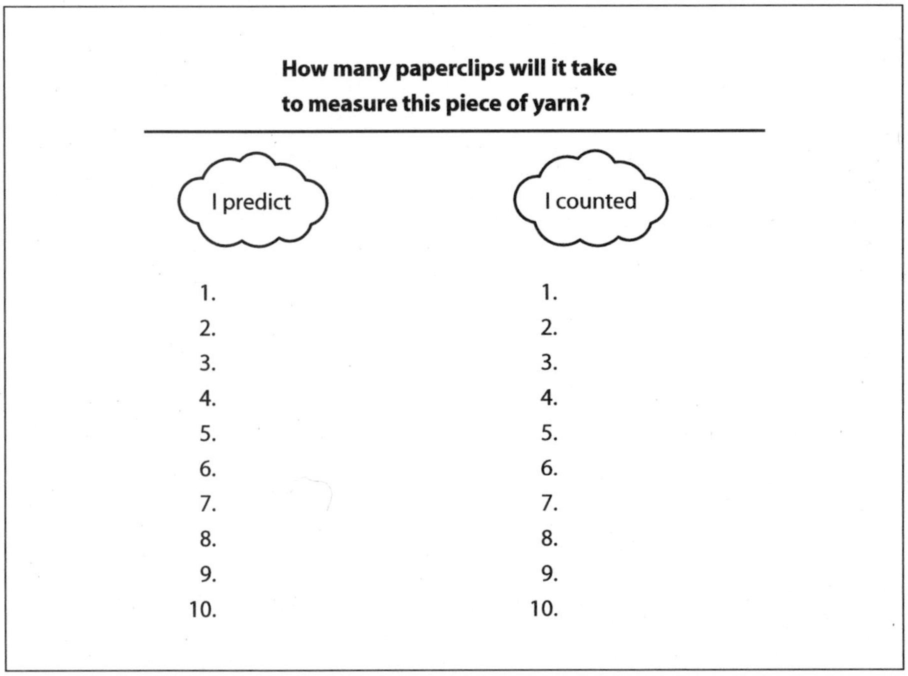

FIGURE 8–2 ◀

Estimation Jar record sheet.

How many paperclips will it take to measure this piece of yarn?

(I predict)   (I counted)

I predict	I counted
1.	1.
2.	2.
3.	3.
4.	4.
5.	5.
6.	6.
7.	7.
8.	8.
9.	9.
10.	10.

If you like to feature a new number every day for which students write equations, consider using the day in the month as your number. Encourage the children to discuss that number in terms of measurements involving length or distance, such as one inch, one centimeter, one foot, one mile. For example, if you've reached the fifth day of the month, use centimeter and/or 1-inch paper, and cut 5 centimeters plus 5 inches so that the children have some reference. These can be taped into math notebooks on the page that is devoted to that particular number of the day. Discuss where you might see measurements such as these. You may also wish to provide two kinds of paper rulers, one showing centimeters and the other inches, which the students can tape into their math notebooks for easy reference. Each school day, the children can color in one more centimeter and one more inch along the rulers, comparing the two as the month progresses.

Maps

Every morning, present a map of the United States or the world and ask for a volunteer to select a place that he or she would like to see on the map. Discuss directionality words such as *up*, *north*, *down*, *south*, *right*, *east*, *left*, and *west*. You may wish to use a piece of yarn or string and extend it from the spot on the map representing where you live to the chosen location on the map. Compare directions and distances. Discuss the fact that maps provide information about distance using units of measurement such as miles. Have the children think about where they have heard about miles during their day-to-day lives.

Poetry

Each week, share a measurement poem. Display the poem on a large piece of chart paper and chant it together every morning that week. Discuss the math ideas in the poems and add any new vocabulary to the *Math Words* poster.

Some examples include:

"One Inch Tall," from *Where the Sidewalk Ends*
"The Longest Nose in the World," also from *Where the Sidewalk Ends*
"Long Mobile" and "Snake Problem" from *A Light in the Attic*

The Mathematics

This chapter describes whole-class, partner, and individual activities that encourage children to actively engage in:

- measuring length and distance.
- using measurement vocabulary.
- working with part/whole relationships and patterns.
- putting numbers together and taking them apart.

The emphases in the activities below progress from nonstandard units of measure to standard units. As in previous chapters, the activities are also organized into literature-based lessons and whole-class/menu lessons that entail the use of manipulates and other materials. I encourage you to pick and choose from the activities in ways that fit the needs of your class.

Literature-Based Lessons

Exploring Units of Measurement

Russo Marisabina's *The Line Up Book* tells the endearing story of a young child who busily places objects next to each other to create a line to the kitchen, where his mother is waiting with his lunch. The little boy's line begins with toys and ends with pretty much anything he can find to complete his task and fill the space. This book can initiate discussions about important aspects of measurement. After reading the story, ask your students some thought-provoking questions; for instance:

"What were some of the things the boy used to create his line?"

"How many objects do you think he used altogether?"

"Do you think the little boy's line would reach across our classroom?"

"Do you think it would take the same number of books as matchbox cars to create a line going across a room? How about if we put a line of blocks across the room: Would the number of blocks be the same as the number of toy cars?"

These kinds of questions can help children begin to think about what it means to measure something. Now look around the room and ask what kinds of things the little boy might use from this classroom to make his line. Discuss what would happen if the children measured the classroom with toys. How many toys might it take to get across the length of the room, or the width of the room?

(The children will likely conclude that the number of toys needed to measure the room will depend on the size of the toys.) Try out some of the students' ideas, such as measuring the room using chairs, blocks, books, or people. Have the children think about what they know and what they don't know about the size of the classroom based on their resulting measurements.

As measurement terms emerge in the conversation, keep your *Math Words* poster handy and record significant vocabulary.

Like all the activities in this chapter, this one requires students to count and keep track of quantities. It also reveals that their chosen unit of measurement—what they use to measure and count—makes a big difference in the information they obtain.

Using Comparative Language

When I Get Bigger by Mercer Mayer explores the major events that mark young children's coming of age. The main character dreams of the day when he'll be able to have a paper route, help "little kids," and stay up late. The story is valuable because it provides an example of multiple meanings of some comparative words. Specifically, in this tale, "When I get bigger" means "When I get older." For children, growing older generally also implies growing bigger, so they often use the two phrases interchangeably.

Read the book to the class, then discuss aspects of getting older that appeal to your students. Write the words *bigger* and *older* on the *Math Words* poster. Cover up the last three letters of each word and ask the children what words they see now. Write the words *big* and *old*. Have children provide examples of things that are big, bigger, and biggest, and old, older and oldest, and include these sets of words on your vocabulary list. Take this opportunity to discuss other equivalent comparisons, such as *little* and *young*. Again, explore patterns in words that end with -*er*, such as *older* and *younger*, then discuss words ending in -*est*; e.g., *oldest* and *youngest*.

Comparing Length

Consider reading Sheila Keenan's *The Biggest Fish* or Margaret Carney's *The Biggest Fish in the Lake* to introduce comparison of length. *The Biggest Fish* is a fictional but realistic-sounding tale about a young girl and her grandfather who enjoy fishing and spending time together. Early one morning, the little girl heads out to the pier all by herself and—much to her amazement—proceeds to hook the biggest fish of all. *The Biggest Fish in the Lake* is a fictional tale about a town caught up in a fishing contest. The story includes comparing nonstandard and standard units of measurement.

Materials

- different colored paper and drawing implements for each child

Instructions

1. Read one of the stories to the class.

2. Discuss what the children know about fishing. Ask if anyone has gone fishing before. Children are usually eager to share stories about this kind of experience. Some of the children may have aquariums, or may have visited a museum with an aquarium. Have these children talk about the smallest and biggest fish they've ever seen.

3. Provide pictures of fish in books or magazines, and invite the children to practice drawing some fish in their math notebooks. After a few attempts, some children will be able and willing to give tips about how to make fish. For example, someone may suggest making an oval and then drawing triangles for the tail and fins. Someone else may advise making a sideways letter *S* to get started.

4. At the chalkboard, use the children's suggestions and model making a variety of fish. Discuss possible shapes and sizes for the fish—long, round, big, little, and so on.

5. Now ask the children to partner up. Tell them they're each going to draw three fish that are all different lengths. Suggest that the partners talk together about how to control the sizes of their fish pictures. Some children may suggest using a measurement tool, like a ruler; others may find it helpful to have different sized paper.

6. Model making dots on the board to indicate the beginning point and ending point of a fish. Draw the fish so that the dots are incorporated into the mouth and tail. (See below.)

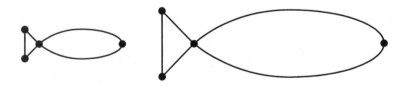

7. Repeat the process of making dots and then drawing a fish three different times, resulting in three distinctly different sized fish.

8. Provide the children paper of varied colors, and let them begin their fish creations.

9. Once the students have drawn and decorated their fish, encourage them to cut them out. Those who get done early can make additional

fish, or can estimate how many fish they think the class will have once everyone has made his or her three pictures.

10. When the fish cutouts are complete, children can work with partners or in small groups to put their fish into order by length.

11. Collect the cut-outs and have the class members discuss how they measured their fish. Most likely, the children used direct comparison by holding one fish up to another. Ask how the children would identify the shortest of two fish if they couldn't hold them up to one another. Some children may suggest an indirect comparison ("This fish is longer than my finger, and the other one is shorter"). Others may think of using standard units of measurement (such as a ruler). Add any new measurement words to the vocabulary list.

12. On another day, have the children sit in a big circle, and give each child one of the large paper fish. Discuss math tools the children could use to compare the fish as fishermen do, when they don't have two fish in the same location to place next to each other. Ask if it would be possible to use hands or fingers to compare the fish. Model using your hand, and have a student use his or her hand. Compare the results. If you've collected measurement tools for the class, look over the collection and try using different tools to measure the paper fish (e.g., a ruler, tape measure, 1-inch cubes, centimeter cubes). Discuss the advantages and disadvantages of these tools. Ask the children if they can think of any other ways that someone might measure real fish in a grocery store.

13. Consider shuffling the different sizes of fish together and putting a handful of them in several bags. These can serve as ordering sets that you can make available during menu time. Partners can grab a bag of fish, spread them out, and arrange them by size. Once they've completed the ordering, Partner A can close his or her eyes, while Partner B removes one fish from the line and pushes the rest back into the line to disguise the space. Partner A then opens his or her eyes and puts the removed fish back in its appropriate spot. The partners can then change roles. As children replace fish in the line, they must think about two things at once: The fish on one side needs to be *smaller* than the fish they're replacing, and the fish on the other side needs to be *bigger*. This relationship has direct bearing on ordinal number (e.g., 5 is bigger than 4, and is smaller than 6). You can use this activity as an assessment for length comparison and language.

You may find it useful to save this fish set and use it for addition and subtraction problems later in the year. These pictures can also make wonderful additions to your bulletin board.

Exploring Length and Height

George Shrinks by William Joyce is a whimsical tale about what the world would be like if you were only a few inches tall. Minimal text and imaginative illustrations communicate the adventures and perils a little boy might experience from such a perspective. The book can provide a context for understanding relative sizes.

Instructions

1. Read the book to the class.

2. Explain that students are going to be exploring ideas involving length and height during the next few weeks. Have them brainstorm ideas for a class book through using framed sentences such as:

    A _____ is longer than a _____ and shorter than a _____.
    A _____ is taller than a _____ and smaller than a _____.

3. Give each child a page with one of the two sentence frames already typed, with blanks for the child's ideas. The children can fill in the blanks and illustrate the page with drawings related to the sentence.

4. Collect the pages into a class book that the children can read and reread during the remainder of the year.

Comparing Length and Width

Jump, Frog, Jump by Robert Kalan is an active tale that children enjoy hearing over and over again. In the story, a frog narrowly escapes as a variety of creatures threaten to capture him. Students enjoy chanting along with the story's refrain, while the frog makes its way to freedom.

Instructions

1. Read the story to the class, encouraging the children to chant along with the refrain.

2. Have the children show you with their hands how far they think a frog can jump. Then ask them to show you with their hands how far they think *they* can jump.

3. Invite the children to make predictions about whether they would be able to jump farther than the length of a chair in the room. How about farther than the length of your desk? Ask the children how many jumps they think it would take for them to cross the entire length of the room. What about the width of the room?

4. Discuss the idea of measuring jumps. Ask the children how they might do this, and develop a plan for measuring jumps in your classroom or in some other space that lends itself to this activity (such as the gym or playground). Perhaps the children will decide to use a tape measure, or maybe they will cut string that measures from a jumper's starting point to his or her ending point. If they are jumping on tarmac outside, they can use chalk to directly mark the starting and ending points of each jump.

5. Discuss ways that you could keep track of this measurement information if you wanted to refer to it over time, as record keepers do in sporting situations. This might be a good opportunity to have the class consult with a physical education teacher or a coach to find out about ways that measurement is used in sports.

6. As you discuss ways to measure the lengths of jumps, record any new measurement vocabulary on your list and make sure the children have a working understanding of that vocabulary.

Understanding Natural Propagation

Eric Carle's *The Tiny Seed* tells the story of natural propagation. In many parts of the world, March is a time to look forward to spring. If you and your students live in a northern part of the United States, spring is a major topic of conversation. Planting some seeds and bulbs indoors at this time of the year can be both educational and exciting for children. Because it will take some time for seeds or bulbs to grow, read *The Tiny Seed* early in the month, to establish a context for planting and measuring. Another longstanding favorite, Ruth Krauss's *A Carrot Seed* is also useful for setting this context.

Materials

- Seeds or bulbs and small pots for planting

Instructions

1. Read one of the above-recommended books to the class.

2. Plant the seeds or bulbs in the small containers, then place them in accessible locations so the children can regularly observe and discuss changes as they take place.

3. Determine how often each pot will need to be watered, and how much water each requires. Designate specific children to take responsibility for watering the plants, and rotate that responsibility. Introduce measuring cups for watering.

4. Point out that, as in many situations, the students don't need to measure out *exact* amounts for watering. You'll find more specifics about measurement and plants later in this chapter.

Encountering Tape Measures

Jim and the Beanstalk by Raymond Briggs offers a charming retelling of the time-honored *Jack and the Beanstalk* fairy tale. Like Jack, Jim awakens one morning to discover a huge, peculiar plant growing outside his bedroom window. He begins to climb up the stalk, to see how far it will take him. Once he reaches the top, he finds an enormous castle and a rather unhappy giant. The older story is a fearful tale that ends in theft, but Jim works to right previous wrongs with consistent generosity. During the course of the story, Jim uses a measuring tape to measure the old giant (the son of the original giant) for gigantic glasses, huge teeth, and an enormous wig. Much to his surprise, Jim receives a thank-you note and a large gold coin from the grateful giant. This story evokes themes of friendship and kindness, as well as measurement.

This story can also serve as an introduction to tape measures.

Materials

- 1 tape measure

Instructions

1. Read the story to the class.

2. Discuss the parts of the giant that Jim measured, and ask whether Jim could have used anything other than a tape measure to determine the size of the giant's face, mouth, and head.

3. Discuss the advantages of tape measures, and demonstrate using one to measure something in the classroom.

4. Invite the to children to ask their parents if they ever need to use this tool. If they do, what do they use it for?

5. Suggest that class members work in pairs to help one another find their own height measurements using available materials—whether they're tape measures, lengths of string or yarn cut to match heights, or some other device. The youngsters could even use connecting cubes, keeping track of how many were needed to record a person's height.

Moving from Nonstandard to Standard Measurement

12 Snails to 1 Lizard by Susan Hightower features Milo the beaver, who is attempting to measure a log in order to repair his dam. With the help of a friend, Milo solves his problem using nonstandard units of measurement in the form of snails and lizards. When he gets less-than-satisfactory results, he uses standard units of measurement.

Materials

- a "mystery measurement kit"—a box filled with various objects that could be used to make measurements (e.g., pencils of different lengths,

Cuisenaire rods, large and small paperclips, Matchbox cars, spoons, Unifix cubes, rulers, tape measures, string)

Instructions

1. Read the story to the class.

2. Present the "mystery measurement kit" to the children. Tell them you're trying to decide which objects would be best for measuring the top of a desk.

3. One by one, pull the items out of the bag. Have the children show "thumbs up" for the objects they think would make useful measuring tools, "thumbs down" if they think an object would present measurement problems, and a flat hand with a little shake if they think that the situation go could either way.

4. Discuss the pros and cons of the various items in the measurement kit.

5. Have children work in small groups or pairs to measure their desktops using materials like those in the kit, and to record their results in their math notebooks. This recording will help them make comparisons and compile data that they can refer to later.

6. Invite the small groups or pairs to share their findings during a whole-class processing discussion. Ask whether they would recommend the object or tool they selected for other measurement tasks. Why or why not?

Using Inches

Inch by Inch by Leo Lionni introduces a standard measurement unit by telling about an inchworm who is attempting to escape from a hungry robin. The tale reveals the usefulness of measuring something by counting the number of times one worm (inch) can be placed and repositioned along a particular surface. In the story, the inchworm makes his way along a variety of surfaces that include bird wings, beaks, tails, and legs. He meets a nightingale who insists that the inchworm measure his song. The worm explains that this is not an appropriate type of measurement for him to take, but when the nightingale threatens to eat him, he decides to give it a try. The nightingale begins to sing, and the inchworm measures inch by inch—until he inches right out of sight.

So far, your students have engaged in measurement activities involving lining up units and then counting the units. These experiences help children understand the importance of a measuring device's placement. If spaces are left between the objects, the measurement won't be accurate. *Inch by Inch* leads students to consider placing one unit (an inch) along one surface over and over again. Children may practice this skill by using paper inchworms (see Figure 8–3 and Blackline Masters) to measure objects such as pencils, books, and surface edges from around the room.

Inch by Inch not only introduces the idea of iteration, or repetition of a single unit, it also invites children to think about how we measure different *kinds* of things. For example, ask your first graders how they would measure the length of a song. Discuss the fact that we measure time in many ways, then ask for examples. Add these ideas to your vocabulary list.

Measuring by Feet

How Big Is a Foot by Rolf Myller tells the story of a king who wishes to give a fabulous gift to the queen on her birthday. He decides to give her a beautiful bed. Unfortunately, beds have not yet been invented—so no one has any idea how large such a piece of furniture should be. The king asks the queen to lie on the floor while he walks carefully around her, counting his steps as he goes. He announces that the bed should be 3 steps wide and 6 steps long. An apprentice who has the task of building the bed thanks

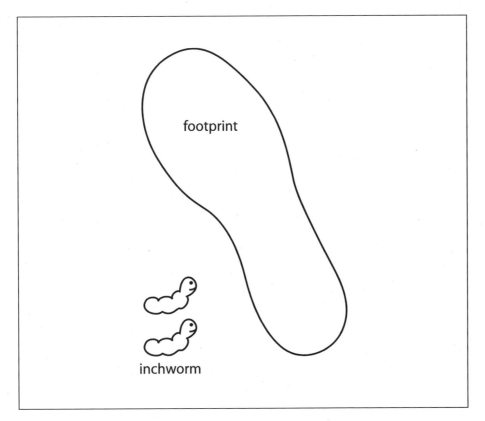

FIGURE 8–3 ◄

Footprint and inchworm measuring device

the king for this information, and carefully walks out the prescribed measurement to construct the bed.

When the bed is delivered to the queen, it is much too small. She is disappointed, and the king is furious. The king sends the apprentice to jail. There, the hapless prisoner realizes that the problem lay in the measurement. As it turns out, the king has much bigger feet than the small apprentice. The apprentice persuades the king to have his foot measured, and a new bed is made using the measurement. The bed is a perfect fit for the queen, and the king rewards the apprentice by declaring him a prince. From that time on, the king's foot is used whenever a foot measurement is needed.

Instructions

1. Read the story to the class.

2. Ask students what they use to measure their feet when they get new shoes. Discuss the ideas of length, width, and shoe size. Inquire whether the children have noticed the markings written on the devices that measure feet.

3. Have the children predict the number of steps (toe to heel) it might take to cross the classroom on foot. Mention a towering sports figure, such as Michael Jordan, and speculate about how many toe-to-heel steps it would take for *him* to cross the room. Discuss whether Jordan or the students would take more steps—and encourage children to share their reasoning.

4. Now have class members walk toe-to-heel across the room. Compare their results with the number of steps that *you* need to take to walk the same length. Using standard one-foot shoe prints created from poster board, measure the room and compare the numbers again. (Refer to Figure 8–3; see also Blackline Masters.) Show the children that the "footprint" matches the length of a 1-foot ruler, and discuss how many inches are in a foot.

Extensions

Have students trace around their own feet with their shoes on, draw a straight line from the toe to the heel on the tracing, and place one-inch cubes on the line. Count and record the number of cubes on the line. Discuss ways the children could keep track of groups of ten as they use the cubes to measure a distance.

Encountering Ruler Increments

Inchworm and a Half by Elinor Pinczes introduces the fractional markings on rulers. Before you read the story, have the children pair up to examine and discuss rulers. List some of their observations. Remind the children of what they learned in *Inch by Inch*, and tell them that the story you are about to read is also about an inchworm.

In this tale, an inchworm becomes frustrated when she discovers that her measurements are not precise. She meets some inchworm friends who happen to be exact fractions of her size. Together, they measure inches, half-inches, thirds, and quarter-inches.

Materials

- overhead projector
- several objects of different lengths: 1 inch, one-half inch, one-third inch, and one-fourth inch
- 1-foot and centimeter rulers; enough for small groups of children to use
- poster-board
- a variety of pictures from magazines

Instructions

1. Read the story to the class.

2. Using the overhead projector, demonstrate for the class how two half-inch-long objects, when put together, are as long as a one-inch-long object. Go through the same process with one-third-inch-long and one-fourth-inch-long objects.

3. Use a ruler to show that these pieces represent the same parts of an inch that are shown on rulers with lines and numbers. These relationships are very complex and will not be particularly relevant to most first-grade students' measurement work. Yet it's useful to offer children an explanation of the markings they encounter on rulers.

4. Make poster-board vegetables resembling those in the story. Have the children use foot-long rulers to measure the vegetables. Then measure the vegetables with centimeter rulers. Compare the results.

5. Display the paper vegetables and their measurements on the wall so the children can discuss the results and symbols.

6. Toward the end of the month, give the children a few new pictures, and ask them to do more measuring. This time the students should work independently, using some of the measurement tools you've discussed in the past few weeks. Ask the children to determine the length of at least one picture by measuring it in some way, and to record their findings on a piece of paper. While the children work, walk around the room and ask them to explain their thinking. Listen for vocabulary that involves making comparisons. Observe the methods and accuracy with which students place objects, take measurements, and make recordings.

7. Collect the papers afterward. These reports will reveal students' preferences and measurement understandings when they encounter an open-ended problem. **Note:** A child's choice of solution does not necessarily mean that he or she doesn't understand the alternatives, but it does tell you what that student finds most comfortable.

Exploring Time

Time to Go by Bruce McMillan uses photography to display analog and digital clocks as readers follow a young boy through the hours of his day. The digital clock displays A.M. and P.M. as well as the numbers indicating the time. Simple text identifies morning, afternoon, evening, and night.

Materials

- about 30 3-by-5-inch index cards

Instructions

1. Read the story to the children.

2. For each time shown in the book, write that time on an index card. Add a small picture demonstrating something that might happen at a particular time; for example, 7:00 A.M. get up; 8:30 P.M. go to bed. Write a descriptive sentence beneath each illustration.

3. Have the children help you sort the cards from earliest to latest time, then display the collection.

4. Talk about the minute as a time-measurement unit. Some students may remember that a minute is sixty seconds long. Discuss the idea of a second, and add these words to the vocabulary list.

5. Tell the children that you would like to try an experiment. Explain that you are going to ask them to rest their heads on their desks for one minute. When they think the minute is up, they can quietly sit up straight.

6. Use a large analog clock that has a second hand to show the children how you will keep time. When the second hand reaches the 12, have the children put their heads down. When the hand returns to the 12, quietly say "One minute."

7. Discuss whether the minute seemed longer than what the children expected, shorter, or about the same.

8. Give the children repeated and varied experiences with the idea of a minute by seeing how many times they can do various tasks in a minute. For instance, have them see how many tally marks they can make in a minute, or how many times they can jump or hop, write numerals,

or write their names or the alphabet. Sing a familiar song, seeing how far you get in a minute. Later, when class members work more closely with the concepts of five minutes, thirty minutes, and sixty minutes, their understanding of one minute will serve as a useful foundation.

Telling Time

Pigs on a Blanket by Amy Axelrod is an entertaining story about a family of pigs who are excited to be heading to the beach. Time ticks by as the pigs get sidetracked while preparing for their outing. Children can relate to the complex and sometimes frustrating process of getting a family from one place to another. As the author keeps track of the time on each page, the pigs get further and further behind schedule. In the end, the poor pigs run out of time. The last pages of the book retell an abbreviated version of the story while keeping track of exact times on the clock. The book also has a chart that provides information about units of time (60 seconds = 1 minute, 60 minutes = 1 hour, and so on).

Materials

- 1 large face clock, or 1 individual clock per student
- 1 paper plate, metal brad, and piece of construction paper per student

Instructions

1. Read the story to your class. While reading the abbreviated version at the end, have the children refer to a large face clock or use individual clocks to retell the times in the story along with you.

2. Invite students to make paper-plate clocks with construction-paper hands they can manipulate. Help them use brads to connect the hands to the center of the paper plate. Make sure the hour hand and the minute hand are significantly different in length. Assist the children in placing dots at the quarter hours on the clock face. Once the dots are in place, have students write the *12, 3, 6,* and *9* on the appropriate dots. This process helps them figure out where the intervening numbers belong.

3. Reenact the story, this time having the children find specific times on their paper-plate clocks.

4. Direct students' attention to the length of time it takes to complete various routine tasks. For instance, ask them how long it takes them to get dressed in the morning, brush their teeth, eat breakfast, get to school, or get ready for bed. Have children practice moving their clock hands to reflect the time required to perform various activities. On the board, write some times during the day when these activities might take place.

Whole-Class/Menu Activities

Height Comparisons

This activity focuses children's attention on comparing heights of different objects.

Materials

■ 5 objects of varying height from around the classroom (e.g., an eraser, piece of chalk, wastebasket, book, and stuffed animal)

Instructions

1. Place the five items where everyone can see them, and invite the children to come and sit with you in a circle around the items.

2. Ask the class members what they notice about the collection of objects you've have gathered.

3. After listening to some responses, tell the class you're interested in measuring these things so you can put them into order by height. Remind the children of the measurement terms they've encountered so far.

4. Ask the children how they would approach putting this collection's objects in order by height. After the children have generated some ideas, use direct comparison to sort the objects by height. Write measurement words such as *height, length, long, longest, tall, tallest, short, shortest, size,* and *order* on the board as you compare the objects.

5. Now ask the children to think about the heights and lengths of other things in the room. Tell them they're going to collect some additional objects and decide which ones are tallest and which are shortest. Explain that they can collect their objects from anywhere in the room, as long as the items can be picked up and carried easily. Let the children know that they will be returning the items to their original places afterward.

6. Invite the children to work in groups of three or four. Each child in a group collects five objects and brings them to his or her group. Then group members work together to compare the objects in their collections. Write the instructions for the activity on the board as you discuss the task:

    a. *Collect five objects and order them by height.*

    b. *Put your objects together with those of the other people in your group.*

c. *Count the objects by fives. How many do you have?*

d. *Order all of your objects by height.*

e. *Be ready to report which object is the longest, and which is the shortest. Are there any objects that are the same height or any that you are not sure about?*

7. Have the groups report their observations, then invite students to walk around the room and view the various collections. Add any new vocabulary words to the *Math Words* poster as you listen to the children discuss the ordered groups of objects.

8. Ask the children how they would compare the height or length of something in their homes with that of something here in the classroom. What would they do if they couldn't place the objects side by side for direct comparison? Discuss possibilities, such as using string to show the length of an object that is in a different location from another object.

9. Ask the children if they keep track of their changing heights and weights at home. If so, how do they do it? Discuss the methods that doctors and parents use to record height and weight.

Family Pictures

Your students have discussed the number of individuals in their families during previous math experiences. This month, they can think about families as a way to understand relative age and height. You might read *Goldilocks and the Three Bears* to initiate this activity.

Materials

- drawing materials for each child

Instructions

1. Tell the children that they're going to make another family picture. But this time, they will be paying particular attention to height as they draw the tallest member of their families, then the next tallest, etc.

2. Ask the class if it is always possible to know who is older based on who is taller. Add the words *age, younger, youngest, older,* and *oldest* to the vocabulary poster as needed.

3. Invite children to draw their family pictures. (See Figure 8–4.)

4. Now ask students to use some comparative terms from the math vocabulary poster to describe the people in their pictures (e.g., "Dad

FIGURE 8–4 ▶

Pia drew five individuals of different heights in her family picture.

My Dad is the oldest, then my Mom. I have an older brother and a younger brother.

is the tallest; I am the smallest. My brother is older; my sister is younger.")

5. Compile the pictures to make a class book.

Extensions

Have the children think about and name books or stories that involve fictional families, such as *The Three Billy Goats Gruff* or *The Berenstain Bears*. Children can use these familiar characters to gain additional practice with comparing heights.

Length Comparisons

This whole-class activity helps students practice comparing objects' lengths through indirect methods.

Materials

- an object from the classroom (e.g., a hefty book) that would not be easy for the children to carry around and use for direct comparison
- 1 recording sheet per student (see Figure 8–5 and Blackline Masters)

Instructions

1. Select an object from the room, and hold it up so everyone can see it.

2. Ask the children to look around the room and find something else that appears to be *shorter* than, *longer* than, and about the *same length (or height)* as the selected object. Discuss the difference between the meaning of the words *length* and *width*, and make sure these terms are on your vocabulary list.

3. Demonstrate making an indirect comparison by cutting a piece of yarn or making a stick of cubes that is the same length as the selected object, and then holding the yarn or stick up to comparison objects suggested by the students.

4. Continue measuring objects selected by the children. Use an overhead projector or chalkboard to show how to record the name of the original object and then list at least two items that are shorter than, longer than, and about the same as the original.

5. Next ask students to pair up. Hand out a copy of a recording sheet to each pair. Have the students list the comparison items in the appro-

Object	Something Longer	Something About the Same Length	Something Shorter

FIGURE 8–5 ◀

Length Hunt record sheet.

priate columns on the recording sheet. Children may report on as many items as they wish.

6. While the children work, walk around the room and ask questions about how they're making comparisons. Listen for comparison terms and make notes that will remind you of specifics so you can assist children who are not yet using this language accurately. Collect the recording papers so you can see who approached the written task with confidence, and who will need more experience with this kind of activity.

Nonstandard Measuring and Counting Units

Previous activities focused on measurement vocabulary and direct and indirect comparisons. This activity features use of nonstandard units of measurement to determine the lengths of various pieces of yarn or ribbon.

Materials

- set of yarn or ribbon pieces cut into 5 or 6 different lengths; pieces of the same length are the same color; 1 set per student
- 1 small bag per set of yarn or ribbon
- small containers of lima beans, toothpicks, paperclips, or other small objects; 1 per student
- overhead projector

Instructions

1. Assemble the sets of yarn or ribbon lengths. Place each set in a small bag for easy storage and access.

2. Give each child (or pair of children) a piece of yarn of identical length and a container filled with the small counting objects. Ask them to stretch the yarn out in a straight line, to place their paperclips or beans alongside the piece, and to record their results in their math notebooks. Assuming there are a variety of results, discuss possible reasons for the range.

3. Use the overhead projector and demonstrate what happens when the beans or paperclips are carefully placed end to end as opposed to when spaces are left between each counting object.

4. Ask the children how they counted the beans or paperclips that are on the overhead, and discuss possibilities that could make that counting process more efficient. If someone suggests counting by 2s, 5s, or 10s, ask students to think about how they might keep track of these number patterns.

5. Make the materials available for menu time. As children select and engage in this activity during menu time, observe them—paying par-

ticularly close attention to how they place and count the units while measuring the yarn.

Measure Me

This partner activity gives students opportunities to measure various aspects of one another's bodies, such as height, head and wrist circumference, etc. You may wish to designate four to six children per day to work as partners during menu time so that this activity is comfortably managed and doesn't become overwhelming.

Materials

- 1 ball of string or yarn
- 1 ruler or tape measure
- 1 professional scale, if available (a scale that measures height and weight)
- 1 infant-sized doll, if available

Instructions

1. Have partners determine one another's height using string or yarn. Encourage the class to experiment with various ways to accomplish this task. Introduce the idea of holding one end of the string at a consistent starting point (e.g., the sole of a person's shoe, or the top of his or her head) and cutting the other end of the string at a consistent ending point.

2. Invite partners to compare their two strings on the floor and identify who is tallest, or whether both are the same height.

3. Discuss the types of standard units of measurement usually used to describe people's height. If possible, use a doll to demonstrate how babies are measured in terms of *length*, and in inches rather than feet. Explain that as the babies grow, the number of inches gets to be so many that they are measured in feet and inches. Point out that once a baby becomes a toddler—and starts being able to stand and walk—we measure his or her *height*, not *length*.

4. Ask the children to think about the scale they stand on during school physicals. If possible, show one of these professional scales, pointing out the height and weight measurement markings on it. Invite volunteers to come up and have their height measured.

5. Show the children how to convert their string measurements into feet and inches using yardsticks or tape measures. Suggest that they measure family members' heights.

Extensions

■ Have students use their string to show half their partner's height, then twice his or her height. Model the process by folding an original string in half and cutting a new piece of string that matches the folded length. Next, attach another piece of string to double the length of the original. The children will likely be especially impressed by the doubled length. They can then take these new strings to the playground and compare their length to those of various pieces of playground equipment. They can also use the strings to measure distances from one piece of equipment to another.

■ Have partners create a poster of personal measurements. Partners can assist one other and use string to measure dimensions such as the length of their arms and the circumference of their waists. For the posters, supply each child with a long, rectangular piece of paper on which they can attach the ends of the measurement strings.

Demonstrate by taking some string measurements of your own body and taping their ends to a piece of paper, labeling the dimensions you measured. (See Figure 8–6.) Intentionally tape the end of a shorter string lower on the paper than an adjacent, longer string, then ask the children if the shorter one is really shorter. The point of this demonstration is to establish the significance of a baseline or consistent starting point for the various measurements. Make a baseline

FIGURE 8–6 ▶

Measure Me diagram.

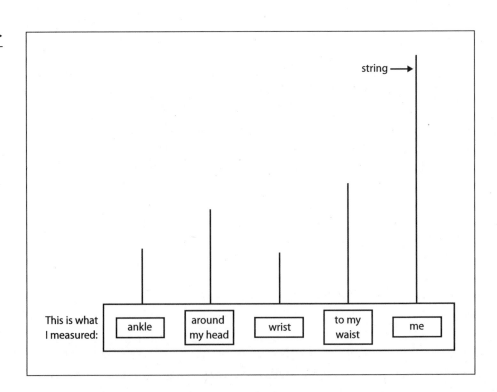

for your measurements by drawing a straight line several inches from the bottom of your paper, or by folding the paper so that the crease goes across the paper. Tape your strings from the baseline up. You may wish to provide each child with pre-drawn baselines on their papers.

When the reports are finished, partners can share their results in small groups.

Measure It

This activity provides practice with using standard and nonstandard measuring tools.

Materials

- a variety of objects that can be measured (books, pencils, crayon boxes, etc.)
- a variety of standard measurement tools (1-inch cubes or tiles, rulers, centimeter cubes, etc.) and nonstandard tools (lima beans, toothpicks, paperclips, etc.)

Instructions

1. Select objects to measure, then demonstrate measuring them with different tools. Ask the children to record and keep track of in their math notebooks which objects were measured, which tools were used, and what results were obtained.

2. Invite students to measure some objects themselves, using *different* tools to measure the *same* object. During whole-class discussions, as well as while students are working, ask children to compare the various measurement units they used, and to describe what they noticed about their results.

Toss and Measure

This is another partner game that invites active participation from students.

Materials

- 1 small object for tossing (e.g., a paperclip or penny) per pair of students
- 3 bowls per pair
- 1 ruler or yardstick per pair
- masking tape or 5–10 stickers per pair

Instructions

1. Identify a starting point on the floor.

2. Have partners use a ruler or yardstick to mark off distances of one foot, two feet, and three feet away from the starting point. Use stickers or small pieces of masking tape to mark the three places.

3. Place a bowl or large margarine container on each of the three marked positions.

4. Partners take turns standing on the starting point and tossing a paperclip or penny into one of the three bowls. Getting the object into the closest bowl wins a student 10 points; the second-closest bowl, 25 points; the farthest bowl, 50 points. Players work together until they get a combined total of 100 points.

Consider introducing this game at recess so everyone has a clear understanding of the directions, then you can use it as an indoor or outdoor activity.

Take Steps

This activity examines the question, "How long is a step?"

Materials

- masking tape or stickers
- 1-inch cubes, 1-inch tiles, or rulers

Instructions

1. Ask students to walk across the room three different times, first by taking "baby steps," then by taking "medium steps," and then by taking "giant steps."

2. Ask questions like: "Did you walk farther using baby steps?" "Did you take more steps using baby steps, medium steps, or giant steps?" "Did the distance across the room change?" "Did the size of your feet change?" "What *did* change?" "How long is our room?" "How wide is our room?"

3. Using easily removed, small pieces of masking tape or stickers, create a starting point on the floor.

4. Invite students to pair up, then ask one player from each pair to take a step of any size from the starting point. Mark that spot using another piece of tape or a sticker.

5. Provide 1-inch cubes, 1-inch tiles, or rulers and have children work with their partners to determine the length of the step taken. Discuss ways to keep track of the cubes and to increase counting efficiency by marking groups of ten tiles or cubes.

6. Suggest that the children record their description of the step's size (baby, medium, or giant) and their measurement findings in their math notebooks.

Plant Growth

This activity has rich possibilities but it needs to unfold over time. You and your students will be doing some planting, so the exact timing of the measurement work will be somewhat unpredictable.

Materials

- two different kinds of seeds that you can plant indoors (e.g., avocado pit, beans, daffodil bulbs)
- potting soil and small pots

Instructions

1. Consider two kinds of seeds for planting. Your geographic area and curriculum may influence what you decide to plant. I always have good luck with avocado pits, which can be placed in soil with half of the pit (or seed) exposed, pointed end up. This large seed will crack and send up a fast-growing, vertical shoot that students can easily measure. Planting anything from bean seeds to daffodil bulbs will provide interesting science connections, as well as growth data.

2. Gather your students together and have them name plants that grow from seeds in your area during the springtime.

3. Explain that observing the growth of living things is a great opportunity for doing some measurement work. Show the children the seeds you have selected. Explain the importance of planting several seeds in case some of them don't sprout.

4. Pass the seeds around so everyone has a chance to inspect them.

5. Make some comparisons: Create two columns on a piece of chart paper and write the name of the two types of seeds at the tops of the columns. Trace around the seeds, so you have a record of their original sizes. Ask the class to make some comparison statements and to record their observations about the two different types of seeds. The children will no doubt mention size and weight differences as well as texture and color.

6. Invite class members to make predictions about how long they think it might take for plants to begin growing from the seeds. Do they expect one type of seed to grow faster than the other type? If they think that there will be a difference, encourage them to share their reasoning.

7. As the children observe, plant the seeds. Label the pots in some way so you can keep track of which ones germinate at a particular time (e.g., *Pot A*, *Pot B*, *Pot C*, and *Pot D*).

8. Have the class help you decide where to place the pots. Discuss what kind of care the seeds will need, and ask students to help you develop a plan for ensuring that the seeds receive of the required sun and water.

9. Indicate on the calendar the exact date that you planted the seeds.

10. Once a seed germinates, note the event and the particular pot on the calendar.

11. At regular intervals—such as every few days, or once a week—measure the growing plants' heights with the class. Create "growth posters" for the various plants. One of the easiest ways to do this is to use yarn to measure, and then glue the yarn to the growth poster, above the date that the plant was measured. You can use separate posters for the different plants, or you can have one large poster for all the plants and use different colors of yarn to represent each plant.

If enough seeds germinate, children can work in small groups to measure the plants, and then cut the yarn to the appropriate lengths. If there are just a couple of plants, the class will enjoy observing you go through this process.

Extensions

Give the children opportunities to compare the lengths of the various pieces of yarn by using inches and centimeters. With your support, first graders can manage this task using rulers. However, the most effective means is to have them place 1-inch or 1-centimeter objects (such as centimeter cubes) next to the yarn and just count them. Also, if possible in your school setting, have the children help you plant some seeds outside and observe the growth during the remainder of the school year.

The Road Traveled

This activity involves using blocks to map the journey of fictional character from a story.

Materials

- a book about a familiar character (for example, Winnie the Pooh)
- 10–20 blocks per student
- several balls of string or yarn, accessible to all students
- 1 ruler per student
- 1 set of 1-inch tiles or cubes per student
- tape

Instructions

1. Read the selected book.

2. Have the children use blocks to represent the path traveled and places visited by the story's main character. For example, if you're reading a Winnie the Pooh story, perhaps Pooh begins at Christopher Robin's house and ends up in a tree, where he hopes to find honey. Or maybe the story involves pirates searching for treasure on an island. The object is to have the children designate a path, or route, that the character uses to get from one place to another.

3. Once they've established the route, have students measure the distance from their route's starting point to the final destination using yarn or string. It may be helpful to use tape to hold the yarn in place.

4. Now ask the children to stretch their string into a straight line and measure it by using the standard units of measure (inches, feet) that they see on rulers. Provide assistance. Many children find the markings and numbers on rulers confusing. (For example, young people frequently assume that the *1* on a ruler indicates where you begin the measurement.) Discuss any areas of confusion.

Extensions

Instead of rulers, have the children use 1-inch tiles or 1-inch cubes to measure the yarn.

Chapter 9

April

MEASUREMENT: AREA, VOLUME, AND WEIGHT

The Learning Environment

With April comes the realization that the school year will soon come to an end. On one hand, the idea of finishing up the year is exciting. On the other, you suddenly think about everything you have to accomplish in the remaining weeks. Now is the ideal time to reflect on the information you have gathered about your students throughout the year. Take a look at your goals and your curriculum. Most important, consider the mathematical development of each child in your class. This is a perfect opportunity to set priorities for the remaining weeks. ▪

During April, you'll continue focusing your students' attention on measurement. But the children will shift to working with area, volume, and weight. They'll also continue combining and rearranging numbers as they make comparisons, keep track of quantities, and determine amounts. Your first graders will be immersed in activities that require them to answer questions about *how much* and *how many*. Even so, you may also want to provide them with more addition and subtraction practice.

Be willing to adjust your weekly schedule to offer a combination of measurement work and practice with adding and subtracting. For instance, you may decide that every Friday the children will spend time playing addition and subtraction games, while the rest of the week is devoted to extending concepts of measurement. To minimize procedural instruction and maximize practice time, you might also select some games and activities that are already familiar to the children. Discuss your reasoning with your students, so they understand your expectations and can anticipate new routines.

This month, real-life contexts such as cooking and building or construction will help children grasp new aspects of measurement. Specifically, students will concentrate on:

- comparing surface areas.
- comparing volumes (e.g., empty, half-full, full).
- comparing weights (light, heavy, heavier, heaviest).
- deepening their understanding of clock time

Routines

Calendar

Days in School

Students will continue the calendar routine of keeping track of the number of days they've been in school. After Day 100, you may have asked them to begin writing the days-in-school number on a large monthly calendar. If so, you've freed up the 1–100 pocket chart for other problem-solving activities. If you gave the children 101–200 charts in March, try this routine:

1. With the class, determine the number of days remaining in the year.

2. Write the total number of school days for your district (e.g., 180) on the chalkboard. Have the children locate that number on their 101–200 charts.

3. Discuss the number of days that students have already been in school this year, and help them find that number on the chart.

4. Next, give the children quiet, independent time to consider how many days of school remain in the year. Let partners or small groups talk about ways to approach this problem. You might simplify things by considering how many days are left in the next two weeks of school.

5. Discuss various strategies the children propose for solving the problem. Some students may count up from today's date, some may count back, others may cluster numbers on the chart, and someone might count the days on the calendar. Still other children may just make a guess.

    Let the children entertain a variety of approaches to solving the problem. Their explorations and the unfolding of their ideas can take place over a period of days or even weeks. Also help them visualize one another's reasoning. Encourage them to use the chalkboard, and perhaps a number chart on the overhead projector, to demonstrate the steps in their thinking.

6. Once the class has reached some agreement on how many days remain in the school year, create a paper chain to represent the number. Arrange the links in groups of ten by color. Hang the chain by the calendar so that students have easy access to it. Each day, have the calendar helpers remove one link to show that there is one less remaining day of school. Discuss the minus-1 pattern that emerges in this routine.

Plants and Seasons

If you planted seeds in March, continue to record the growth of the plants. Consider additional springtime calendar opportunities, such as recording daily temperatures or rainfall amounts.

Time

Keep exploring the topic of time by building on the activities from Chapter 8. If you haven't already done so, create index card pictures that display the minute and hour hands on a face clock. Under each display, write the time as it would appear on a digital clock. Include terms such as A.M., P.M., *morning*, *afternoon*, *evening*, and *night*.

Each morning, ask for a volunteer to pull one of these "mystery cards" and to read the information on it. Discuss the meaning of the time indicated on the card, and ask the child to think of something that he or she might typically do at that time of the day. For instance, if the card shows 10:30 A.M., the student might say something like: "At ten thirty in the morning, I go to the library." Be ready to lend support during this activity. Soon students' confidence will grow as they draw, read, and respond to these cards.

Consider creating a graph of favorite morning, afternoon, and evening activities and a graph indicating class members' preferences regarding sleeping late or getting up early in the morning. Keep using terms like A.M., P.M., *late*, and *early*. Make sure the children offer predictions before you create the graph and that they provide true math statements about the graph afterward.

Estimation Jar

The estimation activities and routines for this month can initiate conversations about area and volume. Each week, provide students with materials and questions that entail covering spaces and filling containers. For example:

Exploring Area

1. Fill a large jar with 1-inch tiles, and place the jar next to a flat, rectangular object, such as a book.

2. Ask the children to make predictions about the number of tiles they think they would need to cover the book. Give a short demonstration by laying a few tiles on the book's cover. Provide a clipboard so the children can record their predictions.

3. Each day, the two children responsible for checking the estimation jar for an exact count can determine an answer to the question by laying tiles on the book's cover. Ask these children to jot their findings in their math notebooks so they can easily refer to their results.

4. On Friday, all of the children who had the estimation job that week can get together and compare their results, and then report their findings to the class. Have the reporters discuss whether their counts matched. If there are any discrepancies, have them speculate about the causes.

5. Ask these students to explain how they approached the job of counting. Trace around the book on an overhead transparency and then use the overhead projector to place tiles on the resulting outline. Use terms like *rows* and *columns* and note any number patterns that emerge as you cover the area and count the tiles. Encourage the children who have already checked this count to share any observations they may have had during the counting process.

Understanding "More Than"

1. Once again, fill a large jar with 1-inch color tiles.

2. Place two box lids of different sizes on the desk next to the jar, and label the lids *A* and *B*.

3. On a clipboard next to the jar, pose questions challenging children to think about how many tiles it might take to cover each of the lids. (See Figure 9–1.)

4. Ask the children to consider which lid will require more tiles and to predict "how many more."

Understanding Volume

1. Fill a large, transparent bag (e.g., a plastic freezer bag) with lentils, corn kernels, or sand. Display it with a small scoop or one-quarter measuring cup.

2. Select a transparent, cylindrical jar that's smaller in volume than the bag. Ask students, "How many scoops do you think it will take to fill this jar with lentils [or corn or sand]?" Have the children write their predictions on a clipboard.

FIGURE 9–1 ▶

Box A and Box B comparison questions.

• Do you think it will take more tiles to cover Box A or Box B?

• If you think there will be a difference, how many more tiles do you think you will need for the larger box?

Make a tally if you think Box A will need more tiles:

Make a tally if you think Box B will need more tiles:

How many more?

How many more?

Box A

Box B

3. Every day, have the estimation-jar leaders determine the number of scoops required. (Be sure to provide a large, flat box or some other protective surface beneath the jar as the children pour.)

4. At the end of the week, discuss the range of estimates and have the reporters share their findings. Ask the class to think about what might cause this type of count to be inaccurate or inconsistent. Discuss the word *full* and show the children scoops that are slightly underfilled or overflowing. Ask how the results might be affected if the jar were not filled just to the top. This conversation sharpens children's awareness that accuracy in their measurement results depends on attention to detail.

5. The following week, place two new jars on the estimation-jar table, along with the same scoop that has already been used. Label the jars *A* and *B*. Write several questions on the clipboard, such as, "How many scoops do you think it will take to fill Jar A? How about Jar B?" "Which jar do you think will hold more scoops? How many more scoops?" Allow space on the page for children to write estimates for both jars.

6. At the end of the week, gather the children and demonstrate filling the jars. Have students count the scoops as you pour them into each jar. Stop periodically to ask if people want to adjust their guesses based on what they're noticing as a jar fills up. As you've done in previous months, remind the children that an estimate is a *best guess*, not the final answer. Reiterate that it's entirely reasonable to change an estimate when we receive more information.

Then ask the children to think about how many scoops of *water* it would take to fill the same two jars. This question could be explored at another whole-group time or during menu activities. Encourage the children to consider these kinds of questions at home as well as at school.

Math Notebooks

This month, your first graders can use their math notebooks to record their thinking about weekly problems. Children's books that are already familiar to your students can serve as convenient sources of problems. When students tackle such problems they deepen their number understandings and supply you with valuable assessment information. Take full advantage of this time by using open-ended problems that allow for multiple responses. You can pose one problem to the whole class.

For instance, consider *The Line Up Book, Biggest Fish in the Lake,* and *Time to Go*—stories you may have read to your class in March. Here are a few problems you could pose based on those stories:

A little girl was lining up toy cars alongside her bed. She used only red and blue cars. When she was done, twelve cars fit along her bed. How many red cars and how many blue cars could she have used?

Wesley and Alex went fishing. When they got home, they had an even number of fish Alex had caught two more fish than Wesley. How many fish could they have caught?

Joe and Mitch went fishing. They each caught the same number of fish. They caught fewer than eighteen fish altogether. How many fish could they have caught individually and together?

Claire liked to get up early. One morning, when Claire's sister got up at seven o'clock, Claire had already been up for an hour and a half. What time did Claire get up?

Write the problem on large chart paper so the children can refer to it during the week. I frequently type a problem on the computer, copy it several times on the same page, then cut each copy into strips for children who like to tape the problem into their math notebooks. Before the children begin the writing process, make sure they can restate the problem *in their own words*. Make manipulatives, number charts, and ten frames available.

Keep encouraging students to record their thinking in their math notebooks. Using their notebooks helps children develop the habits of documenting their reasoning, keeping track of reference information, and reviewing previous work. The notebooks are also ideal for compiling new vocabulary. As you add new terms to the *Math Words* poster, encourage the children to continue building their own measurement vocabulary lists in their notebooks. This month's work extends geometry ideas as well as measurement concepts with terms such as *cover, area, fill, full, cup, teaspoon, weight, ounce, cylinder, cube,* and *sphere.*

The Mathematics

This month's activities develop understandings about area, volume, and weight. As you introduce the activities, use the math vocabulary list to discuss comparative language, and add new words as they come up. Whenever possible, remind the children that organizing quantities of objects (for example, by 10s) can help them count the objects more efficiently. Observe students while they work, and note how each child keeps track of quantities. Ask questions about how they're keeping track, combining, separating, and counting.

As in previous chapters, this month's activities are organized into literature-based lessons and whole-class/menu activities.

Literature-Based Lessons

Opposites

Anne Scheiber's *Slower Than a Snail* uses a variety of comparative terms and can help students make the transition from linear measurement to assessing area, volume, and weight. The text extends the measurement vocabulary from last month. Take time to review the terms you've listed so far. As you read the story, ask the class to listen for and identify new words to add to the list.

Slower Than a Snail highlights contrasting attributes such as *long and short*, and *empty and full*. After reading the story, discuss the idea of opposites. Have the children name opposites they heard in the story. Write these opposites on a large piece of chart paper or poster board. Give each child a piece of paper that has a line or fold down the center. Have the children write contrasting words, or opposites, on the two sides of their papers. Beneath the words, the children can create illustrations for their ideas.

Time

Eric Carle's *The Grouchy Ladybug* begins at 5:00 A.M. as the sun comes up in the sky. Two ladybugs have landed on the same leaf for a breakfast of aphids. One ladybug is in no mood to share and flies off in a huff looking for a fight. Now the adventures begin. At the top right-hand corner of each page are clocks showing the specific times that are being described in the text.

Every hour, the grouchy ladybug encounters a new and slightly larger character. One by one, he challenges these characters to fight. But before the fights can erupt, the ladybug flies off with the disgusted exclamation, "Oh you're not big enough!" Finally, at 5:00 P.M., the ladybug encounters a whale. This whale is so enormous that, every fifteen minutes, the ladybug tries to pick fights with various parts of the whale's body. Eventually, the whale gives the startled ladybug a terrific slap with its tail—sending him careening across the sea and right back to the original leaf, where it's now dinnertime. This experience teaches the ladybug some lessons in manners. He makes an effort to be polite and is rewarded with a pleasant meal and a feeling of cooperation.

Materials

- a series of paper clock faces glued to Popsicle sticks; faces should show all the hours of the day, half-hours, and the written time (see Figure 9–2)

FIGURE 9–2   ▶

**Paper clock faces can be
glued to Popsicle sticks
to make signs.**

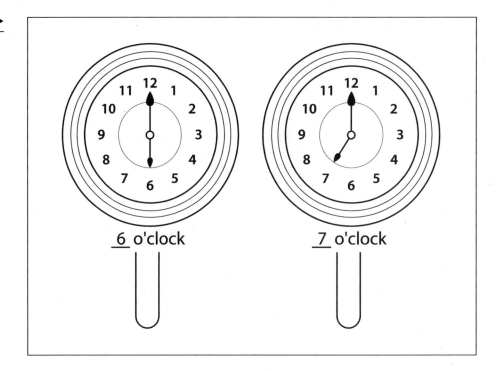

_6_ o'clock   _7_ o'clock

Instructions

1. Show the children the series of paper clock faces, and explain that you'll be asking for volunteers to display the clocks as they listen to the story.

2. Read *The Grouchy Ladybug* to the class without yet using the clocks.

3. Reread the story, this time inviting volunteers to hold up particular clock faces during the appropriate times as they listen. Asking for volunteers gives you information about students' levels of confidence with telling time using analog clocks. As you read, you and your students can chant the repeated text patterns that appear in the book.

4. Have the children sort all the clocks showing hours, from earliest to latest, beginning with 5:00 A.M., and then tape the clocks on the wall. Allow enough space between the clocks to add the half-hour clocks. Leave the display on the wall for a while, so the children can look at the clocks at their leisure and discuss ways to determine hours and half-hours.

Three-Dimensional Shapes

Cubes, Cones, Cylinders, and Spheres by Tana Hoban takes geometry into the realm of three dimensions through wonderful photographs. Your first graders have already studied two-dimensional shapes. This book introduces them to three-dimensional shapes by offering opportunities to fill containers and work with blocks.

Materials

- about 20 balls and other round objects of various sizes
- paper cones with handles (see Figure 9–3 and Blackline Masters)

Instructions
Part 1: Spheres

1. View each page of the book with the class.

2. Define and discuss the word *sphere*. Talk about how spheres are similar to circles, and how they are different.

3. During the week, have the children help you collect balls and other spherical objects of different sizes. Keep these materials in a box or basket, and periodically ask students to make predictions about how many you've collected. As the collection grows, talk about organizing the objects into small groupings whose numbers are easy to recognize (e.g., groups of three or four).

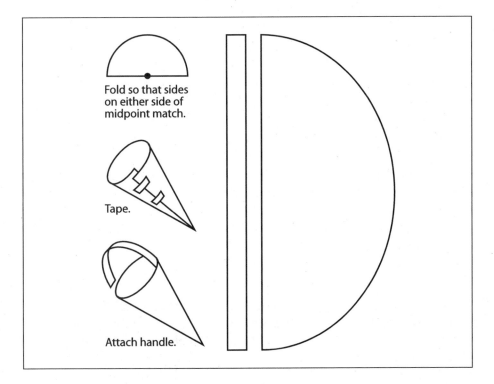

FIGURE 9–3   ◀

Instructions for making cones.

4. Periodically, ask students to sort the balls by some criteria (size or weight). Talk about ways to compare the objects' size so as to be sure of your sorting. If there is a debate about which of two spheres is larger, use a piece of yarn or string to measure the circumference of both. Have the children watch as you cut the string just as it meets the other end around the sphere. Compare the lengths of string and discuss the objects' relative sizes.

5. Play *Which Ball Is Missing?* (This game works best on a carpeted or grassy surface.) After sorting the balls by size, ask the children to close their eyes. Then remove one sphere. Move the remaining balls back together to conceal the gap. Then invite students to open their eyes. Show them the missing ball, ask where it belongs, and ask children to explain their reasoning. See whether anyone points out that the ball on one side of the missing ball needs to be smaller, and the ball on the other side needs to be larger. This is a more complex relationship that a simple comparison of size.

Extensions

Have the class sit in a circle with the collection of balls and roll the balls back and forth to one another. Take time to explore characteristics of spheres. Discuss the ways that attributes such as weight and size affect how easily the balls roll.

Part 2: Cones

Help children make paper cones with handles. Have a popcorn party and use the cones as containers. Ask the children to make predictions about how many scoops of popcorn will be needed to fill a cone.

Construction

There are several books available that can help young readers develop awareness of the role that measurement plays in building construction. Here are some examples:

- *How a House Is Built* by Gail Gibbons
- *Tool Book* by Gail Gibbons
- *The House I'll Build for the Wrens* by Shirley Neitzel

Read any of these books, and consider inviting a builder to come visit your class and talk about construction. If possible, ask your guest to share measurement tools and any visual plans that are relevant to his or her construction efforts.

Cooking

Cooking serves as an ideal context for measurement, though some schools and districts don't allow cooking in classrooms. If that's the case with your school, you can still explore measurement through cooking conversations and simulated activities. Children can also try recipes at home.

Guidelines

If your school does allow projects involving food and cooking in the class-room, keep these guidelines in mind:

- Be aware of any food allergies among students.
- If possible, invite adult volunteers to work with small groups of children in the classroom. The more adults the better. With enough help, children can directly participate in measuring, mixing, and stirring as they make cookies or other treats for a class tasting party.
- Take time to discuss hygiene. Make sure the children wash their hands before a cooking activity begins, and after using the restroom. See that they're working in a clean space, and discourage them from directly touching the ingredients or food.
- Before starting any cooking project, post and compare enlarged versions of the recipes and discuss the units of measurement that will be needed.
- After the cooking is finished, give gifts of the final product to adults who helped. Consider also giving to others who deserve thanks, such as food-service workers at your school, bus drivers, and so forth.
- If you want to keep things simpler, consider using cooking as a menu item. For instance, you could help small groups of children make "Ants on a Log" by spreading several tablespoons of peanut butter onto celery and sprinkling with raisins. Or several students could assist you in mixing ingredients for fruit salad, adding ingredients a half-cup at a time.

Favorite Family Dishes

Fannie in the Kitchen by Deborah Hopkinson gives some historical information about recipes. First graders usually have some awareness of the function of recipes, but they may not realize the significant role measurement plays in cooking instructions. The book's illustrations cue readers that the story takes place in the past.

The main character in this story is a young girl who feels displaced by her family's new baby. When the family hires Fannie, a cook, the child feels even less useful and more isolated. Gradually, a sense of trust develops between the cook and the child, as Fannie teaches the little girl to make several favorite family dishes. When Fannie gets ready to move on to another job, she promises to write down recipes so the girl will be able to create more family favorites.

Fannie's recipes provide measurements as well as advice about cooking, such as ways to determine an egg's freshness. You can also use the book to mention Fannie Merritt Farmer, one of the first cookbook publishers. The original publication, now over 100 years old, is still in use today. If your first graders regularly write or dictate letters to parents, they might enjoy including the book's griddlecake (pancake) recipe—an example of a dish that was as popular a century ago as it is today.

Fannie in the Kitchen introduces measurement words like *recipe* and *ingredients* and provides information about specific cooking quantities. Take time to read the recipe for griddlecakes on the last page. Show the children standardized measuring cups and spoons and compare them with various sized coffee cups and silverware spoons. Discuss the need for standard units of measurement in cooking. Add the new vocabulary (e.g., *cup*, *tablespoon*, *teaspoon*) to your *Math Words* poster.

Ask the children if they ever help in the kitchen at home. Capitalize on this real-life connection by encouraging students to discuss what they know about cooking. Have them dictate or write directions for making a favorite food. For instance, perhaps some children know how to make peanut-butter-and-jelly sandwiches. Maybe others have frequently watched their parents make macaroni and cheese. Ask the children to think about which ingredients must be included in these recipes and how much of each ingredient is needed. Remind them to specify the order in which the ingredients should be put together. This type of activity evokes notions of quantities, amounts, and sequence.

If you're interested in a community-building project, invite families to send favorite recipes to school. Create a class recipe book that children can borrow and share at home.

Chili

Pigs in the Pantry by Amy Axelrod also provides a cooking context. In the story, Mr. Pig and the children decide to help Mrs. Pig recover from a case of the sniffles by taking over in the kitchen and preparing her favorite snack. Though they are extremely enthusiastic in their efforts, they bungle the recipe for "five-alarm chili." Result? A visit from the fire department.

This story includes an actual chili recipe, providing an opportunity for you to present and discuss standard units of measurement. Children enjoy sharing stories about their cooking efforts and adventures. The class could make a list of favorite foods and then create a graph to display the data. This book can also serve as a springboard for discussion of family favorites.

Cookies

The Cookie-Store Cat by Cynthia Rylant tells of a little feline who is adopted by a big-hearted baker. This lucky kitty gets to live in a bakery! As children listen to the story, they hear about a mouth-watering array of cookies. The back pages of the book provide a variety of recipes. After reading this story, students can generate a list of their favorite cookies. The children can also use construction paper to make pretend cookies that they can then display on a graph. After they've completed the graph, remind them to list true math statements about what the graph shows.

Balance and Weight

Who Sank the Boat? by Pamela Allen is a fanciful tale featuring a group of animal friends who decide to take a rowboat ride in a nearby bay—and end up sinking. The story has entertaining illustrations and sets the stage for considerations of balance and weight as young readers try to figure out who sank the boat. The rhyming text is inviting and introduces words like *balance, weight, light,* and *level.*

After reading the story, have students experiment with weighing a variety of objects (cubes, rods, pennies, etc.) on scales. Encourage them to make comparisons and use terms relating to balance.

Weight Comparisons

Just a Little Bit by Ann Tompert provides additional opportunities to explore concepts of balance and weight. In this story, friendship and collaboration emerge on a playground when some appealing animal characters try to solve problems that occur with unequal weight distribution on a seesaw. Placement of the characters on the seesaw and exertion of force are key concepts as the friends try to compensate for and match an elephant's weight.

Children can try their hand at this sort of problem by putting small counting objects on a balance scale while pretending that the scale is a seesaw. Tell stories such as the following: "Once upon a time, five teddy bears went to play on the seesaw. One teddy bear got on one side and the other four got on the other. What do you think happened to the seesaw?" Have the class check their guesses by putting the corresponding number of counters on the scale. Ask the children to make suggestions for balancing the scale.

Here's another idea: Show the children a pair of objects and ask which one they think is heavier. Place the objects on the scale and check the predictions. Offer the children a box of objects and a balance scale for use during menu time, and invite them to balance the objects. Set a limit for the number of objects that can be used at any one time.

Sand

Super Sand Castle Saturday by Stuart Murphy provides a context for sand play and measurement activities. The story features several children at a beach. The children have decided to see who can build the tallest sand castles possible before the tide comes in. Though the approaches vary, each child works hard at this task. Every now and then, the youngsters stop to measure their castles, moats, and walls using a variety of measuring devices—such as shovels, spoons, and footprints. If your students have participated in multiple measurement activities in recent weeks, they will appreciate the difficulties the characters encounter as they attempt to make comparisons using dissimilar measuring tools. A lifeguard helps out by showing up with a tape measure and explaining this tool's advantages.

Instructions

Part 1

1. Read this book with the class gathered around you, so everyone can easily see the pictures.

2. Ask the children to explain the characters' problem in their own words. After the first child shares an explanation, see whether anyone else has something to add or would like to make a similar point but in another way. Perhaps a class member can give another example that is like the one in the story. Most likely, the children will realize that the units of measurement in the story did not match, so the comparisons did not make sense.

3. If the children seem reluctant to share their ideas, have them explain their thinking to a partner. Then ask the whole group to name the characters' problem. You could solicit responses randomly by picking out a name tag from a container and inviting that individual to explain the problem in the story. The child whose name is selected can either share what he or she is thinking or simply say, "Pass," in which case you pull another name.

4. After the class has discussed the story, ask if anyone has ever made a sand castle. Listen as children share their memories of beaches, sandboxes in parks, playgrounds, and backyards. Have the children tell you what kinds of things they've used when building sand castles. You will probably get a list that includes shovels, buckets, bowls, spoons, etc.

5. Ask the children what a beach has that makes building sand castles easy and interesting. If no one mentions water, ask the children to think about what would happen if they filled a container with some nice, dry sand and tried to make a sand castle out of it. Act out the process of packing sand into an imaginary container, and pretend to turn it over and carefully jiggle the container. Ask whether the sand

would come out in the same shape as the container. Most children will realize that sand will not hold a molded form without liquid. But if no one mentions this, pretend that the sand is spilling all over the place. Include dramatic sound effects, too!

Part 2

1. Show the children two differently proportioned, clear cylindrical containers. One of the containers should be as wide as possible; the other, long and narrow.

2. Explain that you're going to use dry sand to figure out which of the two containers can hold more. Ask the children to point to the container that they think will hold the most sand.

3. Show the children a scoop or measuring device that you'll use to fill the containers. Then start filling one of the containers, while the children count as you add scoop after scoop. Stop periodically and discuss whether the container is *more than half full, less than half full,* or *about half full.*

4. When the first container is about half full, take a rubber band and place it at the halfway mark while you discuss the number of scoops that went into the jar. Ask the children if this information helps them to think about how many scoops there might be when you've filled the container all the way. Have children explain their reasoning.

5. Continue filling the rest of the first container, encouraging students to refine their guesses as you go along. Keep the class involved by having them count the scoops and watching to make sure you're filling each scoop just to the top.

6. Write down the number of scoops it took to fill the first jar. This information will provide a reference as you fill the second jar.

7. Again, ask the children how many scoops they think it will take to fill the second container. Start filling that jar while the class counts the number of scoops.

8. When you've filled the jar halfway, mark the place with a rubber band, just as you did with the first container. Ask students if they want to revise their predictions for how many total scoops will be needed.

9. Start filling the rest of the jar. As you're scooping, ask the children if they think that this jar will hold *more, less,* or *about the same amount* as the first jar. Take several ideas, inviting children to explain their thinking. Fill the jar to the top and record how many scoops were needed altogether.

10. Compare the numbers of scoops required to fill each of the jars. Ask, "Which jar needed more scoops? Which one needed fewer?" "How

many more? How many fewer?" "Could we figure out which jar holds more if we didn't have a scoop?" For this last question, invite students to pretend that they have these same two jars in a sandbox or a wading pool. Ask how they might determine which container could hold the most sand or water—"Could it be done without using a scoop?" Wonder out loud whether a container would hold the same amount regardless of whether you're filling it with sand, water, ketchup, dirt, or milk.

Discuss the children's ideas and suggestions, and explain that they'll be able to conduct these kinds of experiments during menu time this month. Remind them to make predictions and ask themselves math questions as they work with and enjoy the materials. Let them know that their observations will be discussed at the end of math menu time. Encourage them to jot down new terms for the *Math Words* poster.

Whole-Class/Menu Activities

Cookie-Cutter Shapes

Cookie cutters are useful for a variety of engaging math activities. Most first graders have experienced the pleasures of Play-Doh and other modeling compounds. If you are able and willing to set aside a spot for a play-dough "station," there are a number of inviting possibilities.

Materials

- Play-Doh or other commercial modeling compound
- 1 rolling pin or similar tool per student
- a variety of cookie cutters
- pencils and paper for tracing
- lima beans (or other small counting objects)
- enamel spray paint (optional)
- 1 recording sheet per student (see Blackline Masters)

Instructions
Part 1

1. Provide the children with the dough, a rolling pin, and cookie cutters of various shapes and sizes.

This is the shape I used:	I estimate I will need this many beans:	I counted this many beans:

2. As the children create their "cookies," encourage conversations that compare quantities and sizes and that explore symmetry.

3. When the class convenes for the processing discussion at the end of math time, ask the children who used these materials to report on their observations. Take time to find out about any stories your students used as they worked with the materials. Children commonly incorporate mathematical ideas during this type of activity, and you may be able to capitalize on contexts that involve size and amount comparisons. For example, you could say, "There were four little bears at the table and each one got two cookies, so we had eight cookies . . . ."

Part 2

You can also help children explore the notion of area through cookie cutters. Here's one idea:

1. Provide students with cutters as well as pencils, paper, lima beans, and a recording sheet.

2. Have the children trace around the cookie cutters on the paper, and then arrange lima beans in the interior of the traced shape. Students could also trace a hand or foot if cookie cutters are not available.

3. Offer a recording sheet that enables class members to document the shape they used, their estimate, and the actual lima-bean count. Your first graders have had many opportunities to estimate and discuss the idea of making a best guess. Thus they'll likely feel comfortable taking some risks of this kind and won't be overly concerned about mismatches between estimates and counts.

Note: If you can offer lima beans that have been painted on one side, children will have a natural means of organizing and grouping the beans by

10s for efficient counting. You can paint lima beans quickly. Do it outside, where you have plenty of ventilation—and preferably on a day that isn't too windy. Place the beans in a box so that one side of each bean is exposed. Using enamel spray paint, which dries quickly, paint one side of the beans.

Yarn Loops

This activity entails comparison of different lengths and strengthens understanding of area and estimation.

Materials

- thick yarn (the kind used in gift wrapping)
- overhead projector
- color tiles, lima beans, or other counting objects

Instructions
Part 1

1. As the class observes, cut several different pieces of yarn that range from one to two feet long. Cut enough so that you will have sufficient quantities for children to double up for the activity.

2. Have the class help you compare the lengths of yarn and sort the pieces in order from shortest to longest.

3. Tell the children that you are going to tie the two ends of each piece of yarn together to make a loop. Then demonstrate this procedure with one of the pieces. Show the loop on the overhead projector.

4. Ask the children to help you think up different shapes you might be able to make with the yarn loop. As the children suggest shapes such as a circle, a square, a rectangle, and a triangle, select one and form that shape with the yarn loop.

5. Ask the children to make predictions about how many tiles or lima beans it would take to fill the interior space of the shape. Demonstrate taping the yarn in a few places so it retains its shape as you position the tiles. If you have overhead-projector color tiles, use more than one color to devise efficient counting techniques (e.g., grouping counters by 2s, 5s, or 10s).

6. Discuss whether the same number of tiles would be needed to fill the area of a different shape. Follow up by repositioning the yarn loop into a different shape, and filling it with tiles.

7. Repeat these steps with a different-sized yarn loop. Using the chalkboard or a piece of chart paper, demonstrate making a recording by

drawing the shape, and writing your estimate and actual count. Explain that the children will be keeping track of this information in their math notebooks.

Part 2

1. While the above instructions are still clear in their minds, ask students to pair up. Give partners yarn loops and tiles or beans and have them repeat the process you demonstrated.

2. After the children have had some experience filling different-sized and -shaped areas with counters, ask them to share what they noticed about the various shapes and the number of tiles that fit inside the shapes. Ask questions such as:

   "Are there particular shapes that fit more tiles?"

   "Are there shapes that fit fewer tiles?"

   "Does the arrangement of the shape (for example, circle versus rectangle) affect how many tiles you can fit?"

3. Ask how the children organized their counters to check the exact number filling the shape. As always, this kind of processing discussion helps children articulate their reasoning and absorb classmates' ideas.

When you feel that students clearly understand the activity, offer it as a menu choice.

Draw a Rectangle

In this activity, students use dice and graph paper to practice creating rectangles.

Materials

- 2 dice
- overhead projector
- marker
- graph paper with grid squares ranging from 2-by-2 centimeters to 1-by-1 inches (see Blackline Masters); several pieces per student

Instructions

1. Show a piece of graph paper on the overhead projector. Place a dot on a "starting-point square" in the upper left-hand corner of the paper.

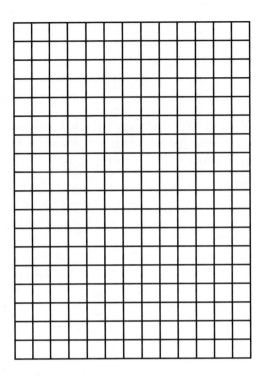

2. Invite a volunteer to roll two dice. Select one die to show the number indicating how many squares to count *over* on the graph paper and the other die to show how many squares to count *down*. Those dimensions will determine the outline of your resulting rectangle.

3. Using a marker, place a dot in each of the small squares within your rectangle as you count each square. For example, if the roll shows a 4 and a 3, you will count over four squares and down three to create a 4-by-3-square rectangle. Demonstrate drawing the rectangle. (See Figure 9–4.)

4. Roll the dice and draw rectangles several more times—asking the children to help supply directions. (Many rectangles can fit on the same sheet of graph paper.)

5. After drawing several rectangles, count the total number of squares in each rectangle and write the number in bold print in the center of the rectangle. If some children begin using pattern counting—by 2s or 5s or 10s—discuss this strategy.

6. Give the children their own graph paper. Roll the dice several more times, and have students draw the resulting rectangles on their papers.

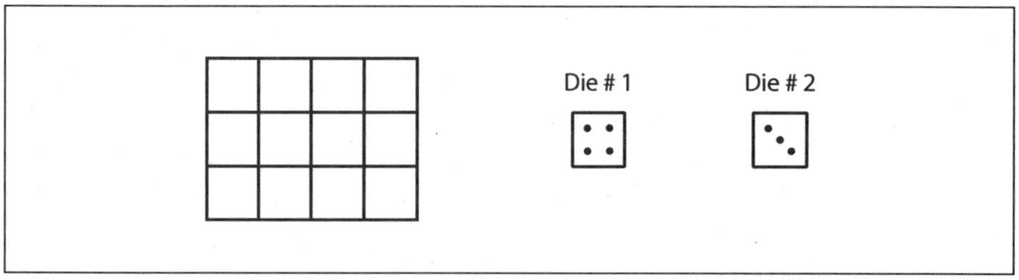

FIGURE 9–4   ◀

Dice roll rectangles.

Extensions

Have the children cut their rectangles out and sort them by size on a piece of construction paper. This gives you an opportunity to discuss the criteria used to arrange the rectangles. For instance, did the children decide on the size of the rectangle by counting the interior squares, or did they look for the longest shape?

Block Traces

Students can use all sorts of blocks to trace and compare shapes. For instance, they can:

- Trace a variety of blocks and then cut out the tracings. Compare dimensions by placing one tracing on top of another.
- Play *Which Block Did I Trace?* by tracing a block privately and then asking a partner to select the correct block from several choices.
- Fill tracings with color tiles and compare counts. (Children may notice that it can be confusing to compare unlike shapes, such as a square and a rectangle. Using some unit of measurement such as tiles or lima beans to fill the interiors can provide a consistent means of comparison.)
- Use geo blocks to create the same sizes and shapes as larger blocks. (Students can experiment with creating a particular shape using a combination of blocks.)
- Use pattern blocks to further explore proportional relationships. For example, make a hexagon shape the same size as the yellow hexagon in the pattern-block set by using combinations of the other pattern blocks. (Have children record their findings in their math notebooks.)
- Use a stipulated number of pattern blocks, such as ten, to make a design. Then make another design of the same shape and size, this time using substitutions for at least some of the pattern blocks. (Children can do this same type of activity using Cuisenaire rods.) Compare

the numbers of blocks in the two designs and record findings in math notebooks. During processing discussions, explore the question "How many more?" in the design with the greatest number of cubes. (Make sure children see that the shape and size remained the same, while the number of blocks required to fill the shape changed.)

Sand and Water

This activity strengthens understandings about volume. It's best used as a menu choice for small groups of children.

Materials

- a sand or water table, or a number of different-sized plastic tubs
- plastic tablecloth or paint drop cloth
- a variety of measuring cups, measuring spoons, and cylinders of varied dimensions that can be used for scooping

Instructions

1. Cover the intended work area with the tablecloth or drop cloth.

2. Invite the children to fill various containers with sand or water and find out how much the different containers can hold. Encourage them to keep track of their findings in some way.

3. During whole-group processing time, ask the children to report what they noticed. Discuss the various methods they used to determine and define how much each container could hold. Someone may report using one container to repeatedly fill a larger container; another person might mention the advantages of using a standard unit of measurement such as a tablespoon or cup.

Through interaction with materials and class discussions, students should grasp the idea that consistent units of measurement are just as important for finding out how much a container can hold as they are for considering length. If no one seems to touch on this idea, explore what happens when you use two very different units to fill a container. For instance, use a one-cup measuring cup and then a tablespoon to fill a bowl as the children keep count. After discussing the sizes of the two measuring devices, alternate the use of the spoon and the cup as if they are interchangeable. When the container is full, ask the children how many scoops were needed. Ask, "Are we talking about tablespoons or cups?"

Rock Sorting

Gathering and sorting collections of rocks, stones, and pebbles can provide a variety of counting and measurement opportunities. Here are some ideas:

- Students compare two rocks' weights by holding one in their hands and then the other, and recording their opinions on paper. (Use a small piece of masking tape to identify the rocks in some way—e.g., Rock A and Rock B.) If balance or other types of scales are available, the children can use them to confirm their impressions.

- Students sort rocks by size. Because many rocks have irregular shapes, determining relative sizes may generate some interesting discussions. Provide paper, pencils, and lima beans so children can trace around the shapes and fill the area with the beans. Of course, tracing around a rock is an imprecise endeavor. The main objective is to have an *approximation* of the rock's area. Have students record the number of beans required to fill the shape. During processing, discuss how the children kept track of the beans as they counted.

- Children love to play "rock shop"—arranging a variety of rocks for "sale." This gives them opportunities to look carefully at the rocks and become familiar with their attributes, including size and weight. It also enables them to revisit the topic of money. To start this activity, use weight or area to determine the rocks' relative value. Mention that, with gems and small, precious stones, bigger doesn't necessarily mean more valuable. But explain that for the purpose of *this* activity, weight or size will determine a rock's "price."

  As the children compare the rocks, have them create price tags. Agree on a top limit (such as $1.00). Organize the play money in advance. Provide the children with a variety of coins placed in an easy-to-manage container, such as an envelope or a 35-millimeter film-roll container. Have partners select five or six rocks to order by weight and by area. Invite students to price the rocks according to either weight or size. After recording their information, have two sets of partners (four children) get together to take turns selling rocks to one another.

Make a Scale

This activity gives children an opportunity to construct their own balance scales.

Materials

- 1 clothes hanger and a handful of paperclips per student
- several 3-by-5-inch index cards per student
- 1 straw per student
- yarn or string

Instructions

1. Hand out a hanger and four paperclips to each child.

2. Using your own set of materials, show students how to attach one paperclip to each end of the bottom portion of a hanger. Then attach a second paperclip to each of the first clips. Hang the bottom-most paperclips such that you can pull out an end to form a kind of hook.

3. Demonstrate how the hanger and paperclips work as a scale: Hold the hanger's top loop lightly between the thumb and forefinger of your left hand, and gently tug on one and then the other paperclip with your right hand.

4. Show the children how to loop additional paperclips over the two hooks so as to conduct weight comparisons.

5. Cut some 3-by-5-inch index cards in half, poke a hole in the centers of the resulting papers, and give them to students to decorate and hang on their scales.

6. As the children manipulate their scales, ask them what they notice. For example, how can they balance the scale if it tips in one direction? What happens if they move one of the first paperclips across the hanger?

Extensions

Have the children make another scale using three paperclips, half a straw, and a piece of yarn or string that is a couple of inches longer that the straw. (See Figure 9–5.)

FIGURE 9–5 ▶

Straw and paper clip mobile scale.

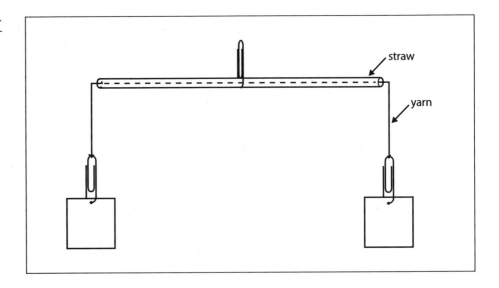

To make this scale, follow these steps:

1. Pass the straw through the widest end of a paperclip, and position the clip in the center of the straw.

2. Pass the yarn through the straw.

3. Tie each end of the yarn to a paperclip.

4. Pull out the ends of the dangling paperclips to form hooks.

5. Hang a variety of objects on the hooks to experiment with the scale.

Addition and Subtraction Revisited

You're introducing students to a lot of new activities and concepts this month. To nurture children's confidence, allow your first graders to engage in some familiar activities as well. Revisit the addition and subtraction activities in Chapter 6, and select some to offer this month. Here's another one to add to your collection:

In or Out

Materials

- 1 foot-long piece of thick yarn
- a handful of lima beans

Instructions

1. Tie the two ends of the yarn together to create a circular loop.

2. Put the loop on the floor or on a tabletop.

3. Ask for a volunteer to select a particular number of lima beans (e.g., five to twelve).

4. The child holds the beans a few inches above the circle and lets them drop.

5. On large chart paper or the chalkboard, record number sentences representing the array of beans. For example, if three beans fell within the circle, and three fell outside, write $3 + 3 = 6$ and $6 - 3 = 3$. (See Figure 9–6.)

6. When children have become familiar with this process, encourage them to play the game independently or with a partner during menu time, and to record their number sentences in their math notebooks.

FIGURE 9–6 ▶

The *In or Out* activity uses yarn and beans to demonstrate addition and subtraction.

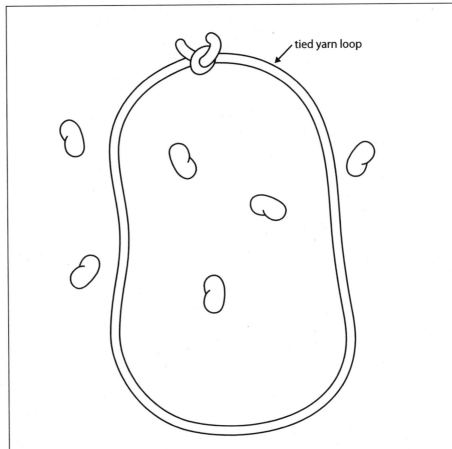

tied yarn loop

Three beans in the loop plus three beans out of the loop makes six beans altogether.

$$3 + 3 = 6$$

I dropped six beans. Three beans landed in the loop. Three beans did not make it inside.

$$6 - 3 = 3$$

Chapter 10

May/June

EXPLORING LARGER NUMBERS

The Learning Environment

The months of May and June are an exhilarating and challenging time of the school year. By now, your students easily work and play with one another. Class members have a sense of how things work and generally understand what needs to be accomplished. At the same time, unless you are in a school that conducts classes year round, everyone is getting excited about the end of the school year and the summer vacation ahead. Getting—and holding—the children's attention requires planning, flexibility, and energy. A balance of novelty, familiar routines, and physical activity—customized to your class and personal preferences—can help to keep learning experiences in the classroom moving along smoothly. ∎

This month, your students will continue to refine their understandings of number combinations to 10. As children move beyond single digits and think about larger numbers, place-value issues inevitably become significant. As children count, combine or separate numbers, and keep track of quantities, they must also develop understandings about the base-ten number system. The activities offered in this chapter require students to use and practice what they know while applying and extending their understandings to steadily increasing quantities. As usual, take advantage of any contextual opportunities, such as seasonal changes, to help children make connections to the real world.

This month's activities focus on:

- efficiency in combining and separating numbers to 10.
- mental and paper-and-pencil computation to 10.
- the ability to combine and separate numbers and groups of numbers to 10 and beyond.
- use of the system of 10s (place value) to organize the digits in multi-digit numbers.

Routines

Calendar

The last six weeks or so of the school year are usually packed with special events such as concerts, field trips, and celebrations. To keep your students focused, help them anticipate changes in routine scheduling. Use the large calendar display or smaller conventional calendar to indicate information about special activities that will take place during the remaining weeks of school. Take this opportunity to *count on* from the present day to a future event and discuss how many days remain until the day of that occasion. During this time of year, many children get involved in sports and other recreational activities outside of school hours. Capitalize on routines of individual class members that draw particular attention to weekend experiences—for example every Saturday morning Yoan has soccer, or on Friday night Megan's family gets pizza and watches a video. These routines help you get to know your students even better.

Acknowledging and celebrating summer birthdays and U.S. holidays (such as the Fourth of July) is a great way to create a focus on the upcoming summer months. Once you've discussed these special events, ask the children to record and illustrate their favorite summer activities on index cards. Invite them to group like activities together into categories, such as "sports," "holidays," or "vacations." Create a graph depicting favorite activities, and elicit true math statements about what the graph shows.

Begin a countdown to the last day of school. The children have already participated in a number of counting-down calendar activities, so ask them to help you decide how this information should be displayed.

Estimation Jar

May and June may be a good time for a change in estimation routines. If you wish to continue using a jar, experiment with unusually shaped containers, such as cubes or rectangular prisms, rather than cylinders. If possible, use objects that relate to a relevant curricular context. For instance, if you've introduced an earth-science topic in class, have the children estimate the number of small objects from the outdoors, such as seeds, rocks, or shells, in the jar. Provide them with mathematical tools like ten frames or place-value mats (described later in this chapter) to help them count the objects.

Food is always a great motivator, so consider putting jelly beans in the jar and asking questions such as, " Do you think there are more than twenty jelly beans in there? Less than twenty? Exactly twenty?" Rather than asking students to take turns counting the jelly beans at the end of each week, have each child take one jelly bean out of the jar. (When you're filling the jar, make sure you use enough jelly beans so that everyone in the room can have one.) Making a one-to-one correspondence between the number of children in the class and the number of jelly beans can serve as a helpful counting strategy. If there turn out to be more jelly beans than students, you can ask, "How many more jelly beans are left over in the jar?"

You could also depart from using estimation jars entirely. For example, consider using a 1–100 chart to play *Guess My Number* (see page 263). Each day, play a round of the game with the class, showing the chart on the overhead projector. Students can keep track of their guesses using the 1–100 charts that they've taped into their math notebooks. You may wish to keep track of the guesses by marking them on an overhead transparency of a 1–100 chart or by making a list. Encourage logical guessing by organizing guesses into the categories *too high* and *too low*. Class members can discuss strategies for making the best possible guesses.

After a couple of weeks, you could raise the challenge a notch by playing the game with the 101–200 chart. Ask the children to predict whether using a different range of numbers will affect how many guesses are needed to hit the target number. Do they think they'll need about the same number of guesses? More? Fewer? Remind the children to explain their thinking.

Math Notebooks

Your first graders' math notebooks are probably bulging with work right about now. For some work, such as weekly or daily problems, students may need to record their thinking on papers that you can collect. This system offers assessment opportunities that are particularly appropriate at this time of the year.

Consider revisiting the idea of exploring equations and combinations for a different number each day. Every morning, invite a different child to select a number from a specified range (e.g., 5–20). Ask your volunteer to see how many different ways he or she can count up to or down from that number. Discuss patterns, such as to get to 20 we can count by 1s or 10s or 5, 10, 15, 20, or by 2s; and number combinations, such as $5 + 0 = 5$, $4 + 1 = 5$, and $3 + 2 = 5$.

In addition to a daily number, you can present students with interesting word problems. Below are some problems about bugs. Be sure to point out that insects have six legs and spiders have eight before you pose these problems. Then post the written problem somewhere handy in the room:

Two spiders were sitting on a web. Each of the spiders had eight legs. How many spider legs were on the web altogether?

Six butterflies were sunning themselves. Each butterfly had two antennae. Two butterflies flew away. How many antennae were left?

Some ants were sitting on a log. How many ants were there if there were eighteen legs altogether?

One spider and one bumblebee were sharing a snack. How many legs did those two friends have altogether?

There were eleven bugs. Some of them were ants, and some of them were ladybugs. How many of each kind of bug could there have been?

Here are some problems about flowers:

I have eight flowers. There are four daisies and the rest are roses. How many roses do I have?

I have nine flowers. Some are red and others are yellow. How many of each could I have?

I have ten flowers. Some are pink and some are blue. I have the same number of each color. How many pink flowers could I have?

I have eleven flowers. Some of them are yellow, and some are orange. I have more yellow than orange. How many yellow ones could I have?

And here are some problems about stones and shells:

I went to the beach and picked up five shells and four stones. I put them in my collection bag. How many things did I put in my bag?

I had ten shells and stones on my windowsill. After I gave three shells to my sister, only the stones were left on the windowsill. How many stones were there?

Julie found eleven white stones at the beach. Then she found six brown stones. How many stones did she find altogether?

Joe is collecting shells. Kaitlyn gave him eight shells, and Claire gave him three more. How many stones did the girls give Joe altogether?

For all these problems, encourage children to explain how they solved the challenge. Did they use words? Pictures? Numbers? A combination of all these?

The Mathematics

The activities described in this chapter center on number relationships, counting, and multi-digit numbers. As in previous chapters, the lessons are organized into literature-based activities and whole-class/menu activities. I encourage you to pick and choose from among the various options to suit your class's needs and personal teaching preferences.

Literature-Based Activities

The Pocket Problem

A Pocket for Corduroy by Don Freeman is an old favorite that can help set the stage for playing *The Pocket Problem*. In this popular investigation, students determine the total number of pockets class members are wearing on a given day (a number that will almost certainly consist of two and possibly even three digits).

The story lays the foundation for the game as Corduroy, a little bear, gets a pocket sewn into his overalls so he can carry some personal identification. Here's how you might conduct the activity:

Instructions

Part 1

1. Read the story, making a point of checking your own clothing for pockets. (To ease any possible discomfort among children who don't

happen to be wearing pockets, avoid wearing pockets on the day you introduce this activity.)

2. Ask the class, "Is there anyone else who does not have *any* pockets on their clothes today?!"

3. You've now established the notion of "fewest pockets." Next ask students to speculate about the *greatest* number of pockets that any one person happens to be wearing that day. Some children will begin patting themselves down or standing up and examining their clothing to find pockets in unlikely places.

4. Once this examination has taken place, ask your students to raise their hands if they think someone in the room has more than four pockets, then more than five, more than six, and so on—until you reach the point at which no one raises a hand. Write the range of guesses across the bottom of the board.

5. Point to each number on the board and have the children who are wearing that particular number of pockets stand briefly while you place an X above the number for each child who has stood up.

6. Discuss the greatest number of pockets worn by any one person, and erase the guesses that exceed that number.

7. Now look at the information on the board and ask the children to tell you what they notice about the graph you've created. The children's comments will likely reflect concepts such as *most, least, same amounts,* and *most common numbers.*

8. Ask the children if they can look at the graph and easily tell you how many pockets there are in the class altogether. Discuss possible ways to solve this problem. Students will realize that the graph shows the number of children with a particular number of pockets, rather than how many pockets in all. Ask them to make some quick predictions about how many pockets there are in the whole class.

9. Now explain that you have a plan for finding out the exact number of pockets in the whole class. Show the children a box or bowl of Snap Cubes that are not snapped together. Distribute the cubes, inviting the children to put one cube in each of their pockets.

10. Ask the children if the cubes have helped them count the total number of pockets. Do they have an idea of how many pockets there might be altogether at this point? Someone will likely explain that you have to count the cubes. To do the count, help the children place their cubes in a long line at the front of the room so everyone can see (for example, on the chalkboard ledge). Then count the cubes by 1s. Though cumbersome, this process offers an opportunity to discuss the fact that counting by 1s gets difficult with larger numbers.

11. Write down your total and compare it with the children's predictions.

Tell the children that you plan to revisit *The Pocket Problem* over time. They may wish to establish a particular day of the week on which to do the activity. It's amazing how many students remember to wear as many pockets as possible on *The Pocket Problem* days! And if you explain the activity in a letter sent home to families, parents may well become interested too—and may do the laundry with an eye toward making pockets available.

Part 2

The next time you revisit *The Pocket Problem*, consider using this process:

1. As in Part 1, identify the range of possible numbers of pockets that individual children might be wearing. Ask children to stand when you call out their number of pockets, and discuss the range and the most common number of pockets. Record this information on the board by writing the numbers and placing an *x* for each student with that number of pockets. Have the children discuss what they notice.

2. Dole out the cubes—but this time, don't have the children put them in their pockets. Instead, instruct the children to snap together the same number of cubes as they have pockets.

3. On the board, write the word *tens*.

4. Ask the children who have five cubes snapped together to stand and hold up their sticks of five. Write *5 + __ = 10* on the board, read the number sentence out loud, and ask the standing children what the missing number is. Someone will likely respond quickly with "Five!"

5. Have two children who are holding sticks of five cubes snap their sticks together to make a stick of ten. Place the new stick below the word *tens* on the chalkboard tray.

6. Ask the other children with five cubes to repeat this process.

7. Invite the children to think of other combinations that would create sticks of ten. Then have children with combinations of ten (1 + 9, 2 + 8, 3 + 7, etc.) connect their sticks and place them on the chalkboard tray under the *tens* label. Keep making 10s until all possibilities have been snapped together. Write the number of 10s the class made (e.g., if you've collected five sticks of ten cubes, write *5* under the *tens* label).

8. Draw a vertical line to the right of the word *tens*. Write the word *ones* at the top of this new column. Record the number of extra single cubes in that column.

9. Now write the number that results from combining the two counts. For instance, if you collected five sticks of ten cubes and eight single cubes, write *58*.

10. Ask what the children notice about this number. For instance, point to the 5 in the number 58, and ask what that means in *The Pocket Problem*. Then discuss the 8. Record the information from the chalkboard on a piece of chart paper so you can compare the data as your class engages in *The Pocket Problem* on other days. Many children enjoy anticipating these comparisons.

Family Sorting

Five Creatures by Emily Jenkins tells the entertaining story of a family of three human beings and two cats. The cheerful child in the story groups and sorts this happy menagerie in a variety of ways. Her categories include everything from how many legs the various creatures have, to how many of them enjoy hiding in boxes.

Instructions

1. Read the story with the children, taking time to enjoy the illustrations.

2. On the board, list all the ways the little girl sorted her family. Ask whether students think this story could be about a real family. Encourage the children to explain their reasoning.

3. Extend the list by inviting additional sorting suggestions from your students. By pretending to be the author and illustrator of a similar book, a child may be able to generate more sorting ideas. For instance, one child may suggest sorting her family into people who love video games and people who don't. Another child might describe sorting his family into those who like to eat dinner in tents made out of blankets, and those who don't.

4. Select a sorting criterion from the extended list, and have your students draw a picture and write a short sorting story of their own based on that criterion.

Extensions

Pose number problems based on sorting criteria. For example, if you use *Five Creatures*' family of two cats and three people, ask questions such as, "How many legs are there in all? How many tails?"

Bug Counting

The Icky Bug Counting Book by Jerry Pellotta is a brightly illustrated book that provides nonfiction information about a wide array of insects. The number of different kinds of insects progresses from one page to the next and steadily increases from 0 to 26. In addition to counting, the book encourages understanding of number relationships, providing information such as, "Elegant crab spiders have eight eyes as well as eight legs" and "Paper wasps could make paper thousands of years before people learned how."

Instructions

1. Read the story.

2. Take a walk around the school with your class. If magnifying glasses are available, have the children bring them. Periodically encourage the children to search for insects. Speculate together about the types of insects that typically live in your environment and might be nearby.

3. When you get back to the classroom, help your students create a list of familiar insects.

4. Use the story or other resources (such as library books or Internet pictures) to assist the children in making simple number drawings of the insects on the list (e.g., one praying mantis, eleven moths, twelve ants). Some insects, such as ladybugs and ants, are relatively easy for most children to draw. Others—such as crickets or walking sticks—may be harder to draw, but may also lead to whimsical depictions that the children enjoy. (See Figures 10–1, 10–2, and 10–3.)

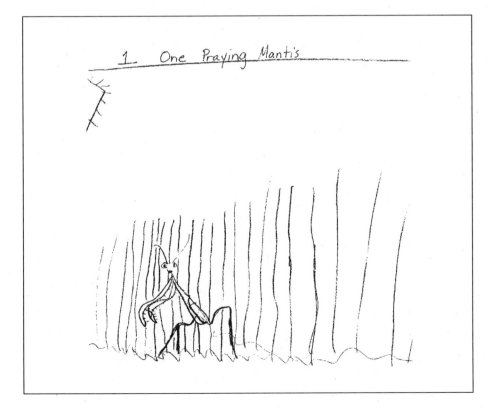

FIGURE 10–1 ◀

Yucheng drew one praying mantis.

FIGURE 10–2   ▶

Tobias drew eleven moths.

FIGURE 10–3   ▶

Irina drew twelve ants.

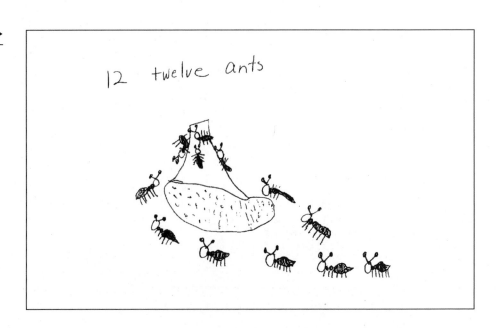

5. When the children have finished their number/insect drawings, collect them and make a class book. If your class gets a visit from next year's first graders, share the book with the visitors.

Extensions

- Have students use their number/insect drawings to create a number-facts book. For instance, they could use ten different insects and make a 1–10 book: one praying mantis, two ladybugs, three beetles, four butterflies, and so on. Each page could also include one true interesting fact about that particular insect.

- Create an insect number book that not only counts insects but also includes numerical information about other details, such as number of legs, on each page.

Finger Counting

Count on Your Fingers, African Style by Claudia Zaslavsky describes ways to keep track of amounts using finger counting. The author explains that sign language can serve as a special form of counting communication. Indeed, throughout Africa, people who speak many different languages use sign language to barter, buy, and sell in the marketplace, and to quickly convey their thoughts and calculations. This book reveals that the need to count and keep track of quantities is universal.

The use of fingers provides another opportunity to discuss the importance of the number 10 in our counting system. Here are some ideas for leveraging the lessons in this book:

- Ask students to share some of the ways they use finger counting to solve problems. Remind them of alternative methods to keep track of numbers, such as tally marks, ten frames, and 1–100 charts. If you have an abacus available, show it and explain that it's another tool that makes use of the base-ten system. If you don't have an abacus, create string arrangements of ten beads on a piece of twine, yarn, or string, or on a pipe cleaner.

- Count by 10s from 1 to 100, then see if the class can count the same numbers backward by 10s.

- Ask some questions involving "ten more" and "ten less" (e.g., "What is ten more than twelve? What is ten less than twelve?" "What is ten more than thirty? What is ten less than thirty?"). Ask everyone to mentally picture a mathematical tool and do some mental math involving 10s.

This focus on 10 develops flexibility with number and increases first graders' awareness of the cross-cultural significance of communicating mathematically. Children are developing the understanding that mathematics is a common language that satisfies a universal human need.

Coins and Jelly Beans

Jelly Beans for Sale by Bruce McMillan begins with a poem about the sale of jelly beans, "One for a penny, ten for a dime. Count them and buy them. You'll have a good time." This beautifully photographed book explores coin values through the context of jelly-bean sales. The pages depict and define pennies, nickels, dimes, and quarters before the story even begins.

The sales are straightforward: Each jelly bean is worth exactly one cent. Throughout the book, sellers and buyers need various combinations of coins for the transactions. Each time a character identifies a quantity of jelly beans, the beans—as well as the required coins to buy them—are arranged in visual clusters that make them easy to count. The detailed photographs show children enjoying their purchases.

At the bottom of each page is an equation expressing the values of the coins used in that particular transaction. The use of the equals sign in the equations provides a springboard for further discussing the meaning of that symbol.

To build on the learning offered by this book, write the following sorts of number sentences on the board:

$$1 + 1 + 1 + 1 + 1 = 5$$

$$1 + 1 + 1 + 1 + 1 + 5 = 10$$

$$1 + 1 + 1 + 1 + 1 + 5 = 5 + 5$$

$$1 + 1 + 1 + 1 + 1 + 1 + 1 + 1 + 1 + 1 = 5 + 5$$

Include some nonexamples as well, such as:

$$1 + 1 + 1 + 1 + 1 = 10$$

$$1 + 1 + 1 + 1 + 1 + 5 = 10 + 5$$

Ask the children whether these sentences represent true statements—that is, whether the two sides are equal. Invite them to generate additional examples.

Combinations of 10

Ten Flashing Fireflies by Philemon Sturges gives children a visual way to explore combinations of the number 10. The story's artful illustrations show addition and subtraction as fireflies move into and out of a jar. Glowing pictures show various part/whole relationships within the number 10. Children can create their own firefly pictures with crayons and watercolors or with black paper and light-colored crayons. You can make this a partner activity by assigning a combination of fireflies that are in and out of the jar, then having partners take turns drawing the corresponding picture.

Materials

- a variety of drawing materials for each child
- black and white construction paper, light-colored crayons, and black or blue watercolor paint for each child

Instructions

1. Read the story with your class.

2. Reread the book, this time encouraging students to help you generate an addition and a subtraction equation for each page. Consider handing out paper with blank equations (e.g., __ + __ = __ and __ − __ = __) so that the children can fill in the blanks.

3. Discuss the children's suggested number sentences to make sure they understand the symbols, and to see whether the numbers match the story on each page.

4. Assign partners to illustrate the number sentences that were generated. Extend the list if you have more children than number sentences. (See Figures 10–4 and 10–5.)

5. See if children want to gather their drawings into a class book.

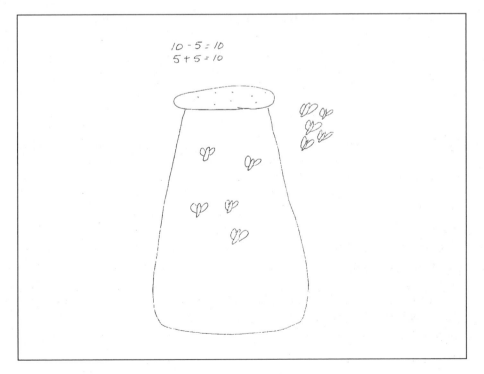

FIGURE 10–4 ◀

Vanessa drew fireflies depicting the equations 10 − 5 = 10 and 5 + 5 = 10.

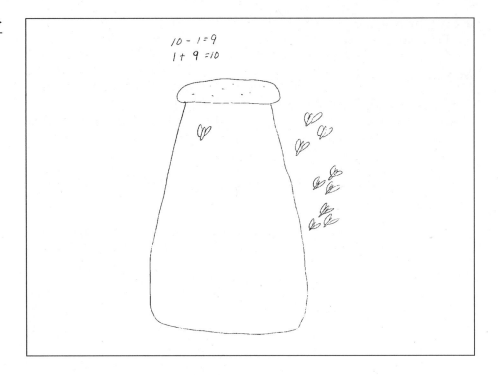

Even when done simply, the illustrations for these ideas enable children to experience a connection with art. You can offer students several simple ways to create their pictures. For example:

■ Provide 9-by-12-inch black construction paper, cut in half, for each student. The children can glue a pre-drawn picture of a jar onto the paper. They can create fireflies with yellow crayons or with small pieces of yellow paper. Give the children time to do some planning before they make their illustrations, and conduct a separate class session for creation of the final class book.

■ Provide white construction paper, light-colored crayons, and dark blue or black watercolor paint. Have the children press down hard with the crayons to draw the jar and fireflies. Then show them how to lightly paint over the drawing with the watercolors to create a "crayon resist" effect. Once each page has dried, place a heavy object (such as a large book) on the artwork so the page doesn't curl.

Regardless of which drawing method your students use, have students attach strips of paper with the number sentences matching their pictures to each page when they're finished. Put the pages order from fewest fireflies in the jar to the most fireflies in the jar. By reading and rereading this class book, your first graders can get repeated practice with number combinations.

Planting in 10s

One Watermelon Seed by Celia Barker Lottridge tells the story of two children who plant one watermelon seed, two pumpkin seeds, three eggplant seeds, and a variety of other types of seeds that increase through the number 10. After they've finished planting, the children care for their plants and then begin enjoying the harvest. The two children in the story pick ten watermelons, twenty pumpkins, thirty eggplants, and so on through the number 100.

Materials

- overhead projector
- grid paper

Instructions

1. Read the story to your class.

2. Ask the children to describe any number patterns they may have noticed. Remind them of past work that involved organizing numbers by creating a T-chart.

3. On the chalkboard, create a T-chart showing the number pairs from the story. (For instance, when the children planted one seed, they got ten fruits, for two seeds they got twenty fruits, etc.) (See below.)

Seeds	Harvest Fruits
1	10
2	20
3	30
4	40

4. Use the overhead projector to show the children how to represent this information in graph form. Plot the pattern on grid paper by showing the number of seeds across the bottom, and the harvest numbers going up the left side of the graph. (See Figure 10–6.)

5. Ask the children to help you place the dots on the graph. Discuss the geometric line that represents the relationship between the seed and the harvest.)

FIGURE 10–6   ▶

Growth for *One Water-melon Seed*

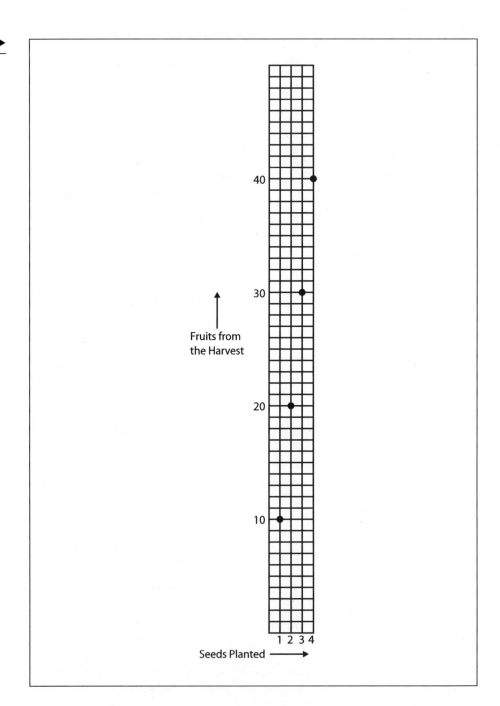

The Number 11

12 Ways to Get to 11 by Eve Merriam uses simple collage illustrations to show twelve different ways that quantities can be grouped to reach the number 11.

Instructions

1. Read the story with the class.

2. Have the children help you write number sentences that match different pages in the book. For instance, one page shows "three sets of triplets in baby carriages, and a pair of twins in the stroller." Students can use their math notebooks to practice writing *3 + 3 + 3 + 2 = 11* as you record the idea on the board. Ask if anyone can think of a subtraction story that would match the page, such as 11 – 2 = 9 Record those number sentences as well.

3. On another day, revisit the story. This time after reading the book, have each child select a number between 5 and 15 and show various combinations of numbers to reach that total. Some children may feel that they've completed the task after offering some quick and superficial responses. If this happens, encourage them to persist. Probe for additional examples. As you look over the children's papers, you will gain insight into their confidence levels and their approaches to the problem.

Numbers from Nature

Counting on the Woods by George Ella Lyon describes and quantifies things found in the natural world. If you can take a field trip to a local natural environment, make the most of the photographic opportunities such a trip affords. Students can take turns using a camera to snap nature photos, or they can gather photos from magazines when they return to the classroom. They can then create their own number-related displays or books by compiling their pictures. The children could also simply draw pictures that identify number-related nature ideas; for instance, drawing flowers with five petals each.

Encourage students to count and quantify things they see whenever they are outside. Take a "How many?" nature walk and have the children count birds, bugs, clouds, trees, flowers, or anything else they see. This kind of experience can help first graders get into the habit of making casual observations involving numbers.

Ways to Make 100

One Hundred Hungry Ants by Elinor Pinczes tells of ants who are marching off, single file, to a picnic. The ants are so hungry that one innovative member of the colony suggests speeding things up by traveling in rows of fifty, twenty-five, twenty, and ten. Though his fellow ants adopt his idea, they don't get to the food any faster. But readers discover new ways to organize, arrange, and count 100 things.

Materials

- 100 cubes or other small counting objects per pair of students

Instructions

1. Write the numbers *100, 50, 25, 20,* and *10* on the board.

2. Have children pair up and use cubes or other small objects to count out 100 things. Children can check their counts by looking for 10 groups of 10.

3. On another day, offer a similar problem, but this time invite the children to divide and arrange the objects by 5s, 20s, or 25s (remind students of nickels and quarters) and experiment with different ways to check the total amount.

4. After the children have had some time to work, encourage everyone to take a "walkabout" and see how other students have organized their materials.

1,000 Things

How Much, How Many, How Far, How Heavy, How Long, How Tall Is 1000? by Helen Nolan helps children conceptualize large numbers. The author provides interesting examples of what 1,000 of something might look like—depending on the sizes of the objects being counted and the space the objects occupy. You can use this book in connection with the perennial favorite *How Much Is a Million?* by David Schwartz, which is lavishly illustrated by Steven Kellogg.

Instructions

1. Read one or both stories.

2. Write the numbers *100, 1,000,* and *1,000,000* on the board.

3. Invite students to view the numbers, and encourage them to make some comparisons. These numbers are so large that first graders will have difficulty grasping what they mean in terms of quantities.

4. Discuss the children's observations about these numbers' similarities and differences.

5. Ask the children to think of places where people might be able to see more than 1,000 or even 1,000,000 of something. For instance, there are more than a million grains of sand on the beach, more than a million stars in the sky, more than a million fish in the sea, and more than a million people on earth.

Extensions

Children are fascinated by large numbers. Consider inviting them to create illustrations of "More Than a Million" for a classroom display or class book.

Whole-Class/Menu Activities

By this time in the school year, things go smoothly if the children have a very clear sense of the procedural and behavioral expectations. Familiar games, such as the ones below (also presented in Chapter 6), provide repeated practice. If needed, the level of difficulty can be increased to provide more of a challenge.

Make Ten

The game of Make Ten is a partner game that requires children to look at combinations of cards and determine when the sum of the cards is ten. This particular partner game involves, removing face cards and jokers, shuffling the cards and putting them in a pile. Remind the children that they can place the cards on the floor and sort of "stir them up" as an easy way to shuffle. Partners take turns turning over one card at a time and placing the cards that have been revealed into a row so that both players can see all of the cards. When a combination of ten is turned over, the player who sees it first says "ten." Sometimes the number 10 itself gets flipped over, usually two cards make the combination. It is also possible to use more than two cards to make the ten. You may wish to instruct the children to place the combinations of ten in one shared pile as a way to reduce feelings of competition. To increase or decrease the level of difficulty of this game, adjust the target number. Children can also play the game using the operation of subtraction. Players specify a number and as they flip the cards, they watch for that difference. For instance, if 2 is the designated number, players are looking for a difference of two between the cards (i.e. 7 and 5). Two cards are flipped simultaneously, players subtract the smaller number from the larger number.

How Many Reds (162)

This is another two-person card game. Children will need 20 playing cards, ace through 10 of a red suit and a black suit. They will need a recording sheet that is divided into ten rectangles. After the cards are thoroughly shuffled, 10 cards are dealt to both partners. Each player will count the number of red cards in their hand. First one player records the number of red cards in both player's hands by placing the two numbers (i.e. 4 + 6) in one of the rectangles on the recording sheet. The cards are then shuffled again, and during this next round, the second player will record how many red cards are in each hand. This game gives children practice with exploring combinations of ten and offers an opportunity for them to use standard notation as they record the combinations. Again the target number can be changed to adjust the level of difficulty.

Addition and Subtraction Spinners

In this activity, students use spinners to explore a wide range of addition and subtraction facts. This game is intended to help children practice mental computation of familiar number facts and numerical relationships. At times, students may require additional support to solve the problems generated by the spinners. Make familiar mathematical tools, such as counters, ten frames, tally marks, and 1–100 charts, available for use as needed. (*About Teaching Mathematics* by Marilyn Burns [2000] has excellent instructions on making spinners.)

Materials

- several different kinds of spinners per group of 3 children

Instructions

1. For each group of students, make one spinner showing four numbers. These numbers will be used to make addition and subtraction equations, so select numbers that reflect a range appropriate for your students, for example, 1 through 12.

2. For each group, make a second spinner showing four different numbers from those shown on the spinners you made in Step 1. For example, the first kind of spinner might have all even numbers, while the second kind has odd numbers. Or one spinner could have numbers between 1 and 6 while the other has multiples of 10.

3. For each group, make a third spinner that is divided down the center and that has an addition sign on the left side and a subtraction sign on the right side.

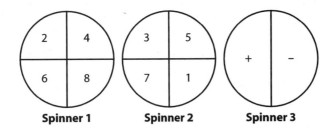

Spinner 1   Spinner 2   Spinner 3

4. To play the game, one student in a threesome spins the addition/sub-traction spinner. The second child spins one of the spinners with the numbers. The third child spins the remaining spinner. The children then solve the resulting addition or subtraction equation. If the sub-traction sign is indicated, the players subtract the smaller number from the larger. All children solve and write (record) the problems.

5. Once students have gained familiarity with the game, have them cre-ate two columns labeled *addition* and *subtraction* in their math note-books and begin recording the equations they solve while playing the game. If your students have not had an opportunity to write and use vertical equations, demonstrate this procedure and encourage them to practice it as they play the game. (See below.)

$$\begin{array}{r} 10 \\ -\ 5 \\ \hline 5 \end{array} \qquad \begin{array}{r} 7 \\ +\ 4 \\ \hline 11 \end{array}$$

6. When the children have finished playing the game, ask them to review the results they recorded in their math notebooks. Ask, "Did some numbers come up more often than others? If so, what were they?" "Did you get more even or odd numbers in your problem answers?" "Were some problems easier or more difficult than others? If so, why?"

In or Out

Chapter 9 introduced one version of *In or Out* that involved using yarn loops and beans. A similar set of materials could be created using an oval piece of construction paper to represent a pond and using small pebbles as counters.

Use a 1-foot piece of thick yarn to create a yarn loop. Select a particu-lar number of tiles or lima beans (5 to 12 depending upon the child's ease with number combinations) hold the beans a few inches above the circle and drop them. Model this process while sitting with the children at circle or using the overhead projector. Use a large chart paper to record horizontal number sentences that show addition and then subtraction.

Children will record how many beans landed inside the circle and how many landed outside the circle and show the total for how many there are altogether __ + __ = __. Students can once again use their math notebooks and record addition and subtraction number sentences. Recording subtraction sentences is generally more challenging for children. It is not uncommon for students to have difficulty with the understanding that they must begin with the total number of beans being dropped and subtract one of the parts. Take the time to review the game and emphasize this subtraction issue.

Addition Tic-Tac-Toe

This partner game further strengthens addition skills.

Materials

- 1 Tic-Tac-Toe game board per pair of students (see Figure 10–7 and Blackline Masters)
- 2 paperclips per pair of students
- 20 cubes of 2 different colors per pair of students; each partner gets 10 cubes of 1 color

Instructions

1. Player 1 chooses two numbers from those listed at the bottom of the game board and places a paperclip on each of those numbers. (The player can opt to place both paperclips on the same number if he or she prefers.)

2. Player 1 then puts a cube on the *sum* of the two numbers in the appropriate spot on the game board.

3. Player 2 moves one of the paperclips to another number. He or she then adds those numbers together and places a different color cube on the resulting sum.

4. Players repeat the process until one player has placed four cubes of his or her color in a row vertically, horizontally, or diagonally. If both players fail to create such a row, the game is a draw.

Place-Value Mats

This activity helps children delineate 10s and 1s by grasping the meaning of place value.

FIGURE 10–7 ◀

Addition Tic-Tac-Toe.

Addition Tic-Tac-Toe

2	7	6	7
8	5	10	8
9	9	7	13
10	11	12	9

1   2   3   4   5   6   7   8   9   10

Materials

- 1 12-by-18-inch construction-paper "mat" per pair of students
- a variety of small counting objects (e.g., beans, beads) per pair of students, or a set of small interlocking cubes per pair
- a small plastic bag of objects for each child
- several tiny paper cups or medical-dosage cups per pair of students (if using beans, beads, and other similar objects)
- overhead projector

Instructions

1. Create one 12-by-18-inch mat per student. For each mat, use one color construction paper for one half of the mat, and a second color paper for the other half. Write *tens* at the top of the left half of the mat and *ones* at the top of the right half. Laminate the mats if you wish to use them several times.

2. For each child, fill a small, transparent bag with beads, beans, or other small counting objects—putting only one kind of object in each bag. Provide small containers. (Students will arrange groups of ten counting objects in these tiny cups as the game unfolds.) Or, provide interlocking cubes instead of beans or beads.

3. Demonstrate the activity: Create an overhead-transparency version of the place-value mats and place it on the overhead projector. Ask a student to give you a number between 1 and 6. Place the corresponding number of counting objects on the 1s section of the mat. Say the number, then say, "Plus one" and place another counter on the 1s side. Discuss how many objects are now on the mat.

4. Repeat the "Plus one" process until you have nine objects on the mat. Each time you add another object, state the total number now showing on the mat. As you go along, organize the objects so they're easy to count, and mention your arrangements to the class.

5. When you reach the number 9, explain that you're at an important point in the activity. Point out that when you add this next object, you will need to put the ten objects in a cup and move the cup over to the 10s side. (Since a cup won't show up clearly on the overhead projector, draw a circle on the 10s side to represent a cup that will contain ten objects.)

6. When you say "Plus one" this time, dramatically add the tenth object, then move ten to the circle on the 10s side of the mat. Say, "One group of tens and zero ones." Write *10* on the board and ask the children to read the number.

7. Continue this process, encouraging students to say "Plus one" each time you add an object. Chant the number of 10s and the number of 1s. Continue until you've placed a total of twenty objects on the mat.

8. Reverse the process by having the children chant "Minus one" as you remove one object at a time from the circles on the 10s side. Again, each time you remove a counter, have the children tell you how many 10s and how many 1s are now on the mat. Take plenty of time to discuss the regrouping process—moving from the tens side to the ones side, and taking the objects out of the cup after removing 1—when you make the transition from ten down to nine objects.

9. The next time you use these materials, have children pair up and share a mat. Repeat your demonstration on the overhead projector, but this time encourage students to work along with you by placing and removing objects on their own mats. Practice until the children feel comfortable and familiar with the procedure.

With practice, students will see place-value mats as another important tool that can help them conceptualize quantities and understand the system of

10s. Later, the children will move beyond showing specific quantities of objects and will begin combining and separating quantities to demonstrate addition and subtraction.

Extensions

Once the children are proficient at using individual counters on the mats, introduce new challenges. For example:

- Use more abstract counting materials, such as pennies and dimes.
- Introduce other patterns, such as "Plus two" or "Minus five."
- Add a third color of construction paper to the left of the 10s place and label this section *hundreds*. Count to high enough numbers to use the 100s column.
- Instead of starting the game with anywhere from one to six counters, begin with a double-digit number. (Children can use their 1–100 charts to think up starting numbers.)
- Generate addition and subtraction problems: Students select *two* starting numbers instead of one. They place the larger quantity on the mat and then remove the smaller quantity. Suggest that they record the problems and results in their math notebooks.

Silly Sentences

Chapter 6 describes a version of this game (*How Much Is Your Word Worth?*). In the version below, players create silly sentences and assign values to three categories of words: nouns, verbs, and adjectives. Children enjoy this connection with reading and enthusiastically select this option from the math menu.

Materials

- One large piece of 12-by-18-inch construction-paper rectangles for each of three different colors

Instructions

1. Make 3-by-5-inch construction-paper rectangles of three different colors, at least 15 of each kind of word.
2. Ask students to help you generate a list of living things, such as *dogs, cats, elephants, spiders, flowers,* and *trees.*
3. Number these words in the order in which they appear on the list. These numbers will become the worth of their corresponding words.
4. Next have the children brainstorm a list of descriptive words, such as *fun, purple, silly, loud, polka-dotted,* and *spooky.* Once again, number the words on the list.

5. Write each noun from Step 5 on an individual rectangle of a particular color. Include the number that you assigned to each word.

6. Write the descriptive words and their numbers on a second color of paper rectangles.

7. Tell the children that you're going to write a "connecting word" on a third color of rectangular paper. Write the words *are* and *can be* on individual cards of the third color rectangle. Create the same number of cards that you have used for the nouns and adjectives. For example, if you have ten noun cards and ten adjective cards, make ten connecting-word cards. On each of these "verb cards," write *10*.

8. Shuffle each of the three piles of word cards while keeping the colors separate. Then position the three piles face down in the following order: nouns, verbs, and adjectives. Invite volunteers to come up and turn over one card from each pile and then read the resulting silly sentence. Volunteers can then add up the numbers from their three cards to come up with a total number of points for their silly sentence.

9. As a class, discuss the best ways to total the numbers. (It helps to record the numbers on the board or on large chart paper so that everyone can see.) For instance, suppose your first volunteer draws "Trees" (3 points) "are" (10 points) "polka-dotted" (8 points). In this case, some children might prefer to combine the 3 with the 8 to make 11 and then add the remaining 10. Others might use 2 from the 3 to turn the 8 + 2 into another 10 (10 + 10 = 20) and then add on the remaining 1 from the 3. Still others might prefer to calculate 8 + 10 = 18 and then *count on* to include the remaining 3.

10. Once the class is comfortable with the activity, have students pair up and play during menu time. Player 1 draws a silly sentence and calculates its total points. Then Player 2 does the same. Ask children to record their number sentences in their math notebooks.

Ten Frames

You've given your students experience with ten frames earlier in the year. This month, have them generate addition and subtraction ideas to be demonstrated with counters on the frames. Decide on an appropriate range of numbers (e.g., 1–30), then ask the children to draw number cards from an envelope to generate addition and subtraction problems. For example, 8 + 3 or 9 – 7. Once they've generated a problem, students can demonstrate the resulting calculation on their ten frames. Meanwhile, you can model writing horizontal and vertical equations on the board. Once children feel comfortable with the procedures, partners can use laminated ten frames as a menu option and write their own equations in their math notebooks.

Additional Ideas for 1–100 Charts

Students benefit from plenty of opportunities to revisit and explore 1–100 charts.

Materials

- 1 overhead transparency of a 1–100 chart
- overhead projector
- 10 transparent color tiles in 2 colors, or overhead markers of 2 colors

Instructions
Part 1: Guess My Number

1. Put the overhead transparency of a 1–100 chart on the projector. Cover up all numbers higher than 10 on the chart.

2. Ask for a volunteer to come and whisper a secret number from 1 to 10 your ear.

3. Jot down the secret number on a slip of paper and put it in your pocket or some other safe place.

4. Explain that you're going to ask for volunteers to guess the secret number. State that if a guess is too low, you will place a red (for example) tile on the number that was guessed (or use a marker to write a red *X* on that number). If the guess is too high, you will put a blue (for example) tile on the number that was guessed (or make a blue *X* on the number).

5. Begin playing the game. Stop after the first couple of guesses to ask what the children are noticing as the numbers get covered up.

6. Play additional rounds of the game using numbers 1–20, then 1–50, and finally 1–100.

7. On another day, play one more round of the game with your class. This time, have a volunteer take your place at the overhead projector.

Partners can play *Guess My Number* using paper number charts and squares of two different colors to cover numbers that are too low or too high. Cubes tend to stay in place and work well to cover the numbers. Construction-paper squares also adequately serve this purpose. If you have laminated 1–100 charts, the children can use crayons or dry-erase markers to draw their *X*s directly on the charts. In this case, supply tissues, paper towels, or soft cloths so children can clean the charts after each round.

It's not uncommon for some children to struggle with the concepts behind this game. Observe the children while they work, to assess understanding and provide individual support as needed. You can also send the game home with some students to provide additional playing time.

Race for a Quarter

This activity further strengthens addition skills.

Materials

- small bags containing 30 play or real pennies, 10 nickels, 10 dimes, and 1 quarter; 1 bag per pair of children
- 1 die per pair of children

Instructions

1. Have children pair up.

2. Player 1 rolls the die to determine the number of pennies to take out of the bag. If the number is fewer than five, play passes to Player 2. But if Player 1 rolls a 5, he or she exchanges the pennies for a nickel.

3. With every roll, each player assesses his or her coins to see whether they can be exchanged for a nickel or dime. The first player who can accumulate enough coinage value to exchange for a quarter wins.

Extensions

Have the children play *Race for a Dollar*.

Riddles

Many children find riddles interesting and motivating. This activity enables them to immerse themselves in riddles.

Materials

- 10–15 tiles of 3 different color configurations in a paper bag (e.g., 1 bag contains 2 different colors; another, 3 different colors); 1 bag per student

Instructions

1. Demonstrate the activity: Show students the bag containing tiles of two different colors. On an index card, write clues to the bag's contents. (See examples below.)

I have 11 yellow and green tiles in my bag.

I have 1 more than twice as many yellow tiles as green tiles.

How many yellow tiles do I have in my bag?

How many green tiles?

I have 11 yellow and green tiles in my bag.

I have 11 – 6 green tiles.

How many tiles are green and how many are yellow?

2. Now show the bag containing three different tile colors. Again, write clues on index cards.

   I have red, yellow, and green tiles in my bag.

   I have 2 + 3 red tiles.

   I have 6 + 1 yellow tiles.

   I have 1 + 2 green tiles.

   How many tiles are in my bag?

3. Invite the children to sit with you at circle or wherever your whole-group gatherings take place. Paperclip the index cards to your "mystery bags," and let students take a closer look at the bags and clues.

4. Ask if anyone can explain what a riddle is. Hold up an index card and tell the class that you are going to share several riddles for the children to solve.

5. Explain that soon the students will be writing their own riddles. Mention that this activity can get very exciting. Suggest that students think up answers to the riddles silently in their own minds and share them only after you've asked them to. Ask what happens when someone calls out an answer to a question before everyone has had time to think about it.

6. Read the riddles from the index cards while showing the clues on a piece of chart paper. After a moment, invite solutions to the riddles. Ask students to explain how they used the clues to solve the riddles.

7. Suggest that the children help you write some new riddles. Create a list of ideas that could be included in the riddles, such as *half, twice as many, more, less, same number, addition,* and *subtraction.* Have the children help you count out the appropriate number of tiles for the new riddles and create additional riddle bags. Attach the riddles to the tops of the bags.

After the initial riddle session, some children may be ready to partner up with another classmate and begin creating riddles using up to fifteen tiles of three colors. Others may wish to continue working with you so as to get more practice. Accommodate both preferences. Eventually, however, give each child an opportunity to create at least one riddle. Check the riddles for accuracy, then have the children trade to solve one another's riddles. Offer this activity as a menu option.

Afterword

It is late in May as I write this. We're winding down the school year and after all these months, the children are in the habit of asking questions and discussing their work. Yesterday one of my students raised her hand after being given a written math problem about the total number of markers there would be if you had two boxes of twelve markers. Julia said, "I can read the words in this problem, and I understand those numbers, but I still don't know what the problem means." I told Julia that I thought it was really important that she was able to realize that the problem wasn't making sense to her yet.

We talked about some things that might help her get a better idea about the meaning of the problem. For instance, she might draw a picture, or use some objects like markers and count them. Julia decided that she didn't want to do either of those things, she wanted to pretend to act it out with me. So she directed and we pretended to each have a box of twelve markers. I asked Julia if she had any idea how many markers we would have if we counted them one at a time. She said we both had our own box and that both of the pretend boxes had twelve markers in them. I asked her how we could figure out how many there were in all and she said that it was easier for her to think of 10 + 10, and then add the twos because 10 + 10 = 20, and then 2 + 2 = 4. "Put the twenty together with the four and we've got twenty-four markers." I asked her to put those ideas on paper and she happily went to work.

Two things struck me after this exchange. First, I was impressed with Julia's assumption that the problem needed to make sense. She could have simply added to the two numbers (2 and 12) together to give herself the illusion of being "done." Of course she would have gotten the wrong answer, but I've seen children resort to manipulating numbers in this way. The second thing that made an impression on me was Julia's personal decision about how she wanted to approach the problem. I have to say that my first impulse was to ask (direct) her to use counters or a draw a picture so that she would have a visual representation and could count the markers. As I watched and listened, I realized that Julia needed to experience the action of addition, the actual motion of putting things together, in order to make sense of what was happening with the quantities. She then used the distributive property to make the numbers more manageable. Her final solution was more sophisticated and abstract than the one that I would have suggested.

This exchange with Julia made me curious about the problem solving preferences of my other students. Later that day I asked the class to think about things that they find to be most helpful when they are learning math. We looked through their math notebooks and talked about some of the math explorations and math tools that we had experienced together during the past year.

I gave the children several minutes and then I asked them to share their thoughts. Here's what they said:

"I like to use counting to figure things out."

"Me too, and faster counting, like counting on from a number or using number patterns like 2s and 10s to count and sometimes it even helps to count backwards."

"I learn by paying attention to numbers in the world, like channels on TV, and prices and speed limit signs."

"You can find out about big numbers when you learn math words like *digits*."

"Flashbacks!" [I asked for clarification on this and John said, "You know remembering when you've seen something before, like you're seeing it again in your mind!"]

"Using little things like beans or cubes for counters."

"Acting things out."

"Getting good at reading the math signs for plus, take away, and equals—so you know what you're supposed to do with a problem and you don't get mixed up."

"I always like to use tally marks."

"The 1–100 chart helps me see where the numbers are."

"Flash cards so you can get really fast with problems."

"The calendar because I'm so used to looking at it."

"Number lines."

"Games that you play with somebody else because then you try really hard and sometimes your partner can teach you stuff."

"Practice, practice, practice!" [The children all laughed at that one, because "Practice, practice, practice!" is my standard advice for everything from shooting a basketball to reading.]

I was warmed by the richness of this list and the ease with which the children shared their ideas. As teachers, our classroom efforts focus on helping first graders to achieve and become proficient with specific skills. Seeing math as accessible, useful, and interesting will help to place children on a path to successful learning. I wish you the very best in this complex endeavor and sincerely hope that you will enjoy some of the possibilities that I've passed along in this book.

Blackline Masters

Weekly Planning Chart

Teacher's Name: Date: Curricular Focus or Unit of Study:

Math Priorities:

Monday	Tuesday	Wednesday	Thursday	Friday

Weekly Routines: Needed Materials and Literature:

The important thing about

_____

is _____.

She _____

and _____.

But the important thing about

_____

Is that she _____.

The important thing about

_____

is _____.

He _____

and _____.

But the important thing about

_____

Is that he _____.

1–100 Chart

1	2	3	4	5	6	7	8	9	10
11	12	13	14	15	16	17	18	19	20
21	22	23	24	25	26	27	28	29	30
31	32	33	34	35	36	37	38	39	40
41	42	43	44	45	46	47	48	49	50
51	52	53	54	55	56	57	58	59	60
61	62	63	64	65	66	67	68	69	70
71	72	73	74	75	76	77	78	79	80
81	82	83	84	85	86	87	88	89	90
91	92	93	94	95	96	97	98	99	100

Pattern Menu

T Shirt Patterns

_____ **date**

_____ **date**

Paper Tube Patterns

_____ **date**

_____ **date**

Pattern Block Caterpillars

_____ **date**

_____ **date**

Code Patterns

_____ **date**

_____ **date**

Roll and Extend

_____ **date**

_____ **date**

T-Shirt Pattern 1

T-Shirt Pattern 2

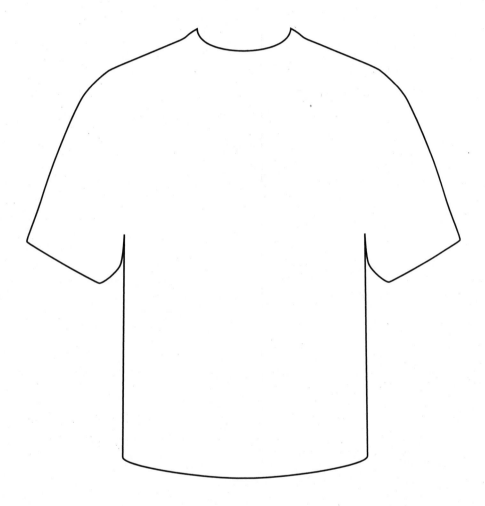

tens	ones

Tangram

Cut tangram pieces out of cardstock or plastic.

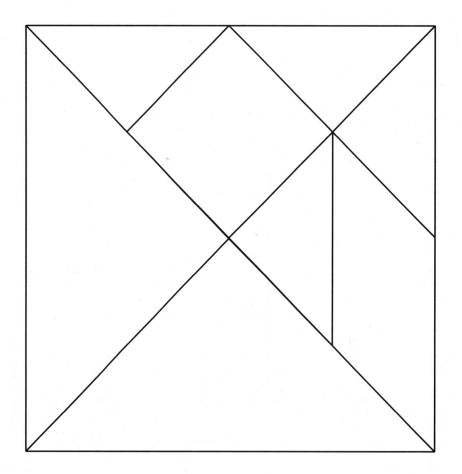

Tangram House Puzzle

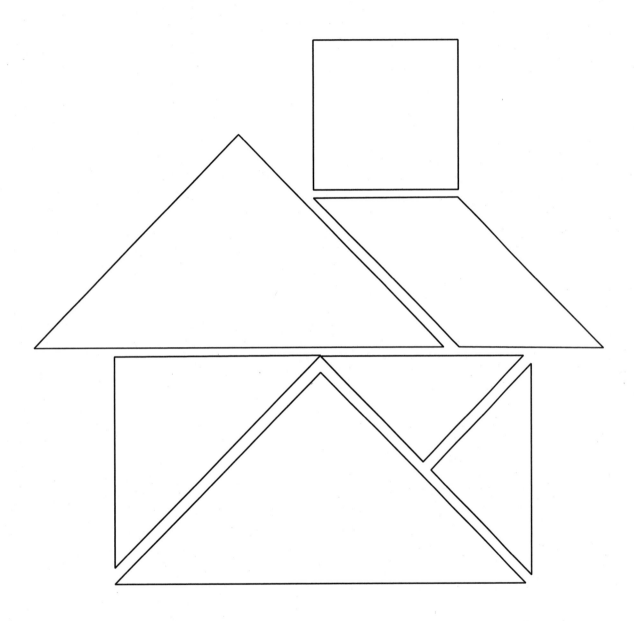

Mobile Shapes

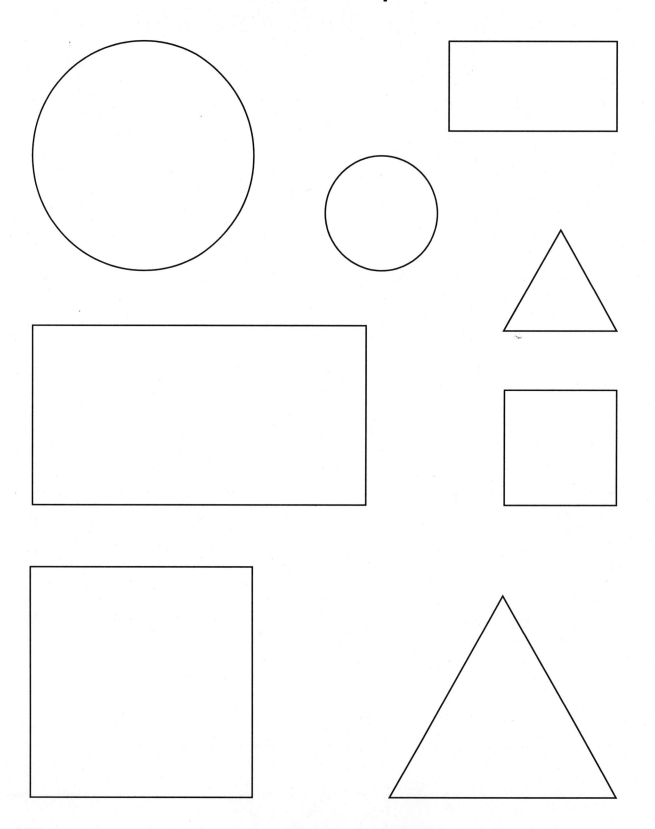

Ten Rectangle Record Sheet

Roll Two Dice

2	3	4	5	6	7	8	9	10	11	12

Finish Line

Calendar Countdown

101	102	103	104	105	106	107	108	109	110
111	112	113	114	115	116	117	118	119	120
121	122	123	124	125	126	127	128	129	130
131	132	133	134	135	136	137	138	139	140
141	142	143	144	145	146	147	148	149	150
151	152	153	154	155	156	157	158	159	160
161	162	163	164	165	166	167	168	169	170
171	172	173	174	175	176	177	178	179	180
181	182	183	184	185	186	187	188	189	190
191	192	193	194	195	196	197	198	199	200

Estimation Jar Record Sheet

How many _____ will it take to measure _____?

I predict

I counted

1.

1.

2.

2.

3.

3.

4.

4.

5.

5.

6.

6.

7.

7.

8.

8.

9.

9.

10.

10.

From *First-Grade Math: A Month-to-Month Guide* by Vicki Bachman. © 2003 Math Solutions Publications

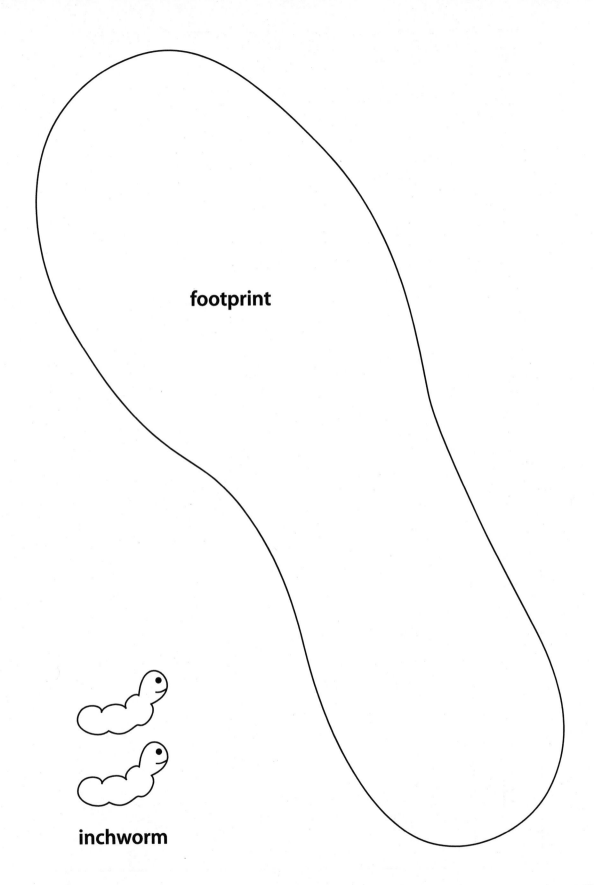

footprint

inchworm

From *First-Grade Math: A Month-to-Month Guide* by Vicki Bachman. © 2003 Math Solutions Publications

289

Length Hunt Record Sheet

Object	Something Longer	Something About the Same Length	Something Shorter

Cone Pattern

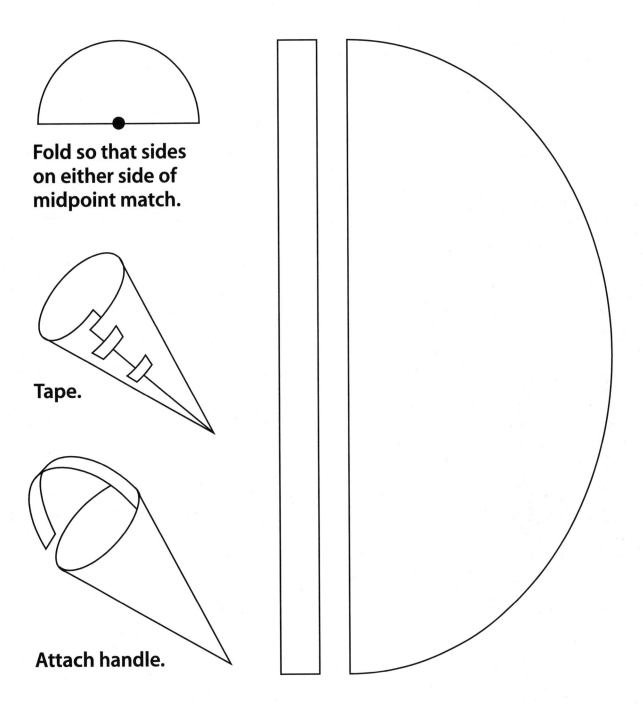

Fold so that sides on either side of midpoint match.

Tape.

Attach handle.

Shape Record Sheet

This is the shape I used:	I estimate I will need this many beans:	I counted this many beans:

One Watermelon Seed Squares

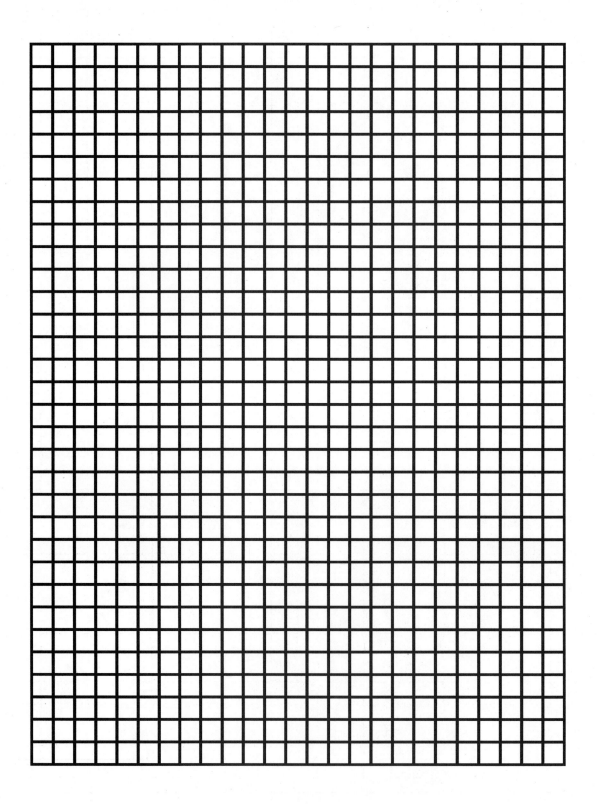

Addition Tic-Tac-Toe

2	7	6	7
8	5	10	8
9	9	7	13
10	11	12	9

1 2 3 4 5 6 7 8 9 10

From *First-Grade Math: A Month-to-Month Guide* by Vicki Bachman.© 2003 Math Solutions Publications

References

Audio Resources

Diamond, Charlotte. 1986. "The Days of the Week." *Diamond in the Rough.* Hug Bug Music compact disk.

Jean, Dr., and Friends. 1998. *Days of the Week.*

Professional Resources

Burns, Marilyn. *About Teaching Mathematics: A K–8 Resource.* 2d ed. Sausalito, CA: Math Solutions Publications.

Copley, Juanita. 2000. *The Young Child and Mathematics.* Washington, DC: National Association for the Education of Young Children.

Crawford, Jane. 1996. *Math By All Means: Money, Grades 1–2.* Sausalito, CA: Math Solutions Publications.

Investigations in Number, Data, and Space Series. Palo Alto, CA: Dale Seymour Publications.

Sheffield, Stephanie. 1995. *Math and Literature (K–3): Book Two.* Sausalito, CA: Math Solutions Publications.

Tank, Bonnie. 1996. *Math By All Means: Probability, Grades 1–2.* Sausalito, CA: Math Solutions Publications.

Tank, Bonnie, and Lynne Zolli. 2001. *Teaching Arithmetic: Lessons for Addition and Subtraction, Grades 2–3.* Sausalito, CA: Math Solutions Publications.

Children's Literature

Allen, Pamela. 1982. *Who Sank the Boat?* New York: Putnam and Gosset Gracy.

Anno, Mitsumasa. 1986. *Anno's Counting Book.* New York: Harper Trophy.

Atherlay, Sara. 1995. *Math in the Bath: And Other Fun Places, Too!* Illus. Megan Halsey. New York: Simon & Schuster.

Axelrod, Amy. 1994. *Pigs Will be Pigs: Fun with Math and Money.* Illus. Sharon McGinley-Nally. New York: Simon & Schuster.

———. 1996a. *Pigs in the Pantry: Fun with Math and Cooking.* Illus. Sharon McGinley-Nally. New York: Simon & Schuster.

———. 1996b. *Pigs on a Blanket: Fun with Math and Time.* Illus. Sharon McGinley-Nally. New York: Simon and Schuster.

Aylesworth, Jim. 1990. *One Crow: A Counting Rhyme.* Illus. Ruth Young. New York: HarperTrophy.

Borden, Louise. 1999. *A. Lincoln and Me.* Illus. Ted Lewin. New York: Scholastic.

Briggs, Raymond. 1970. *Jim and the Beanstalk.* New York: Coward-McCann.

Brown, Margaret Wise. 1949. *The Important Book.* Illus. Leonard Weisgard. New York: HarperTrophy.

Burns, Marilyn. 1994. *The Greedy Triangle.* New York: Scholastic.

Carle, Eric. 1970, 2001. *The Tiny Seed.* New York: Simon & Schuster.

———. 1972. *Roosters Off to See the World.* New York: Scholastic.

———. 1977. *The Grouchy Ladybug.* New York: HarperCollins.

Carney, Margaret. 2001. *The Biggest Fish in the Lake.* Illus. Janet Wilson. Toronto: Kids Can Press.

Coats, Lucy. 2000. *Neil's Numberless World.* New York: DK Publishing.

Crews, Donald. 1995. *Ten Black Dots.* New York: Mulberry Books.

de Beer, Hans. 1999. *Little Polar Bear.* Trans. Rosemary Lanning. New York: North-South Books.

Donnell, Rubay. 1998. *Stickeen: John Muir and the Brave Little Dog.* Illus.

Christopher Canyon. Nevada City, CA: Dawn Publications.

Ehlert, Lois. 1990. *Fish Eyes: A Book You Can Count On.* New York: Harcourt.

Freeman, Don. 1978. *A Pocket for Corduroy.* New York: The Viking Press.

Gibbons, Gail. 1982. *Tool Book.* New York: Holiday House.

———. 1989. *Monarch Butterfly.* New York: Holiday House.

———. 1990. *How a House Is Built.* New York: Holiday House.

———. 1995. *The Reasons for the Seasons.* New York: Holiday House.

———. 2000. *Polar Bears.* New York: Holiday House.

Hamm, Diane Johnston. 1991. *How Many Feet in the Bed?* Illus. Kate Salley Palmer. New York: Simon & Schuster.

Henkes, Kevin. 1991. *Chrysanthemum.* New York: Greenwillow.

Hightower, Susan. 1997. *Twelve Snails to One Lizard: A Tale of Mischief and Measurement.* Illus. Matt Novak. New York: Simon & Schuster.

Hill, Eric. 1980. *Where's Spot?* New York: Putnam.

Hoban, Tana. 2000. *Cubes, Cones, Cylinders, and Spheres.* New York: Greenwillow Books.

Holtzman, Caren. 1995. *A Quarter from the Tooth Fairy.* Illus. Betsy Day. Hello Math Reader Series. New York: Scholastic.

Hong, Lily Toy. 1993. *Two of Everything: A Chinese Folktale.* Morton Grove, IL: Albert Whitman.

Hopkinson, Deborah. 2001. *Fannie in the Kitchen.* Illus. Nancy Carpenter. New York: Atheneum.

Intrater, Roberta Grobel. 1995. *Two Eyes, a Nose, and a Mouth.* New York: Scholastic.

Jenkins, Emily. 2001. *Five Creatures.* Illus. Tomek Bogacki. New York: Frances Foster Books.

Johnston, Tony, and Tomie dePaola. 1985. *The Quilt Story.* New York: Putnam.

Jonas, Ann. 1995. *Splash.* New York: Greenwillow Books.

Joyce, William. 2000. *George Shrinks*. New York: Laura Geringer Books.

Kalan, Robert. 1989. *Jump, Frog, Jump!* Illus. Byron Barton. New York: Mulberry Books.

Kalman, Bobbie. 2001. *The Life Cycle of a Butterfly*. Illus. Margaret Amy Reiach. New York: Crabtree.

Keenan, Sheila. 1996. *The Biggest Fish*. Illus. Holly Hannon. Hello Math Reader Series. New York: Scholastic.

Krauss, Ruth. 1989. *The Carrot Seed*. Illus. Crockett Johnson. New York: HarperTrophy.

Krudwig, Vickie Leigh. 1998. *Cucumber Soup*. Illus. Craig McFarland Brown. Golden, CO: Fulcrum.

Kvasnosky, Laura McGee. 1998. *Zelda and Ivy*. Cambridge, MA: Candlewick Press.

Lewin, Ted. 1996. *Market!* New York: Lothrop, Lee & Shepard.

Lionni, Leo. 1960, 1995. *Inch by Inch*. New York: HarperTrophy.

Lobel, Arnold. 1971. *Frog and Toad Are Friends*. New York: HarperTrophy.

Long, Lynette. 1996. *Domino Addition*. Watertown, MA: Charlesbridge.

Lottridge, Celia Barker. 1997. *One Watermelon Seed*. Illus. Karen Patkau. Toronto: Stoddart.

Lyon, George Ella. 2000. *Counting on the Woods*. New York: DK Publishing.

Maccarone, Grace, with Marilyn Burns. 1998. *Three Pigs, One Wolf, and Seven Magic Shapes*. Illus. David Neuhaus. Hello Math Reader Series. New York: Scholastic.

MacKinnon, Debbie. 2000. *Eye Spy Shapes*. Illus. Anthea Sieveking. Watertown, MA: Charlesbridge.

Mayer, Mercer. 1999. *When I Get Bigger*. New York: Golden Books.

McMillan, Bruce. 1989. *Time to Go*. New York: Scholastic.

———. 1996. *Jelly Beans for Sale*. New York: Scholastic.

Medearis, Angela Shelf. 1996. *The 100th Day of School*. Illus. Joan Holub. Hello Math Reader Series. New York: Scholastic.

Melmed, Laura Krauss. 1992. *The Rainbabies*. Illus. Jim LaMarche. New York: Lothrop, Lee and Shepard.

———. 1997. *Little Oh*. Illus. Jim LaMarche. New York: Lothrop, Lee and Shepard.

Merriam, Eve. 1993. *12 Ways to Get to 11*. Illus. Bernie Karlin. New York: Trumpet Club.

Miller, Margaret. 1988. *Whose Hat?* New York: Mulberry Books.

———. 1998. *Where Does It Go?* New York: Mulberry Books.

Miranda, Anne. 1997. *To Market, to Market*. Illus. Janet Stevens. New York: Harcourt.

Modell, Frank. 1987. *One Zillion Valentines*. New York: William Morrow.

Morozuma, Atsuko. 1990. *One Gorilla: A Counting Book*. New York: Farrar, Straus and Giroux.

Morris, Ann. 1989. *Hats, Hats, Hats*. New York: Lothrop, Lee and Shepard.

Murphy, Stuart J. 1999. *Super Sand Castle Saturday*. Illus. Julia Gorton. New York: HarperTrophy.

Myller, Rolf. 1962, 1990. *How Big Is a Foot?* New York: Dell Yearling.

Neitzel, Shirley. 1997. *The House I'll Build for the Wrens*. Illus. Nancy Winslow Parker. New York: Greenwillow.

Neye, Emily. 2000. *Butterflies*. Illus. Ron Broda. New York: Grosset and Dunlap.

Nikola-Lisa, W. 1995. *Bein' with You This Way*. Illus. Michael Bryant. New York: Lee and Low Books.

Nolan, Helen. 1997. *How Much, How Many, How Far, How Heavy, How Long, How Tall Is 1000?* Illus. Tracy Walker. Toronto: Kids Can Press.

Pallotta, Jerry. 1992. *The Icky Bug Counting Book*. Illus. Ralph Maisello. Watertown, MA: Charlesbridge.

Paul, Ann Whitford. 1991. *Eight Hands Round: A Patchwork Alphabet*. Illus. Jeanette Winter. New York: Harper-Collins.

Pinczes, Elinor J. 1993. *One Hundred Hungry Ants*. Illus. Bonnie MacKain. New York: Houghton Mifflin.

———. 2001. *Inchworm and a Half*. Illus. Randall Enos. New York: Houghton Mifflin.

Pluckrose, Henry. 1988. *Look at Teeth*. New York: Franklin Watts.

Rathmann, Peggy. 1995. *Officer Buckle and Gloria*. New York: G. P. Putnam.

Reid, Margarette S. 1990. *The Button Box*. Illus. Sarah Chamberlain. New York: Puffin Books.

Russo, Marisabina. 1986. *The Line Up Book*. New York: Greenwillow.

Rylant, Cynthia. 1999. *The Cookie-Store Cat*. New York: The Blue Sky Press.

Schwartz, David M. 1985. *How Much Is a Million?* Illus. Steven Kellogg. New York: Mulberry Books.

Sendak, Maurice. 1962, 1990. *Chicken Soup with Rice: A Book of Months*. New York: HarperTrophy.

Schreiber, Anne. 1995. *Slower Than a Snail*. Illus. Larry Daste. Hello Math Reader Series. New York: Scholastic.

Slate, Joseph. 1998. *Miss Bindergarten Celebrates the 100th Day of Kindergarten*. Illus. Ashley Wolff. New York: E. P. Dutton.

Sloat, Teri. 1991. *From One to One Hundred*. New York: E. P. Dutton.

Slobodkina, Esphyr. 1940, 1987. *Caps for Sale: A Tale of a Peddler, Some Monkeys and Their Monkey Business*. New York: HarperTrophy.

Sturges, Philemon. 1995. *Ten Flashing Fireflies*. Illus. Anna Vojtech. New York: North-South Books.

Tompert, Ann. 1990. *Grandfather Tang's Story*. Illus. Robert Andrew Parker. New York: Random House.

———. 1993. *Just a Little Bit*. Illus. Lynn M. Munsinger. New York: Houghton Mifflin.

Wells, Rosemary. 2001. *Yoko's Paper Cranes*. New York: Hyperion.

Wildsmith, Brian. 1970. *Brian Wildsmith's Circus*. New York: Franklin Watts.

Williams, Vera. 1984. *A Chair for My Mother*. New York: Mulberry Books.

Zaslavsky, Claudia. 2000. *Count on Your Fingers African Style*. Illus. Wangechi Mutu. New York: Black Butterfly Books.

Index